A Pocket Guide to Public Speaking

THIRD EDITION

Getting Started ■ Development ■ Organization
■ Starting, Finishing, and Styling ■ Delivery ■
Presentation Aids ■ Types of Speeches ■ The
Classroom and Beyond ■ Citation Guidelines

Dan O'Hair
University of Oklahoma

Hannah Rubenstein

Rob Stewart
Texas Tech University

Bedford/St. Martin's   Boston ◆ New York

For Bedford/St. Martin's

Executive Editor for Communication: Erika Gutierrez
Executive Developmental Editor: Simon Glick
Developmental Editor: Lai T. Moy
Editorial Assistant: Mae Klinger
Production Editor: Bill Imbornoni
Production Supervisor: Andrew Ensor
Marketing Manager: Adrienne Petsick
Art Director: Lucy Krikorian
Text Design: Claire Seng-Niemoeller
Copy Editor: Hilly van Loon
Indexer: Leoni Z. McVey
Cover Design: Donna L. Dennison
Composition: Macmillan Publishing Solutions
Printing and Binding: Quebecor World Eusey Press

President: Joan E. Feinberg
Editorial Director: Denise B. Wydra
Director of Development: Erica T. Appel
Director of Marketing: Karen R. Soeltz
Director of Editing, Design, and Production: Marcia Cohen
Assistant Director of Editing, Design, and Production: Elise S. Kaiser
Managing Editor: Shuli Traub

Library of Congress Control Number: 2009933859

Manufactured in the United States of America.

4 3 2 1 0 9
f e d c b a

For information, write: Bedford/St. Martin's, 75 Arlington Street,
Boston, MA 02116   (617-399-4000)

ISBN-10: 0-312-55404-4
ISBN-13: 978-0-312-55404-0

Acknowledgments
Acknowledgments and copyrights appear at the back of the book
on page 322, which constitutes an extension of the copyright page.

How to Use This Book

A Pocket Guide to Public Speaking, Third Edition, is designed to provide quick, clear answers to your questions about public speaking — whether you're in a public speaking class, in a course in your major, on the job, or in your community. Here, you will find the tools you need to prepare and deliver a wide range of speeches and presentations.

In Parts 1 through 6 you will find chapters covering all the steps necessary to create a speech — from planning, research, and development to organization, practice, and delivery. Chapters beginning in Part 7 contain guidelines for creating three of the most commonly assigned speeches in public speaking classes: *informative, persuasive,* and *special occasion.* For specific guidelines on speaking in other college classes, in small groups, and on the job, see Part 8.

Finding What You Need

TABLES OF CONTENTS.   Browsing through the brief table of contents inside the front cover will usually guide you to the information you need. If not, consult the more detailed table of contents included inside the back cover.

INDEX.   If you can't locate what you need in either set of contents, consult the index at the back of the book, beginning on page 323. This can be especially useful if you're looking for something specific and you know the word for it. For example, if you need to prepare a sales presentation for a business course, you could simply look under "sales presentations" in the index and then go to the designated pages.

LISTS OF FEATURES.   On pages 336–39 (just before the end of the book), you'll find a quick guide to some of the most often consulted parts of this book: the Checklists, Quick Tips, Visual Guides (illustrated explanations of key points), and full-length model speeches.

SPEAKING BEYOND THE SPEECH CLASSROOM.   In Part 8, "The Classroom and Beyond," you'll find detailed directions for speaking in a range of college classes — including courses in the social sciences, arts and humanities, education, business, science and mathematics, engineering and architecture, and nursing and allied health — plus chapters on presenting successfully as a team and communicating effectively in groups.

GLOSSARY.   For definitions of key terms highlighted in the book, see pages 290–308.

Quick Speech Preparation

If you have to prepare a speech quickly (as in giving a first speech early in the semester), consult Chapters 1–3 in *A Pocket Guide:*

* Chapter 1, "Becoming a Public Speaker," provides a brief discussion of public speaking basics.
* Chapter 2, "From A to Z: Overview of a Speech," offers quick guidance on each step in the speechmaking process, from selecting a topic to delivery.
* Chapter 3, "Managing Speech Anxiety," provides techniques that will help you overcome any fears you may have.

For more on specific types of speeches, consult Chapters 23–25 on informative, persuasive, or special occasion speeches, or the appropriate chapter in Part 8.

Other Useful Tools

CITATION GUIDELINES.   Appendix A (pp. 268–82) contains guidelines for documenting sources in the following styles: *Chicago,* American Psychological Association (APA), Modern Language Association (MLA), Council of Science Editors (CSE), and Institute of Electrical and Electronics Engineers (IEEE).

TIPS FOR NON-NATIVE SPEAKERS OF ENGLISH.   Appendix D (pp. 286–89) addresses the most common ESL challenges, including difficulty pronouncing words and problems in being understood.

Preface

A Pocket Guide to Public Speaking, Third Edition, represents our belief in offering a truly effective speech resource that is comprehensive yet brief, affordable and student friendly, with solid scholarship and an emphasis on the rhetorical tradition. This guide is designed to be useful in the widest possible range of situations, from the traditional speech classroom and courses across the curriculum to applications on the job and in the community.

In developing *A Pocket Guide,* our goal has always been to meet the needs of speech instructors who find mainstream, full-size introductory speech texts either too overwhelming or too constraining for their classes. In addition, we hope to satisfy instructors in other disciplines who want an easy and affordable tool for teaching basic presentation skills that is also manageable enough to allow them to focus on their own course material.

Happily, *A Pocket Guide to Public Speaking* seems to have struck a chord. Since the first edition published in 2003, over 150,000 instructors and students across the academic spectrum — from courses in speech and the humanities to education, engineering, and business — have embraced the book, making it the most successful pocket-size speech text available. We have used their generous feedback to create this third edition.

Features

A Pocket Guide to Public Speaking addresses all of the topics and skills typically covered in an introductory speech text. And because the book is meant to be used throughout students' academic careers and in a wide variety of classroom settings, examples are drawn from a broad range of speech situations and disciplines. Part 8, "The Classroom and Beyond," gives guidelines for creating the kinds of presentations that students are likely to deliver in their majors and on the job, and has been reorganized and streamlined in this new edition to make it even more useful. (For more information, see the "New to This Edition" section on the next page.)

Throughout the text, users will find many tools to help them focus on key public speaking concepts: charts and

tables that summarize salient points; Checklists that reinforce critical content; insightful Quick Tips that offer succinct and practical advice; Visual Guides that illustrate the
steps for accomplishing challenging speech tasks; and appen-
dices offering citation guidelines, help with question-and-
answer sessions and mediated communication, and support
for non-native speakers of English.

New to This Edition

Based on feedback from hundreds of instructors about the
challenges of teaching public and presentational speaking,
this revised third edition is designed to help students master
basic skills and apply what they learn in class from the text to
their *own* speeches.

- **Reorganized and expanded Part 1 gets students speaking effectively, right from the start.** The chapter "From A
  to Z: Overview of a Speech" has been moved up to offer
  students even more help with giving a successful speech
  early in the semester. Also moved up is the chapter "Managing Speech Anxiety," with new, concrete advice *for* students *from* students on overcoming public speaking
  jitters.

- **Three new Visual Guides.** Building on the success of the
  previous edition's four visual research guides, these new
  visual tutorials walk students through key steps in the
  speechmaking process: selecting and narrowing a topic,
  demonstrating source credibility, and incorporating
  effective transitions.

- **More on orally citing sources.** To help students accurately and effectively use supporting material in their
  speeches, the third edition offers a full new chapter on
  orally citing sources (Chapter 11) and expands coverage
  in appropriate sections throughout.

- **Three new full-text annotated sample speeches** (five
  total). New student speeches include an informative
  speech about a promising new cancer treatment and a
  persuasive speech on significant challenges facing emergency healthcare in the United States; the new professional speech is a humorous and heartwarming wedding
  toast.

- **Improved coverage of speaking beyond the speech
  classroom.** This edition includes a full new chapter on
  team presentations (Chapter 34), expanded coverage of

communicating in groups (Chapter 35), and treatment of business and professional presentations now streamlined into a single chapter (Chapter 33).

Supplements

Resources for Students

- *Speech Central* at bedfordstmartins.com/speechcentral. Here, students will find an abundance of free study tools to help them excel in class, including help with speech topics, tutorials for evaluating sources and avoiding plagiarism, exercises for speaking in other college courses, and more. In addition, students can access *VideoCentral* (described below).

- *VideoCentral: Public Speaking* at bedfordstmartins .com/speechcentral. The most extensive video offering available for the public speaking course, *VideoCentral* provides 120 brief speech clips and eighteen full student speeches that model key speech concepts. Access to *VideoCentral* also connects students with additional premium resources, including the *Bedford Speech Outliner 2.0* and the *Relaxation Audio Download*. To package *VideoCentral* with the print book at a special discount, use ISBN-10: 0-312-62184-1 or ISBN-13: 978-0-312-62184-1. Students can also purchase stand-alone access at bedfordstmartins.com/speechcentral.

- *Video Theater 3.0 Interactive CD-ROM.* This CD-ROM offers seven full student speeches — informative, persuasive, special occasion, and demonstration — with analysis and guidance for each speech, plus twenty professional speech clips. These video examples work not just as models but as powerful teaching tools. Available at a discount rate, you can package the CD-ROM with the book using ISBN-10: 0-312-62185-X, ISBN-13: 978-0-312-62185-8.

- *The Essential Guides.* These brief yet comprehensive and affordable print booklets focus on a range of topics and are designed to supplement a main text in a public speaking course. These guides are available to be packaged with *A Pocket Guide to Public Speaking* for a very low price. Versions include *The Essential Guide to Rhetoric* by William M. Keith and Christian O. Lundberg; *The Essential Guide to Presentation Software* by Allison Ainsworth and Rob Patterson; *The Essential Guide to Intercultural Communication* by Jennifer Willis-Rivera; *The Essential*

Guide to Interpersonal Communication by Dan O'Hair and Mary O. Wiemann; and *The Essential Guide to Group Communication* by Dan O'Hair and Mary O. Wiemann. For more information about packaging the *Essential Guides,* please contact your local publisher's representative or visit us online at bedfordstmartins.com/pocketspeak/catalog.

Resources for Instructors

- *Instructor's Resource Manual.* Paula Baldwin, George Mason University; Elaine Wittenberg-Lyles, University of North Texas; and Melinda M. Villagran, George Mason University. This comprehensive manual offers useful guidance for new and experienced instructors, and outlines and activities for every chapter in the main text. The manual is available for download from bedfordstmartins.com/pocketspeak/catalog.

- *Test Bank* (**print and electronic versions**). Paula Baldwin, George Mason University; Elaine Wittenberg-Lyles, University of North Texas; and Merry Buchanan, University of Central Oklahoma. **Print:** ISBN-10: 0-312-60485-8, ISBN-13: 978-0-312-60485-1. **Electronic:** ISBN-10: 0-312-60483-1, ISBN-13: 978-0-312-60483-7.

- *ESL Students in the Public Speaking Classroom: A Guide for Teachers.* Robbin Crabtree and Robert Weissberg, New Mexico State University. To request a copy, please contact your local publisher's representative.

- **Professional Speeches.** In DVD and VHS formats, multiple volumes of the Great Speeches series are available to adopters, along with more videos from the Bedford/St. Martin's Video Library.

- **Student Speeches.** Three volumes of student speeches in DVD and VHS formats. For more on receiving copies of our professional and student speech collections, please visit bedfordstmartins.com/pocketspeak or contact your local publisher's representative.

- **Content for Course Management Systems (CMS).** A variety of student and instructor resources for this textbook are ready for use in systems such as Blackboard/WebCT/Angel, Desire2Learn, and Moodle. To access CMS content, go to bfwpub.com/cms.

Acknowledgments

We would like to thank all our colleagues at Bedford/St. Martin's; we are especially grateful for the many contributions of Editor Lai T. Moy who expertly guided us through every step of this revision.

Thanks to all the instructors who participated in reviews for the third edition: Barry Antokoletz, *NYC College of Technology*; Donna Baker, *Community College of Vermont*; Karl D. Chambers, *Northern Essex Community College*; Carolyn Clark, *Salt Lake Community College, South City Campus*; Kristopher Copeland, *Florida Community College, Jacksonville*; Deborah Craig-Claar, *Metropolitan Community College, Penn Valley*; Maureen Ebben, *University of Southern Maine*; Amber Erickson, *University of Cincinnati*; Beth Eschenfelder, *University of Tampa*; Keith Forrest, *Atlantic Cape Community College*; David C. Gaer, *Laramie County Community College*; Susan Gilpin, *Marshall University*; Kent Goshorn, *Adams State College*; Lynn L. Greenky, *Syracuse University*; Nancy Jackson, *Community College of Aurora*; Kimberly Korcsmaros, *Bridgewater College*; Paul Luby, *Seminole Community College*; Scott MacLaughlin, *Cowley County Community College*; Linda Norris, *Indiana University of Pennsylvania*; Amy J. Poteet, *Ashland Community and Technical College*; Richard Shawn Queeney, *Bucks County Community College*; James W. Reed, *Glendale Community College*; Holly J. Susi, *Community College of Rhode Island*; Paula Marie Usrey, *Umpqua Community College*; Gretchen Weber, *Horry-Georgetown Technical College*; Dennis Wemm, *Glenville State College*.

Part 1
Getting Started

1 Becoming a Public Speaker

Whether in the classroom, workplace, or community, the ability to speak confidently and convincingly before an audience is empowering. This pocket guide offers the tools you need to create and deliver effective speeches, from brief presentations to fellow students, co-workers, or fellow citizens to major addresses. Here you will discover the basic building blocks of any good speech and acquire the skills to deliver presentations in a variety of specialized contexts—from the college psychology class to business and professional situations.

Gain a Vital Life Skill

The ability to speak confidently and convincingly in public is a valuable asset to anyone who wants to take an active role in the world. Now, more than ever, public speaking has become both a vital life skill and a secret weapon in career development.[1] Recruiters of top graduate school students report that what distinguishes the most sought-after candidates is not their "hard" knowledge of finance or physics, but the "soft skills" of communication.[2] Dozens of surveys of managers and executives reveal that ability in oral and written communication is the most important skill they look for in a college graduate. In a recent survey of employers, for example, oral communication skills ranked first in such critical areas as teamwork, interpersonal competence, and analytical skills.

SKILLS EMPLOYERS SEEK
1. Communication skills (verbal and written)
2. Strong work ethic
3. Teamwork skills (works well with others)
4. Initiative
5. Interpersonal skills (relates well to others)

Source: Job Outlook 2009, a survey conducted by the National Association of Colleges and Employers, 2009.

Learn Practical and Transferable Knowledge

Perhaps more than any other course of study, public speaking offers extraordinarily useful practical knowledge and skills that lead to satisfying personal and professional development. For example, public-speaking training sharpens your ability to reason and think critically. As you study public speaking, you will learn to construct claims and then present evidence and reasoning that logically support them.

As you practice organizing and outlining speeches, you will become skilled at structuring ideas and identifying and strengthening the weak links in your thinking. These skills are valuable in any course that includes an oral-presentation component, from engineering to art history, or in any course that requires writing, researching topics, analyzing audiences, supporting and proving claims, and selecting patterns for organizing ideas. These skills will also serve you well throughout your career and beyond.

QUICK TIP

Public Speaking Leads to Career Success

According to a report titled What Students Must Know to Succeed in the 21st Century, *"Clear communication is critical to success. In the marketplace of ideas, the person who communicates clearly is also the person who is seen as thinking clearly. Oral and written communication are not only job-securing, but job-holding skills."*[3]

Find New Opportunities for Engagement

While public speaking skills contribute to both career advancement and personal enrichment, they also offer you ways to enter the public conversation about social concerns and become a more engaged citizen.

Climate change, energy, social security, immigration reform—such large civic issues require our considered judgment and action. Yet today too many of us leave it up to politicians, journalists, and other "experts" to make decisions about critical issues such as these. Today, only about 35 percent of people in the United States regularly vote. When citizens speak up in sufficient numbers, change occurs. Leaving problems such as pollution and global warming to others, on the other hand, is an invitation to special interest groups who may or may not act with our best interests in mind.

As you study public speaking, you will have the opportunity to research topics that are meaningful to you, consider alternate viewpoints, and if appropriate, choose a course of action.[4] You will learn to distinguish between argument that advances constructive goals and uncivil speech that serves merely to inflame and demean others. You will learn, in short, the "rules of engagement" for effective public discourse.[5]

Build on Familiar Skills

Learning to speak in public can be less daunting when you realize that you can draw on related skills that you already have. In several respects, for example, planning and delivering a speech resemble engaging in a particularly important conversation. When speaking with a friend, you automatically check to make certain you are understood and then adjust your meaning accordingly. You also tend to discuss issues that are appropriate to the circumstances. When a relative stranger is involved, however, you try to get to know his or her interests and attitudes before revealing any strong opinions. These instinctive adjustments to your audience, topic, and occasion represent critical steps in creating a speech. Although public speaking requires more planning, both the conversationalist and the public speaker try to uncover the audience's interests and needs before speaking.

Preparing a speech also has much in common with writing. Both depend on having a focused sense of who the audience is.[6] Both speaking and writing often require that you research a topic, offer credible evidence, employ effective transitions to signal the logical flow of ideas, and devise persuasive appeals. The principles of organizing a speech parallel those of organizing an essay, including offering a compelling introduction, a clear thesis statement, supporting ideas, and a thoughtful conclusion.

Develop an Effective Oral Style

Although public speaking has much in common with everyday conversation and with writing, it is, obviously, "its own thing." More so than writers, successful speakers generally use familiar terms, easy-to-follow sentences, and transitional words and phrases. Speakers also routinely repeat key words and phrases to emphasize ideas and help listeners follow along; even the briefest speeches make frequent use of repetition.

Spoken language is often more interactive and inclusive of the audience than written language. The personal pronouns *we*, *I*, and *you* occur more frequently in spoken than in written text. Audience members want to know what the speaker thinks and feels and that he or she recognizes them and relates the message to them. Yet, because public speaking usually occurs in more formal settings than everyday conversation, listeners generally expect a more formal style of communication from the speaker. When you give a speech, listeners expect you to speak in a clear, recognizable, and organized fashion. Thus, in contrast to conversation, in order to develop an effective oral style you must practice the words you will say and the way you will say them.

Become an Inclusive Speaker

Every audience member wants to feel that the speaker has his or her particular needs and interests at heart, and to feel recognized and included in the message. To create this sense of inclusion, a public speaker must be able to address diverse audiences with sensitivity. No matter how passionately they believe in an issue, our most admired public speakers strive to respect differing viewpoints. When planning and delivering their speeches, they try to take audience members' sensitivities related to culture, ethnicity, gender, age, disability, and other relevant characteristics into account.

Striving for inclusion and adopting an audience-centered perspective throughout will bring you closer to the goal of every public speaker—establishing a genuine connection with the audience.

Public Speaking as a Form of Communication

Public speaking is one of four categories of human communication: dyadic, small group, mass, and public speaking. **Dyadic communication** happens between two people, as in a conversation. **Small group communication** involves a small number of people who can see and speak directly with one another. **Mass communication** occurs between a speaker and a large audience of unknown people who usually are not present with the speaker, or who are part of such an immense crowd that there can be little or no interaction between speaker and listener.

In **public speaking**, a speaker delivers a message with a specific purpose to an audience of people who are present during the delivery of the speech. Public speaking always includes a speaker who has a reason for speaking, an audience that gives the speaker its attention, and a message that is meant to accomplish a specific purpose.[7] Public speakers address audiences largely without interruption and take responsibility for the words and ideas being expressed.

Shared Elements in All Communication Events

In any communication event, including public speaking, several elements are present. These include the source, the receiver, the message, the channel, and shared meaning (see Figure 1.1).

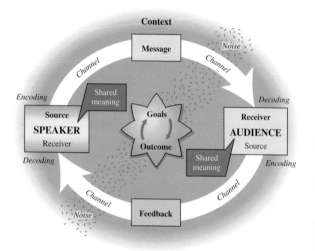

FIGURE 1.1 The Communication Process

The **source**, or sender, is the person who creates a message. Creating, organizing, and producing the message is called **encoding**—the process of converting thoughts into words.

The recipient of the source's message is the **receiver**, or audience. The process of interpreting the message is called **decoding**. Audience members decode the meaning of the message selectively, based on their own experiences and attitudes. **Feedback**, the audience's response to a message, can be conveyed both verbally and nonverbally.

The **message** is the content of the communication process: thoughts and ideas put into meaningful expressions, expressed verbally and nonverbally.

The medium through which the speaker sends a message is the **channel**. If a speaker is delivering a message in front of a live audience, the channel is the air through which sound waves travel. Other channels include the telephone, television, computers, and written correspondence. **Noise** is any interference with the message. Noise can disrupt the communication process through physical sounds such as cell phones ringing and people talking, through psychological distractions such as heated emotions, or through environmental interference such as a frigid room or the presence of unexpected people.

Shared meaning is the mutual understanding of a message between speaker and audience. The lowest level of shared meaning exists when the speaker has merely caught the audience's attention. As the message develops, a higher degree of shared meaning is possible. Thus listener and speaker together truly make a speech a speech—they "co-create" its meaning.

Two other factors are critical to consider when preparing and delivering a speech—context and goals. **Context** includes anything that influences the speaker, the audience, the occasion—and thus, ultimately, the speech. In classroom speeches, the context would include (among other things) recent events on campus or in the outside world, the physical setting, the order and timing of speeches, and the cultural orientations of audience members. Successful communication can never be divorced from the concerns and expectations of others.

Part of the context of any speech is the situation that created the need for it in the first place. All speeches are delivered in response to a specific **rhetorical situation**, or a circumstance calling for a public response.[8] Bearing the context and rhetorical situation in mind ensures that you remain **audience centered**—that is, that you keep the needs, values, attitudes, and wants of your listeners firmly in focus.

A clearly defined *speech purpose* or goal is a final prerequisite for an effective speech. What is it that you want the audience to learn or do or believe as a result of your speech? Establishing a speech purpose early in the speechmaking process will help you proceed through speech preparation and delivery with a clear focus in mind.

The Classical Roots of Public Speaking

Originally the practice of giving speeches was known as **rhetoric** (also called **oratory**). Rhetoric flourished in the Greek city-state of Athens in the fifth century B.C.E. and referred to making effective speeches, particularly those of a persuasive nature.

Athens was the site of the world's first direct democracy, and its citizens used their considerable skill in public speaking to enact it. Meeting in a public square called the **agora**, the Athenians routinely spoke with great proficiency on the issues of public policy, and to this day their belief that citizenship demands active participation in public affairs endures. Later, in the Roman republic (the Western world's first-known representative democracy), citizens spoke in a public space called a **forum**.

From the beginning, public speakers, notably Aristotle (384–322 B.C.E.), and later, the Roman statesman and orator

Cicero (106–43 B.C.E.), divided the process of preparing a speech into five parts, called the **canons of rhetoric**. *Invention* refers to adapting speech information to the audience in order to make your case. *Arrangement* is organizing the speech in ways best suited to the topic and audience. **Style** is the way the speaker uses language to express the speech ideas. *Memory* and **delivery** are the methods of rehearsing and presenting the speech so that you achieve the most effective blend of content, voice, and nonverbal behavior.

Although such founding scholars as Aristotle and Cicero surely didn't anticipate the omnipresent PowerPoint slideshow that accompanies contemporary speeches, the speechmaking structure they bequeathed to us as the canons of rhetoric remain remarkably intact. Often identified by terms other than the original, these canons nonetheless continue to be taught in current books on public speaking, including this pocket guide.

QUICK TIP

Voice Your Ideas in a Public Forum

The Greeks called it the agora; the Romans the forum. Today, the term **public forum** *denotes a variety of venues for the discussion of issues of public interest, including traditional physical spaces such as town halls as well as virtual forums streamed to listeners online. Participation in forums offers an excellent opportunity to pose questions and deliver brief comments, thereby providing exposure to an audience and building confidence. To find a forum in your area, check with your school or local town government, or check online at sites such as the National Issues Forum (www.nifi.org/index.aspx).*

---

2   From A to Z: Overview of a Speech

Novice speakers in any circumstances, whether at school, at work, or in the community, will benefit from preparing and delivering a first short speech. An audience of as few as two people will suffice to test the waters and help you gain confidence in your ability to "stand up and deliver."

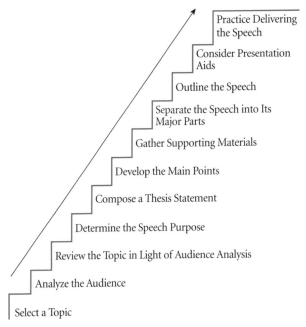

Practice Delivering the Speech

Consider Presentation Aids

Outline the Speech

Separate the Speech into Its Major Parts

Gather Supporting Materials

Develop the Main Points

Compose a Thesis Statement

Determine the Speech Purpose

Review the Topic in Light of Audience Analysis

Analyze the Audience

Select a Topic

FIGURE 2.1 Steps in the Speechmaking Process

This chapter presents a brief overview of the process of preparing a first speech or presentation (see Figure 2.1). Subsequent chapters expand on these steps.

Select a Topic

The first step in creating a speech involves finding something to speak about. Unless the topic is assigned, let your interests—your passions—be your guide. What deeply engages you? What are your areas of expertise? Your hobbies? Be aware, however, that even though personal interest is important, *your topic must be of interest to the audience.* Selecting an appropriate topic requires knowledge of who is in the audience and what their interests are.

Analyze the Audience

Audiences have personalities, interests, and opinions all their own, and these factors will determine how receptive an audience will be toward a given topic. You must therefore learn all you can about your audience—what they share in common, and what may divide them.

Audience analysis is a systematic process of getting to know your listeners. It involves studying the audience through techniques such as interviews and questionnaires (see Chapter 6). For a brief speech, consider some general variables:

- Begin with some fairly easily identifiable *demographic characteristics*: the ratio of males to females; racial and ethnic differences represented in the group; noticeable age variations; and the proportion of the group that is from out of state or from another country.

- Consider how different people (e.g., older and younger, men and women, international and native-born) might think or feel differently about your topic.

Determine the Speech Purpose

Decide what you wish to convey about your topic and why. For any given topic, you should direct your speech toward one of three *general speech purposes*—to *inform*, to *persuade*, or to *mark a special occasion*.

An **informative speech** provides an audience with new information, new insights, or new ways of thinking about a topic. Its general purpose is to increase the audience's awareness by imparting knowledge. Sample topics might include trends in video gaming or advances in electric cars.

A **persuasive speech** intends to influence the attitudes, beliefs, values, or acts of others. For example, a speaker might attempt to convince listeners that state universities should not charge tuition or argue that the child foster-care system is in disarray.

A **special occasion speech** (also called *ceremonial* speech) marks a special event, such as a wedding, funeral, commencement, or banquet. This type of speech can be either informative or persuasive and is often a mix of both. However, depending on the occasion, its underlying purpose is to entertain, celebrate, commemorate, inspire, or set a social agenda.

Your speech should also have a *specific purpose*—a single phrase—usually left unsaid in the speech itself—stating specifically what you expect the speech to accomplish:

- If the general speech purpose about campus security is *to inform*, the specific purpose might be "to inform the audience of how the administration plans to implement its new safety and security measures this fall."

- If the general speech purpose about campus security is *to persuade*, the specific purpose might be "to persuade the audience that the administration's safety and security measures are inadequate to address current threats."

Compose a Thesis Statement

Next, compose a thesis statement that clearly expresses the central idea of your speech. While the specific purpose focuses your attention on what *you* want to achieve with the speech, the *thesis statement* concisely identifies for your audience, in a single sentence, what the speech is about:

GENERAL PURPOSE:	To inform
SPECIFIC PURPOSE:	To inform my audience about the privacy policy of the social networking site Facebook.
THESIS STATEMENT:	Facebook collects a wide variety of information about its users, and utilizes it for diverse and some times surprising purposes.

Wherever you are in the planning stage, always refer to the thesis statement to make sure that you are on track to illustrate or prove the central idea of your speech.

Develop the Main Points

Organize your speech around two or three *main points*. These points are your primary pieces of knowledge (in an informative speech) or your key arguments (in a persuasive speech). If you create a clear thesis statement for your speech the main points will be easily identifiable, if not explicit:

THESIS: Rather than censorship, concerns about the potential for clogging its computer system drove the U.S. military's decision to block service members from accessing YouTube, MySpace, and ten other popular sites.

    I. The military based their selection of sites to block on highest-volume use.

    II. In key war zones, limited infrastructure reduces the amount of bandwidth that is available to the military's network.

    III. Most deployed forces can still access the blocked sites using commercial Internet cafes and providers.

Gather Supporting Materials

Supporting materials illustrate speech points by clarifying, elaborating, and verifying your ideas. They include the entire world of information available to you—from personal experiences to every conceivable kind of print and electronic source. A speech is only as good as its supporting materials, which provide evidence for your assertions and lend credibility to your message (see Chapters 9–11).

Separate the Speech into Its Major Parts

Every speech has three major parts: *introduction, body*, and *conclusion*. Develop each part separately, then bring them together using transition statements (see Chapter 12).

The *introduction* serves to introduce the topic and the speaker and to alert the audience to your specific speech purpose. A good introduction should catch the audience's attention and interest (see Chapter 15). Just like the body of a written essay, the speech *body* contains the speech's main points and subpoints, all of which support the speech's thesis. The *conclusion* restates the speech purpose and reiterates how the main points confirm it (see Chapter 15).

MAJOR SPEECH PARTS
INTRODUCTION
• Arouse the audience's attention with a quotation, short story, example, or other kind of attention-getting device.
• Introduce the topic and purpose of the speech.
• Preview the main points.
• Use a transition to signal the start of the speech body.
BODY
• Clearly state the thesis.
• Develop the main points using a structure that suits the topic, audience, and occasion.
• Use a transition to signal the conclusion.
CONCLUSION
• Restate the thesis and reiterate how the main points confirm it.
• Leave the audience with something to think about or challenge them to respond.
• Be prepared to answer questions.

Outline the Speech

An outline provides the framework upon which to arrange main points in support of your thesis and subordinate points in support of your main points. Outlines are based on the principle of *coordination and subordination*—the logical placement of ideas relative to their importance to one another. *Coordinate points* are of equal importance and are indicated by their parallel alignment. *Subordinate points* are given less weight than the main points they support and are placed to the right of the points they support. (For a full discussion of outlining, see Chapters 12 and 14.)

COORDINATE POINTS

I. Main Point 1

II. Main Point 2

SUBORDINATE POINTS

1. Main Point 1
    A. First level of subordination
        1. Second level of subordination
        2. Second level of subordination
            a. Third level of subordination
            b. Third level of subordination

As your speeches become more involved, you will need to select an appropriate *organizational pattern* (see Chapter 13). You will also need to familiarize yourself with developing both working and speaking outlines (see Chapter 14). *Working outlines* contain points stated in complete sentences, whereas *speaking outlines* (also called "presentation outlines") are far briefer and use either short phrases or key words. Speaking outlines are printed out on separate sheets or written on 4" × 6" index cards for use during the speech.

Consider Presentation Aids

Presentation aids that summarize and highlight information, such as charts and graphs, often can help the audience retain ideas and understand difficult concepts. They also can provide dramatic emphasis that listeners will find memorable (see Chapter 20).

Practice Delivering the Speech

The success of any speech depends on how well prepared and practiced you are. So practice your speech—often. It has been suggested that a good speech is practiced at least six times. For a four- to six-minute speech, that's only thirty to forty minutes (figuring in restarts and pauses) of actual practice time.

Vocal Delivery

Vocal delivery includes speech volume, pitch, rate, variety, pronunciation, and articulation. As you rehearse, do the following:

- Pay attention to how loudly or softly you are speaking.
- Pay attention to the rate at which you speak. Aim to speak neither too fast nor too slowly.
- Avoid speaking in a monotone.
- Decide how you want to phrase your statements, and then practice saying them.
- Pronounce words correctly and clearly.

Nonverbal Delivery

Beyond noticing the words of a speech, audiences are highly attuned to a speaker's nonverbal speech behavior—facial expression, gestures, general body movement, and overall physical appearance. As you rehearse, do the following:

- Practice smiling and otherwise animating your face in ways that feel natural to you. Audiences want to feel that you care about what you are saying, so avoid a deadpan, or blank, expression.
- Practice making eye contact with your listeners. Doing so will make audience members feel that you recognize and respect them.
- Practice gestures that feel natural to you, steering clear of exaggerated movements.

3   Managing Speech Anxiety

Everyone, even the most experienced speakers, often feel jittery before they give a speech. According to one study, at least 75 percent of students in public-speaking courses approach the course with anxiety.[1] It turns out that feeling nervous is not only normal but desirable! Channeled properly, nervousness may actually boost performance.

The difference between seasoned public speakers and the rest of us is that the seasoned speakers know how to make their nervousness work *for* rather than *against* them. They use specific techniques, described in this chapter, to help them cope with and minimize their tension.

> I focus on the information. I try not to think about being graded. I also practice my speech a ton to really make sure I do not speak too quickly. I time myself so that I can develop an average time. This makes me more confident [in dealing] with time requirements. And, because I know that I am well prepared, I really try to just relax.
> — *Kristen Obracay, student*

Identify What Makes You Anxious

Lacking positive public-speaking experience, feeling different from members of the audience, or feeling uneasy about being the center of attention—each of these factors can lead to the onset of **public-speaking anxiety,** that is, fear or anxiety associated with either actual or anticipated communication to an audience as a speaker.[2] Identifying at which stage you become anxious can help you lessen your fear.

Lack of Positive Experience

If you have had no exposure to public speaking or have had unpleasant experiences, anxiety about what to expect is only natural. And with no positive experience to fall back on, it's hard to put these anxieties in perspective. It's a bit of a vicious circle. Some people react by deciding to avoid making speeches altogether. Although they avoid the anxiety of speechmaking, they also lose out on the considerable rewards it brings.

Feeling Different

Novice speakers often feel alone—as if they were the only person ever to experience the dread of public speaking. The prospect of getting up in front of an audience makes them extra-sensitive to their personal idiosyncrasies, such as having a less-than-perfect haircut or an accent. Novice speakers may think that no one could possibly be interested in anything they have to say.

As inexperienced speakers, we become anxious because we assume that being different somehow means being inferior. Actually, everyone is different from everyone else in many ways. And, just as true, nearly everyone experiences nervousness about giving a speech.

> I control my anxiety by mentally viewing myself as being
> 100 percent equal to my classmates.
>
> —*Lee Morris, student*

Being the Center of Attention

Certain audience behaviors—such as lack of eye contact
with the speaker or conversing with a neighbor—can be dis-
concerting. Our tendency in these situations is to think we
must be doing something wrong; we wonder what it is and
whether the entire audience has noticed it.

Left unchecked, this kind of thinking can distract us
from the speech itself, with all our attention now focused
on "me." As we focus on "me," we become all the more sensitive to things that might be wrong with what we're
doing—and that makes us feel even more conspicuous,
which increases our anxiety! In fact, an audience generally
notices very little about us that we don't want to reveal,
especially if our speeches are well developed and effectively
delivered.

> It's always scary to speak in front of others, but you just have
> to remember that everyone's human. . . . Nobody wants you
> to fail; they're not waiting on you to mess up.
>
> —*Mary Parrish, student*

Pinpoint the Onset of Nervousness

Different people become anxious at different times during
the speechmaking process. Depending on when it strikes, the
consequences of public-speaking anxiety can include everything from procrastination to poor speech performance. But
by pinpointing the onset of speech anxiety, you can address
it promptly with specific anxiety-reducing techniques (see
strategies to boost confidence on pp. 18–20).

Pre-preparation Anxiety

Some people feel anxious the minute they know they will be
giving a speech. **Pre-preparation anxiety** at this early stage
can have several negative consequences, from reluctance to
begin planning for the speech to becoming so preoccupied
with anxiety that they miss vital information necessary to
fulfill the speech assignment. If this form of anxiety affects
you, use the stress-reducing techniques described in this
chapter early on in the process.

Preparation Anxiety

For a minority of people, anxiety arises only when they actually begin to prepare for the speech. At that point, they might feel overwhelmed at the amount of time and planning required. They might hit a roadblock that puts them behind schedule, or be unable to locate support for a critical point. These kinds of preparation pressures produce a cycle of stress, procrastination, and outright avoidance. All contribute to **preparation anxiety**. If you find yourself feeling anxious during this stage, defuse the anxiety by taking short, relaxing breaks.

Pre-performance Anxiety

Some people experience anxiety when they rehearse their speech. At this point, the reality of the situation sets in: Soon they will face an audience of people who will be watching and listening only to them. As they rehearse, they might also realize that their ideas don't sound as focused or as interesting as they should. Knowing that time is short, they begin to get nervous. If this **pre-performance anxiety** is strong enough and is interpreted negatively, they might even decide to stop rehearsing.

> I got really scared the first time I rehearsed my last presentation—it just didn't seem interesting enough. I spent a few hours trying to strengthen it and make it more interesting, then I rehearsed again. The second time around felt much better, and the speech went well.
> —*Hallie Klein, student*

Performance Anxiety

For the majority of people, anxiety levels tend to be highest just before they begin speaking.[3] This is true even of actors, who report that their worst stage fright occurs just as they walk on stage to begin their performances. **Performance anxiety** in speechmaking is probably most pronounced during the introduction phase, when we utter the first words of the speech and are most aware of the audience's attention. As might be expected, audiences we perceive as hostile or negative usually cause us to feel more anxious than those we sense are positive or neutral.[4] However, experienced speakers agree that if they control their nervousness during the introduction, the rest of the speech will come relatively easily.

Regardless of when anxiety about a speech strikes, the important thing to remember is to manage your anxiety and not let it manage you—by harming your motivation, or by causing you to avoid investing the time and energy required to prepare and deliver a successful speech.

Use Proven Strategies to Boost Your Confidence

A number of proven strategies exist to help you rein in your fears about public speaking, from meditation and visualization to other forms of relaxation techniques. The first step in taming speech anxiety is to have a clear and thorough plan for each presentation.

Prepare and Practice

If you are confident that you know your material and have adequately rehearsed your delivery, you'll feel far more confident in front of an audience than otherwise. Preparation should begin as soon as possible after a speech is assigned. Once you have prepared the speech, be sure to rehearse it several times.

QUICK TIP

Rehearse to Build Confidence
Making progress on any task increases confidence. Preparing your speech in advance will lessen your nervousness considerably. Remember, just as sitting around wishing you were in better physical shape won't firm you up, merely wishing your speech will be a success won't make it so. To ensure a positive result, prepare the speech well in advance and rehearse it several times.

Modify Thoughts and Attitudes

Negative thoughts about speechmaking increase speech anxiety.[5] A positive attitude, on the other hand, actually results in lowered heart rate and reduced anxiety during the delivery of the speech.[6] As you prepare for and deliver your speech, regard it as a valuable, worthwhile, and challenging activity. Remind yourself of all the reasons that public speaking is helpful personally, socially, and professionally. Think positively about public speaking, and remind yourself that it is an opportunity toward, not a threat to, personal growth.

Just before a speech those feelings of anxiety undoubtedly try to sneak in. The way I keep them from taking over is to not let my mind become negative. As long as I keep positive thoughts of confidence in my head, anxiety doesn't stand a chance!

—*Morgan Verdery, student*

QUICK TIP

Envision Your Speech as a Conversation
Altering your thinking about public speaking from a "performance" to a "communication" can significantly increase confidence.[7] Try thinking of your speech as an extension of an ordinary conversation. Doing so might help you feel more relaxed about the process, and with each successive speech experience, your attitude toward public speaking will grow more positive.

Visualize Success

Visualization is a highly effective way to reduce nervousness.[8] The following is a script for visualizing success on a public speaking occasion. This exercise requires you to close your eyes and visualize a series of positive feelings and reactions that will occur on the day of the speech.

Close your eyes and allow your body to get comfortable in the chair in which you are sitting. Take a deep, comfortable breath and hold it . . . now slowly release it through your nose. Now take another deep breath and make certain that you are breathing from the diaphragm . . . hold it . . . now slowly release it and note how you feel while doing this. Now one more deep breath . . . hold it . . . and release it slowly . . . and begin your normal breathing pattern.

Now begin to visualize the beginning of a day in which you are going to give an informative speech. See yourself getting up in the morning, full of energy, full of confidence, looking forward to the day's challenges. You are putting on just the right clothes for the task at hand that day. Dressing well makes you look and feel good about yourself, so you have on just what you want to wear, which clearly expresses your sense of inner well-being. As you are driving, riding, or walking to the speech setting, note how clear and confident you feel, and how others around you, as you arrive, comment positively regarding your fine appearance and general demeanor. You feel thoroughly prepared for the target issue you will be presenting today.

Now you see yourself standing or sitting in the room where you will present your speech, talking very comfortably and confidently with others in the room. The people to whom you will be presenting your speech appear to be quite friendly and are very cordial in their greetings and conversations prior to the presentation. You feel absolutely sure of your material and of your ability to present the information in a forceful, convincing, positive manner.

Now you see yourself approaching the area from which you will present. You are feeling very good about this presentation and see yourself move eagerly forward. All of your audiovisual materials are well organized, well planned, and clearly aid your presentation.[9]

Activate the Relaxation Response

Before, during, and sometimes after a speech you may experience rapid heart rate and breathing, dry mouth, faintness, freezing-up, or other uncomfortable sensations. These are automatic physiological reactions that result from the "fight-or-flight" response. Research shows that you can counteract these sensations by activating the relaxation response[10] using techniques such as meditation and controlled breathing.

Briefly Meditate

You can calm yourself considerably with this brief meditation exercise:

1. Sit comfortably in a quiet space.
2. Relax your muscles, moving from neck to shoulders to arms to back to legs.
3. Choose a word, phrase, or prayer that is connected to your belief system (e.g., "Namaste," "Om," "Hail Mary Full of Grace"). Breathe slowly and say it until you become calm (about ten to twenty minutes).

Use Stress-Control Breathing

When you feel stressed, the center of your breathing tends to move from the abdomen to the upper chest, leaving you with a reduced supply of air. The chest and shoulders rise, and you feel out of breath. With *stress-control breathing*,[11] you will feel more movement in the stomach than in the chest. Try stress-control breathing in two stages.

STAGE ONE   Inhale air and let your abdomen go out. Exhale air and let your abdomen go in. Do this for a while until you get into the rhythm of it.

STAGE TWO   As you inhale, use a soothing word such as "calm" or "relax," or use a personal mantra, such as the following: "Inhale calm, abdomen out, exhale calm, abdomen in." Go slowly. Each inhalation and exhalation of stress-control breathing takes about three to five seconds.

Start stress-control breathing *several days* before you're scheduled to speak. Then, once the speaking event arrives, use it while you wait your turn and just before you start your speech.

> I have two ways to cope with my nervousness before I'm about to speak. I draw a couple of deep breaths from my stomach; I breathe in through my nose and out through my mouth. This allows more oxygen to the brain so you can think clearly. I also calm myself down by saying, "Everything will be okay, and the world is not going to crumble before me if I mess up."
>
> —*Jenna Sanford, student*

QUICK TIP

Stretch Away Stress
You can significantly lessen pre-speech jitters by stretching. A half-hour to one-hour session of whole body stretches and Yoga poses, combined with deep breathing, will help discharge nervous energy.

Use Movement to Minimize Anxiety

During delivery, you can use controlled movements with your hands and body to release nervousness.

Practice Natural Gestures

Practice some controlled, natural gestures that might be useful in enhancing your speech, such as holding up your index finger when stating your first main point. Think about what you want to say as you do this, instead of thinking about how you look or feel. (See Chapter 19 for tips on practicing natural gestures.)

Move as You Speak

You don't have to stand perfectly still behind the podium when you deliver a speech. Walk around as you make some of your points. Movement relieves tension and helps hold the audience's attention.

QUICK TIP

Seek Pleasure in the Occasion
Most people ultimately find that giving speeches can indeed be fun. It's satisfying and empowering to influence people, and a good speech is a sure way to do this. Think of giving a speech in this way, and chances are you will find pleasure in it.

Learn from Feedback

When you've finished your speech, welcome feedback as an opportunity to do even better next time. Although you can learn a great deal from your own evaluation, research suggests you can learn even more from the objective evaluations of others.[12] Feedback is given in the spirit of helping you to present your speech to the best of your ability.

 CHECKLIST: Steps in Gaining Confidence

Prepare and practice often.

✓ Modify thoughts and attitudes—think positively.

✓ Accept your nervousness as normal—work with it rather than against it.

✓ Concentrate on your message, not on yourself.

✓ Visualize success.

✓ Breathe deeply and stretch.

✓ Use mind-focusing and relaxation techniques.

✓ Seek pleasure in the occasion.

✓ Learn from your experience.

4   Ethical Public Speaking

When we have an audience's attention, we are in a unique position to influence or persuade listeners and, at times, to move them to act—for better *or* worse. With this power to affect the minds and hearts of others comes *responsibility*— "a charge, trust, or duty for which one is accountable."[1] Taking responsibility for your message lies at the heart of being an ethical speaker.

Earn Your Listeners' Trust

Ethics is derived from the Greek word **ethos**, meaning "character." As Aristotle first noted so long ago, audiences listen to and trust speakers if they demonstrate *positive ethos*, or good character. Speakers in Ancient Greece were regarded positively if they were well prepared, honest, and respectful toward their audience. Today, surprisingly little has changed. Modern research on **speaker credibility** reveals that people place their greatest trust in speakers who:

- Have a solid grasp of the subject.
- Display sound reasoning skills.
- Are honest and unmanipulative.
- Are genuinely interested in the welfare of their listeners.[2]

Respect Audience Values

Our ethical conduct is a reflection of our *values*—our most enduring judgments or standards of what's good and bad in life, of what's important to us. Like the individuals who hold them, values can conflict and clash. The more diverse the society, the greater these conflicts tend to be. One only has to think of the so-called *values divide* in the United States between "red states" (representing conservative values) and "blue states" (representing liberal values).

Conflicting values make it difficult to speak about certain topics without challenging cherished beliefs. The United States is a country of immigrants, for example, but half of the population with only a high school education believe that immigrants threaten traditional U.S. values, while only a quarter of college-educated Americans agree.[3] As you prepare speeches on controversial topics, anticipate that audience members will hold a range of values that will differ not only from your own, but from each other's. Demonstrate respect for your audience's values, even when you do not share them. (See Chapter 6 on identifying audience members' values.)

Use Your Rights of Free Speech Responsibly

Codes of ethical speech are built on moral rather than legal principles. Thus the **First Amendment**, which guarantees freedom of speech, assures protection both to speakers who treat the truth with respect and to those whose words are inflammatory and offensive.

Though often legally protected, racist, sexist, homophobic, pornographic, and other forms of negative speech clearly are unethical and should be avoided at all cost. *Be aware that certain types of speech are actually illegal:*

- Speech that provokes people to violence ("incitement" or "fighting words")
- Speech that can be proved to be **defamatory,** or that potentially harms an individual's reputation at work or in the community
- Speech that invades a person's privacy, such as disclosing information about an individual that is not in the public record.

How can you tell if your speech contains defamatory language? If you are talking about public figures or matters of public concern, you will not be legally liable unless it can be shown that you spoke with a **reckless disregard for the truth**—that is, if you knew that what you were saying was false but said it anyway. If your comments refer to private persons, it will be easier for them to assert a claim for defamation. You will have the burden of proving that what you said was true.[4]

Contribute to Positive Public Discourse

An important measure of ethical speaking is whether it contributes something positive to **public discourse**—speech involving issues of importance to the larger community, such as the need to implement green practices on campus or to take action to slow climate change.

Perhaps the most important contribution you can make to public debates of this nature is the *advancement of constructive goals.* An ethical speech appeals to the greater good rather than narrow self-interest. It steers clear of **invective,** or verbal attacks designed to unfairly discredit, demean, and belittle those with whom you disagree. Ethical speakers avoid arguments that target a person instead of the issue at hand (*ad hominem* attack) or that are built upon other fallacies of reasoning (see Chapter 24).

QUICK TIP

Follow the Rules of Engagement

Verbal attacks, irrational arguments, and other so-called **conversation stoppers** *breach the acceptable "rules of engagement" for public conversations. Originally used as a military term to describe how soldiers may use their weapons, the concept can also be applied to the ways we relate to one another in the public arena. Here, the* **rules of engagement** *oblige us to "speak the truth, to disclose one's purposes, to respond to others, to listen, and to understand."*[5]

Observe Ethical Ground Rules

Whether your speech focuses on a sensitive social issue or a dispassionate, factual matter, follow these ground rules for ethical speaking.

The qualities of *dignity* and *integrity* should infuse every aspect of a speech. **Dignity** refers to ensuring that listeners feel worthy, honored, or respected as individuals.[6] **Integrity** signals the speaker's incorruptibility—that he or she will avoid compromising the truth for the sake of personal expediency.[7]

Speaking ethically also requires that we adhere to certain "pillars of character."[8] These include being *trustworthy*, *respectful, responsible*, and *fair* in our presentations.

Trustworthiness is a combination of honesty and dependability. It includes revealing your true purpose to your audience—and not sacrificing the truth to it. Trustworthy speakers don't offer misleading, deceptive, or false information.

Respect is demonstrated by addressing audience members as unique human beings and refraining from any form of personal attack. The respectful speaker focuses on issues rather than on personalities and allows the audience the power of rational choice.

Responsibility means being accountable for what you say. For example, will learning about your topic in some way benefit listeners? Do you use sound evidence and reasoning? Do you offer emotional appeals because they are appropriate rather than to shore up otherwise weak arguments?

Fairness refers to making a genuine effort to see all sides of an issue and acknowledging the information listeners need in order to make informed decisions.[9] Few subjects are black and white; rarely is there only one right or wrong way to view a topic.

Avoid Offensive Speech

To be an ethical speaker, you must scrupulously avoid expressions of ethnocentrism, stereotypes, or outright prejudice. **Hate speech** is any offensive communication—verbal or nonverbal—that is directed against people's racial, ethnic, religious, gender, or other characteristics. This kind of speech is never acceptable.

CHECKLIST: An Ethical Inventory

✓ Have you distorted any information to make your point?

✓ Have you acknowledged each of your sources?

✓ Does your speech focus on issues rather than on personalities?

✓ Have you tried to foster a sense of inclusion?

✓ Is your topic socially constructive?

✓ Do any of your arguments contain fallacies of reasoning? (see pp. 197–199)

✓ Is the content of your message as accurate as you can make it?

✓ Do you avoid speech that demeans those with whom you disagree?

Avoid Plagiarism

Crediting sources is a crucial aspect of any speech. **Plagiarism**—the passing off of another person's information as one's own—is as unethical in a speech as it is elsewhere. To plagiarize is to use other people's ideas or words without acknowledging the source. You are obviously plagiarizing when you simply "cut and paste" material from sources into your speech and represent it as your own. But it is also plagiarism to copy material into your speech draft from a source and then change and rearrange words and sentence structure here and there to make it appear as if it were your own.[10] Whether it's done intentionally or not, plagiarism is stealing.

Orally Acknowledge Your Sources

The rule for avoiding plagiarism as a public speaker is straightforward: *Any source that requires credit in written form should be acknowledged in oral form.* These sources include direct quotations, as well as paraphrased and summarized information—any facts and statistics, ideas, opinions, theories, gathered and reported by others. The source of any information that was not gathered by you should always be cited in your speech. For each source that requires citation, you need to include the *type of source* (magazine, book, personal interview, Web site, etc.), the *author or origin of the source*, the *title or a description of the source*, and the *date of the source*.

Oral presentations need not include the full bibliographic reference (including full names, dates, titles, volume, and page numbers). However, you should include a complete reference in a bibliography page or at the end of the speech outline. (For more on creating a written bibliography for your speeches, see Appendix A.)

One exception to sources needing citation is the use of **common knowledge**—information that is likely to be known by many people (though such information must *truly* be widely disseminated). For example, it is common knowledge that terrorists flew two planes into the World Trade Center towers on September 11, 2001. It is not common knowledge that the towers were 1,368 and 1,362 feet high. These facts require acknowledgment of a source—in this case, the Port Authority of New York and New Jersey, the owners of the World Trade Center.[11]

Citing Quotations, Paraphrases, and Summaries

When citing other people's ideas, you can present them in one of three ways:

- **Direct quotations** are statements made verbatim—or word for word—by someone else. Direct quotes should always be acknowledged in a speech.

- A **paraphrase** is a restatement of someone else's ideas, opinions, or theories in the speaker's own words.[12] Because paraphrases alter the *form* but not the *substance* of another person's ideas, you must acknowledge the original source. After all, they are not your ideas.

- A **summary** is a brief overview of someone else's ideas, opinions, or theories. While a paraphrase contains approximately the same number of words as the original source material stated in the speaker's own words, a summary condenses the same material, distilling only its essence.

Note how a speaker could paraphrase and summarize, *with credit,* the following excerpt from an article titled "The Age of Nutritionism" by Nir Rosen, published January 28, 2007, in the *New York Times Magazine*:

ORIGINAL VERSION:

It was in the 1980s that food began disappearing from the American supermarket, gradually to be replaced by "nutrients," which are not the same thing. Where once the familiar name of recognizable comestibles—things like eggs or breakfast cereal or cookies—claimed pride of place on the brightly colored packages crowding the aisles, now new terms like "fiber" and "cholesterol" and "saturated fat" rose to large-type prominence. More important than mere foods, the presence or absence of these invisible substances was now generally believed to confer health benefits on their eaters.

Compare the original version of the excerpt to how it could be properly quoted, paraphrased, or summarized in a speech. Oral citation language is bolded for easy identification.

DIRECT QUOTATION:

As Nir Rosen states in an article titled "The Age of Nutritionism," published in the January 28, 2007, issue of the *New York Times Magazine, and I quote,* "It was in the 1980s that food began disappearing from the American supermarket, gradually to be replaced by 'nutrients,' which are not the same thing."

ORAL PARAPHRASE:

In an article titled "The Age of Nutritionism" published in the January 28, 2007, issue of the *New York Times Magazine,* Nir Rosen says that we have taken our focus off real food and put it on its chemical composition—on the nutrients in it. **Rosen claims that** rather than the actual food we eat—things like eggs or apples, breakfast cereal or chicken breasts—we now believe it is the unseen substances within those foods such as cholesterol, saturated fat, and fiber, that make us healthy or sick.

ORAL SUMMARY:

In an article titled "The Age of Nutritionism" published in the January 28, 2007, issue of the *New York Times Magazine,* Nir Rosen argues that we have shifted our focus from real food to unseen substances such as cholesterol and saturated fat. We decide whether a food is healthy or not solely on the basis of how much or how little of these substances a food contains.

For detailed directions on crediting sources in your speech, see Chapter 11, "Citing Sources in Your Speech."

CHECKLIST: Correctly Quote, Paraphrase, and Summarize Information

✓ If *directly quoting* a source, repeat the source word for word and acknowledge whose words you are using.

✓ If *paraphrasing* someone else's idea, restate the ideas in your own words and acknowledge the source.

✓ If *summarizing* someone else's ideas, briefly describe their essence and acknowledge the source.

Fair Use, Copyright, and Ethical Speaking

Copyright is a legal protection afforded the original creators of literary and artistic works.[13] When including copyrighted materials in your speeches—such as reproductions of charts or photographs, a downloaded video clip, and so forth— you must determine when and if you need permission to use such works. For information on integrating media (such as downloaded videos and sound recordings) into your speech while respecting the laws of copyright, see Chapter 22, "A Brief Guide to Microsoft PowerPoint."

When a work is copyrighted, you may not reproduce, distribute, or display it without the permission of the copyright holder.[14] For any work created from 1978 to the present, a copyright is good during the author's lifetime, plus 50 years. After that, unless extended, the work falls into the **public domain**, which means anyone may reproduce it. Not subject to copyright are federal (but *not* state or local) government publications, common knowledge, and select other categories.

An exception to the prohibitions of copyright is the doctrine of **fair use**, which permits the limited use of copyrighted works without permission for the purposes of scholarship, criticism, comment, news reporting, teaching, or research.[15] This means that when preparing speeches for the classroom, you have much more latitude to use other people's creative work without seeking permission, but *with* credit in all cases, including display of the copyright symbol (©) on any copyrighted handouts or visual aids you include in your speech. Different rules apply to the professional speaker, whose use of copyrighted materials is considered part of a for-profit "performance." (For more information, see www.copyright.gov.)

Creative Commons is an organization that allows creators of works to decide how they want other people to use their copyrighted works. It offers creators six types of licenses, three of which are perhaps most relevant to students in the classroom: *attribution* (lets you use the work if you give credit the way the author requests); *noncommercial* (lets you use the work for *noncommercial purposes* only); and *no derivative works* (lets you use only verbatim—exact—versions of the work).

The rules of fair use apply equally to works licensed under Creative Commons and the laws of copyright. Student speakers may search the Creative Commons Web site for suitable materials for their speech at creativecommons .org.

Avoiding Internet Plagiarism

The rules for copyright, Creative Commons, and fair use apply equally to print and online sources. As with print sources, you must accurately credit direct quotations, paraphrased information, facts, statistics, or other information posted online that was gathered and reported by someone other than yourself. For specific guidelines on how to record and cite sources found on Web sites, see "From Source to Speech" on pages 80–81.

5   Listeners and Speakers

Most of us understand that giving a speech involves preparation and practice, but few recognize the hard work that listening to a speech requires. Rather than being a passive activity that simply "happens" to us, **listening** is the conscious act of *receiving, comprehending, interpreting, evaluating,* and *responding* to messages.[1]

Recognize That We Listen Selectively

In any given situation, no two audience members will process the information in exactly the same way. The reason lies in **selective perception**—people pay attention selectively to certain messages while ignoring others. Several factors influence what we listen to and what we ignore:

- We pay attention to what we hold to be important.
- We pay attention to information that touches our experiences and backgrounds.
- We sort and filter new information on the basis of what we already know (i.e., one way we learn is by analogy).[2]

With these principles in mind, try to:

- Identify what's important to your listeners, including their interests, needs, attitudes, and values.
- Show them early on what they stand to gain from listening to you.
- Touch upon their experiences and backgrounds.
- Use analogies to help listeners learn new ideas.
- Build repetition of key ideas into the speech.
- When appropriate, use presentation aids to visually reinforce your message.

QUICK TIP

Beat the Odds by Listening

Each of us devotes about 40 percent of our daily lives to listening. Executives dedicate even more time to this highly valued skill, upwards of 50 percent.[3] Yet if asked to recall a message immediately following a listening event, the average person can only summon up about half of what was said. One day later, the figure drops to about 35 percent.[4] Those who actively develop listening skills beat the averages, and these people tend to be successful in school and at work.

Listen Responsibly

As a speaker, you have the power of the podium; but as a listener, you also have considerable power that you can wield constructively or destructively. As listeners, we are ethically bound to refrain from disruptive and intimidating tactics—such as heckling, name-calling, or interrupting—that are meant to silence those with whom we disagree. If we find the arguments of others morally offensive, we are equally bound to speak up appropriately in refutation.

Strive for the Open Exchange of Ideas

In contrast to monologue, in which we try merely to impose what we think on another person or group of people, **dialogic communication** is the open sharing of ideas in an atmosphere of respect.[5] For the speaker, this means approaching a speech not as an argument that must be "won," but as an opportunity to achieve understanding with audience members. For listeners, it means maintaining an open mind and listening with empathy.

Anticipate the Common Obstacles to Listening

Active listening—listening that is focused and purposeful—isn't possible under conditions that distract us.[6] As you listen to speeches, try to identify and overcome some common obstacles.

Minimize External and Internal Distractions

A **listening distraction** is anything that competes for the attention we are trying to give to something else. Distractions can originate outside of us, in the environment (external distractions), or within us, in our thoughts and feelings (internal distractions).

To minimize *external listening distractions*, such as the din of jackhammers or competing conversations, try to

CHECKLIST: Dealing with Distractions While Delivering a Speech

✓ *Problem*: *Passing distractions* (chatting, entry of latecomers)

✓ *Solution*: Pause until distraction recedes

✓ *Problem*: *Ongoing noise* (construction)

✓ *Solution:* Raise speaking volume

✓ *Problem*: *Sudden distraction* (collapsing chair, falling object)

✓ *Solution:* Minimize response and proceed

✓ *Problem*: *Audience interruption* (raised hand, monologue)

✓ *Solution:* Acknowledge audience reaction and either follow up or defer response to conclusion of speech[7]

anticipate and plan for them. If you struggle to see or hear at a distance, arrive early and sit in the front. To reduce *internal listening distractions*, avoid daydreaming, be well rested, monitor yourself for lapses in attention, and consciously focus on listening.

Guard against Scriptwriting and Defensive Listening

When we engage in *scriptwriting*, we focus on what we, rather than the speaker, will say next.[8] Similarly, people who engage in **defensive listening** decide either that they won't like what the speaker is going to say or that they know better. When you find yourself scriptwriting or listening with a defensive posture, remind yourself that effective listening precedes effective rebuttal.[9] Try waiting for the speaker to finish before devising your own arguments.

Beware of Laziness and Overconfidence

Laziness and overconfidence can manifest themselves in several ways: We may expect too little from speakers, ignore important information, or display an arrogant attitude. Later, we discover we missed important information. Never assume that you already know exactly what a speaker will say; you'll seldom be right.

Work to Overcome Cultural Barriers

Differences in dialects or accents, nonverbal cues, word choice, and even physical appearance can serve as barriers to listening, but they need not if you keep your focus on the message rather than the messenger. Consciously refrain from judging a speaker on the basis of his or her accent, appearance, or demeanor; focus instead on what is actually being said. Whenever possible, reveal your needs to him or her by asking questions.

When speaking, the following will minimize confusion:

- Watch for **idioms**, or colloquial expressions such as "apple of his eye," that non-native speakers might not know. Either eliminate or define them.

- Speak at a rate that is neither too fast nor too slow. Pay particular attention to pronunciation and articulation.

- Be alert to nonverbal cues that suggest that listeners may not comprehend you, and clarify points when indicated.

Practice Active Listening

Taking the following practical steps can help you listen actively:

- Set listening goals and state them in a way that encourages action: "In my colleagues' presentation, I will learn why it took them six months to complete the last phase."
- Listen for the speaker's main ideas and take note of key points.
- Watch for the speaker's nonverbal cues.
- Try to detect the speaker's organizational pattern.

STEPS IN SETTING LISTENING GOALS
Identify Need: "I must know Suzanne's speech thesis, purpose, main points, and type of organization in order to complete and hand in a written evaluation."
Indicate Performance Standard: "I will get a better grade on the evaluation if I am able to identify and evaluate the major components of Suzanne's speech."
Make Action Statement (Goal): "I will minimize distractions and practice the active listening steps during Suzanne's speech. I will take careful notes during her speech and ask questions about anything I do not understand."
Assess Goal Achievement: "Before I leave the classroom, I will review my notes carefully to make sure that I covered everything."

Evaluate Evidence and Reasoning

As you listen to speeches, use your critical faculties to do the following:

- *Evaluate the speaker's evidence.* Is it accurate? Are the sources credible?
- *Analyze the speaker's assumptions and biases.* What lies behind the speaker's assertions? Does the evidence support or contradict these assertions?
- *Assess the speaker's reasoning.* Does it betray faulty logic? Does it rely on fallacies in reasoning? (See Chapter 24.)
- *Consider multiple perspectives.* Is there another way to view the argument? How do other perspectives compare with the speaker's?
- *Summarize and assess the relevant facts and evidence.*

> **QUICK TIP**
>
> ***Use the Thought/Speech Differential to Listen Critically***
> *Did you know that we listen at a much faster rate than we speak? We listen at 90–200 words per minute, but think at 500–600 words per minute.* [10]
>   *This differential between "thought speed" and "speech speed" is one reason we can be easily distracted. But you can also use the differential to your advantage. When you find yourself "thinking ahead" of the speaker, use the time to focus on questions that foster critical thinking:*
>   *What does the speaker really mean? Why is he or she presenting this material? Is the speaker leaving anything out? How can I use what the speaker is telling me?*

Offer Constructive and Compassionate Feedback

Follow these guidelines when evaluating the speeches of others:

- *Be honest and fair in your evaluation.*
- *Adjust to the speaker's style.* Don't judge the content of a speaker's message by his or her style.
- *Be compassionate in your criticism.* Always start by saying something positive, and focus on the speech, not the speaker.
- *Be selective in your criticism.* Make specific rather than global statements. Rather than statements such as, "I just couldn't get into your topic," give the speaker something he or she can learn from: "I wanted more on why the housing market is falling . . ."

Part 2
Development

6 | Analyzing the Audience

Advertisers are shrewd analysts of people's needs and wants, extensively researching their buying habits to identify what motivates them. To engage your listeners and bring them to your point of view, you too must investigate your audience. **Audience analysis** is the process of gathering and analyzing information about audience members' attributes and motivations with the *explicit aim of preparing your speech in ways that will be meaningful to them.* This is the single most critical aspect of preparing for any speech.

Maintaining an **audience-centered** approach to all phases of the speech preparation process—from treatment of the speech topic to making decisions about how you will organize, word, and deliver it—will help you prepare a presentation that your audience will want to hear.

Adapt to Audience Psychology: Who Are Your Listeners?

As you prepare your speeches, try to uncover the audience's attitudes, beliefs, and values—their feelings and opinions—toward (1) the topic of your speech, (2) you as the speaker, and (3) the speech occasion. This "perspective taking" will help you learn more about your audience and see things from their point of view.

Taking the measure of the audience is critical because people tend to evaluate messages in terms of their own, rather than the speaker's, perspective. You may want classmates to support a four-day school week, but unless you know how they feel and what they know about the proposal, you won't know how to adapt your presentation accordingly.

Attitudes, beliefs, and values, while intertwined, reflect distinct mental states that reveal a great deal about us. **Attitudes** are our general evaluations of people, ideas, objects, or events.[1] To evaluate something is to judge it as relatively good or bad, useful or useless, desirable or undesirable, and so on. People generally act in accordance with their attitudes (although the degree to which they do so depends on many factors).[2]

Attitudes are based on **beliefs**—the ways in which people perceive reality.[3] Beliefs are our feelings about what is true. The less faith listeners have in the existence of something—UFOs, for instance—the less open they are to hearing about it.

Both attitudes and beliefs are shaped by **values**—our most enduring judgments about what's good and bad in life,

37

as shaped by our culture and our unique experiences within it. Values are more long-lasting than attitudes or beliefs and are more resistant to change. Values usually align with attitudes and beliefs.

As a rule, people are more interested in and pay greater attention to topics toward which they have positive attitudes and that are in keeping with their values and beliefs. The less we know about something, the more indifferent we tend to be. It is easier (though not simple) to spark interest in an indifferent audience than it is to turn negative attitudes around.

Appeal to Listeners' Attitudes, Beliefs, and Values

Evoking some combination of your listeners' attitudes, beliefs, and values in a speech can make it more personally relevant and motivating. For example, the Biodiversity Project counsels its speakers to appeal directly to the values its members hold about the environment as seen in this example:

> You care about your family's health, and you feel a responsibility to protect your loved ones' quality of life. The local wetland provides a sanctuary to many plants and animals. It helps clean our air and water and provides a space of beauty and serenity. All of this is about to be destroyed by irresponsible development.[4]

Gauge Listeners' Feelings toward the Topic

Try to learn what your listeners know about the topic. What is their level of interest? Do they hold positive, negative, or neutral attitudes toward it? Once you have this information, adjust the speech accordingly:

If the topic is *new* to listeners,

- Start by showing why the topic is relevant to them.
- Relate the topic to familiar issues and ideas about which they already hold positive attitudes.

If listeners know *relatively little* about the topic,

- Stick to the basics and include background information.
- Steer clear of jargon, and define unclear terms.
- Repeat important points, summarizing information often.

If listeners are *negatively disposed* toward the topic,

- Focus on establishing rapport and credibility.
- Don't directly challenge listeners' attitudes; instead begin with areas of agreement.
- Discover why they have a negative bias in order to tactfully introduce the other side of the argument.
- Offer solid evidence from sources they are likely to accept.
- Give good reasons for developing a positive attitude toward the topic.[5]

If listeners hold *positive attitudes* toward the topic,

- Stimulate the audience to feel even more strongly by emphasizing the side of the argument with which they agree.
- Tell stories with vivid language that reinforce listeners' attitudes.[6]

If listeners are a *captive audience,*

- Motivate listeners to pay attention by stressing what is most relevant to them.
- Pay close attention to the length of your speech.

QUICK TIP

Custom-Fit Your Message

Audience members like to feel that the speaker recognizes them as unique individuals. You can do this by making positive references to the place where you are speaking and the group to whom you are addressing your comments. Personalize the speech by applying relevant facts and statistics in your speech directly to the audience. If your topic is hurricanes, for example, you could note that "Right here in Carla, Texas, you endured and survived a Category 4 hurricane in 1961."

Gauge Listeners' Feelings toward You as the Speaker

How audience members feel about you will have significant bearing on their responsiveness to the message. A speaker who is well liked can gain an initial hearing even when listeners are unsure what to expect from the message itself.

To create positive audience attitudes toward you, first try to display the characteristics of speaker credibility (ethos) described in Chapter 4. Listeners have a natural desire to identify with the speaker and to feel that he or she shares their perceptions,[7] so establish a feeling of commonality, or **identi-fication**, with them. Use eye contact and body movements to include the audience in your message. Relate a relevant personal story, emphasize a shared role, focus on areas of agreement, or otherwise stress mutual bonds. Even your physical presentation can foster a common bond. Audiences are more apt to identify with speakers who dress in ways they find appropriate.

CHECKLIST: Analyze the Audience as You Speak

As you deliver your speech, read the audience for signs of how they are receiving your message. Look for bodily clues that indicate interest or disengagement:

✓ Large smiles and eye contact suggest a liking for and agreement with the speaker.

✓ Arms folded across the chest may signal disagreement.

✓ Averted glances, slumped posture, and squirming usually indicate disengagement.

Engage with the audience when it appears they aren't with you:

✓ Invite one or two listeners to relate briefly their own experiences about the topic.

✓ Share a story linked to the topic to increase identification.[8]

Gauge Listeners' Feelings toward the Occasion

Depending on the speech occasion, people will bring different sets of expectations and emotions to it. Members of a **captive audience**, who are required to hear the speaker, may be less positively disposed to the occasion than members of a **voluntary audience** who attend of their own free will. Failure to anticipate the audience's expectations risks alienating them.

QUICK TIP

Be Authentic

*Being audience centered does not mean that you must cater to the audience's whims and abandon your own convictions. This practice, called **pandering,** will only undermine your credibility in the eyes of the audience. Just as you might do with a new acquaintance, use audience analysis as an opportunity to get to know and establish common ground with your listeners. The more you find out about someone, the more you can discover what you share in common and how you differ.*

Adapt Your Message to Audience Demographics

Demographics are the statistical characteristics of a given population. At least six such characteristics are typically considered in the analysis of speech audiences: age, ethnic or cultural background, socioeconomic status (including income, occupation, and education), religion, political affiliation, and gender. Any number of other traits—for example, group membership, physical disability, sexual orientation, or place of residence—may be important to investigate as well.

Knowing where audience members fall in relation to audience demographics will help you identify your **target audience**—those individuals within the broader audience whom you are most likely to influence in the direction you seek. You may not be able to please everyone, but you should be able to establish a connection with your target audience.

Age

Each age group has its own concerns and, broadly speaking, psychological drives and motivations. In addition to sharing the concerns associated with a given life stage, people of the same generation often share a familiarity with significant individuals, local and world events, noteworthy popular culture, and so forth. Being aware of the audience's age range and generational identity, such as the Millennials (those born between 1977 and 1995), allows you to develop points that are relevant to the experience and interests of the widest possible cross section of your listeners.

Ethnic or Cultural Background

An understanding of and sensitivity to the ethnic and cultural composition of your listeners are key factors in delivering a successful (and ethical) speech. Some audience members may have a great deal in common with you. Others may be fluent in a language other than yours and must struggle to understand you. Some members of the audience may belong to a distinct **co-culture**, or social community whose perspectives and style of communicating differ significantly from yours. (See p. 44, "Adapt to Cultural Differences.")

Socioeconomic Status

Socioeconomic status (SES) includes income, occupation, and education. Knowing roughly where an audience falls in terms of these key variables can be critical in effectively targeting your message.

INCOME   *Income* determines people's experiences on many levels. It directly affects how they are housed, clothed, and fed, and determines what they can afford. Beyond this, income has a ripple effect, influencing many other aspects of life. For example, depending on income, health insurance is either a taken-for-granted budget item or an out-of-reach dream. The same is true for travel and leisure activities. Given how pervasively income affects people's life experiences, insight into this aspect of an audience's makeup can be quite important.

OCCUPATION   In most speech situations, the *occupation* of audience members is an important and easily identifiable demographic characteristic. The nature of people's work has a lot to do with what interests them. Occupational interests are tied to several other areas of social concern, such as politics, the economy, education, and social reform. Personal attitudes, beliefs, and goals are also closely tied to occupational standing.

EDUCATION   Level of *education* strongly influences people's ideas, perspectives, and range of abilities. If the audience is generally better educated than you are, your speech may need to be quite sophisticated. When speaking to a less-educated audience, you may choose to clarify your points with more examples and illustrations.

Religion

The *Encyclopedia of American Religions* identifies more than 2,300 different religious groups in the United States,[9] from Seventh-Day Adventists to Zen Buddhists, so don't assume that everyone in your audience shares a common *religious heritage*. Furthermore, don't assume that all members of the same religious tradition will agree on all issues. For example, Catholics disagree on birth control and divorce, Jews disagree on whether to recognize same-sex unions, and so forth.

Political Affiliation

Beware of making unwarranted assumptions about an audience's *political values and beliefs*. Some people like nothing better than a lively debate about public-policy issues. Others avoid anything that smacks of politics. Many people are very serious, and others are very touchy, about their views on political issues. Unless you have prior information about the audience's political values and beliefs, you won't know where your listeners stand.

Gender

Gender is another important factor in audience analysis, if only as a reminder to avoid the minefield of gender stereotyping. Distinct from the fixed physical characteristics of biological sex, **gender** is our social and psychological sense of ourselves as males or females.[10] Making assumptions about the preferences, abilities, and behaviors of your audience members based on their presumed gender can seriously undermine their receptivity to your message.

QUICK TIP

Be Sensitive to Disability When Analyzing an Audience
One out of every five people in the United States has some sort of physical or mental disability;[11] 14 percent of those enrolled in college and graduate school are counted as disabled. Problems range from sight and hearing impairments to constraints on physical mobility and employment.[12] Thus you must ensure that your speech reflects language that accords dignity, respect, and fairness to persons with disabilities (PWD).

Adapt to Cultural Differences

In the United States, at least 30 percent of the population belongs to a racial or ethnic minority group, and 34 million people, or 11 percent, are foreign-born.[13] California leads the nation, with 27 percent of its residents foreign-born; New York, New Jersey, and Hawaii follow close behind. Worldwide, there are more than two hundred recognized countries, and many more distinct cultures within these countries.[14] These statistics suggest that audience members will hold different cultural perspectives and employ different styles of communicating that may or may not mesh with your own.

How might you prepare to speak in front of an ethnically and culturally diverse audience, including that of your classroom? In any speaking situation, your foremost concern should be to treat your listeners with dignity and to act with integrity. Since values form the basis of people's attitudes and actions, identifying those of your listeners with respect to your topic can help you to avoid ethnocentrism and deliver your message in a culturally sensitive manner.

Consider Cross-Cultural Values

In the United States, researchers have identified a set of core values, including *achievement and success, equal opportunity, material comfort, hard work, practicality and efficiency, change and progress, science, democracy,* and *freedom.*[15] A survey of several Asian societies reveals such core values as the spirit of *harmony, humility toward one's superiors, awe of nature,* and a *desire for prosperity.*[16]

People in every culture also possess values related to their personal relationships, religion, occupation, and so forth. Table 6.1 illustrates some of these values in China, India, Mexico, and Iraq.

Focus on Universal Values

As much as possible, it is important to try to determine the attitudes, beliefs, and values of audience members. At the same time, you can focus on certain values that, if not universally shared, are probably universally aspired to in the human heart. These include love, truthfulness, fairness, freedom, unity, tolerance, responsibility, and respect for life.[17]

TABLE 6.1 • CORE VALUES IN CHINA, INDIA, MEXICO, AND IRAQ

CHINA	INDIA
• Modesty	• Family orientation
• Tolerance	• Material success and creativity
• Filial piety	• Fatalism
• Stoicism	• Do-it-yourself mentality
• Respect for hierarchy	• Honor of family and group
• Pride (not losing face)	• Problem-solving
• Wisdom	

MEXICO	IRAQ
• Group loyalty	• Devoutness
• Mañana (cyclical time)	• Hospitality
• Machismo	• Gender inequality
• Family closeness	• Values rhetoric
• Saving face at all costs	• Pride in ancient heritage
• Deference to age	• Moralism
• Mysticism, fatalism	

Source: Adapted from material in Richard D. Lewis, *When Cultures Collide: Leading across Cultures,* 3rd ed. (Boston: Intercultural Press-Nicholas Brealey International, 2005).

CHECKLIST: Reviewing Your Speech in the Light of Audience Demographics

✓ Does your speech acknowledge potential differences in values and beliefs and address them sensitively?

✓ Have you reviewed your topic in light of the age range and generational identity of your listeners? Do you use examples they will recognize and find relevant?

✓ Have you tried to create a sense of identification between yourself and audience members?

✓ Are your explanations and examples at a level appropriate to the audience's sophistication and education?

✓ Do you make any unwarranted assumptions about the audience's political or religious values and beliefs?

✓ Does your topic carry religious or political overtones that are likely to stir your listeners' emotions in a negative way?

✓ Is your speech free of generalizations based on gender?

✓ Does your language reflect sensitivity toward people with disabilities?

Seek Out Information about Your Audience

How do you actually uncover information about your audience? Unlike a professional pollster, you cannot survey thousands of people and apply sophisticated statistical techniques to analyze your results. On a smaller scale, however, you can use the same techniques. These include surveys, interviews, and published sources. Often, it takes just a few questions to get some idea of where audience members stand on each of the demographic factors.

Survey Audience Members

Surveys can be as informal as a poll of several audience members or as formal as the pre-speech distribution of a written survey, or **questionnaire**—a series of open- and closed-ended questions.

Closed-ended questions elicit a small range of specific answers supplied by the interviewer:

"Do you or did you ever smoke cigarettes?"

Answers will be either "Yes," "No," or "I smoked for X number of years." Closed-ended questions may be either fixed-alternative or scale questions. **Fixed-alternative questions** contain a limited choice of answers, such as "Yes," "No," or "Sometimes." **Scale questions**—also called attitude scales — measure the respondent's level of agreement or disagreement with specific issues:

"Flag burning should be outlawed":

Strongly Agree _____ Agree _____ Undecided _____
Disagree _____ Strongly Disagree _____

Scale questions can be used to measure how important listeners judge something to be and how frequently they engage in a particular behavior:

"How important is religion in your life?"

Very important _____ Important _____ Moderately
Important _____ Of Little Importance _____
Unimportant _____

Open-ended questions allow respondents to elaborate as much as they wish:

"How do you feel about using the results of DNA testing to prove innocence or guilt in criminal proceedings?"

A mix of open- and closed-ended questions can reveal a fairly clear picture of the backgrounds and attitudes of the members of your audience. Closed-ended questions are especially helpful in uncovering the shared attitudes, experiences, and knowledge of audience members. Open-ended questions are particularly useful for probing beliefs and opinions.

Conduct Interviews

Interviews, even brief ones, can reveal a lot about the audience's interests and needs. You can conduct interviews one-on-one or in a group, in person or by telephone or e-mail. Consider interviewing a sampling of the audience, or even just one knowledgeable representative of the group that you will address.

- *Prepare questions for the interview.* Plan the questions you will ask well in advance of the actual interview date.
- *Word questions carefully.* The wording of a question is almost as critical as the information it seeks to uncover.
- Avoid *vague questions*, those that don't give the person being interviewed enough to go on. He or she must either guess at what you mean or spend time interviewing you for clarification.
- Avoid *leading questions*, those that encourage, if not force, a certain response and reflect the interviewer's bias (e.g., "Like most intelligent people, are you going to support candidate X?"). Likewise, avoid *loaded questions*, those that are phrased to reinforce the interviewer's agenda or that have a hostile intent (e.g., "Isn't it true that you've never supported school programs?").
- Aim to create *neutral questions*, those that don't lead the interviewee to a desired response. Usually this will consist of a mix of open, closed, primary, and secondary questions.

Begin by establishing a spirit of collaboration. Briefly summarize your topic and informational needs:

- Acknowledge the interviewee, and express respect for his or her expertise.
- Briefly summarize your topic and informational needs.
- State a (reasonable) goal, such as what you would like to accomplish in the interview, and reach agreement on it.
- Establish a time limit for the interview and stick to it.

Pose substantive questions. Listen to what the subject is saying, not just to what you want to hear. Strive to use the active listening strategies described in Chapter 5:

- Don't break in when the subject is speaking or interject with leading comments.
- *Paraphrase* the interviewee's answers when appropriate in order to establish understanding.
- Ask for *clarification* and *elaboration* when necessary.

End the interview by rechecking and confirming:

- Check that you have covered all the topics (e.g., "Does this cover everything?").
- Briefly offer a positive summary of important things you learned in the interview.
- Offer to send the results of the interview to the interviewee.

Investigate Published Sources

Yet another way to learn about audience members is through published sources. Organizations of all kinds publish information describing their missions, operations, and achievements. Sources include Web sites and online articles, brochures, newspaper and magazine articles, and annual reports.

You might also consider consulting *published opinion polls* that report on trends in attitudes. (See, for example, the Pew Research Center Web site at people-press.org.) To hone in on how audience members from other cultures might view specific issues, consider consulting cross-cultural polls such as the World Values Survey (www.worldvaluessurvey.org) and the International Social Survey Program (ISSP) (www.issp.org/data.shtml). Although the polls won't specifically reflect your particular listeners' responses, they can provide valuable insight into how a representative state, national, or international sample feels about the issue in question.

Assess the Speech Setting and Context

As important as analyzing the audience is assessing and then preparing for the setting in which you will give your speech — size of audience, location, time, seating arrangement, and rhetorical situation:

1. Where will the speech take place?
2. How long am I expected to speak?
3. How many people will attend?
4. Will I need a microphone?
5. How will any equipment I plan to use in my speech, such as an LCD projector, function in the space?
6. Where will I stand or sit in relation to the audience?
7. Will I be able to interact with the listeners?
8. Who else will be speaking?
9. Are there special events or circumstances of concern to my audience that I should acknowledge (the rhetorical situation)?

7   Selecting a Topic and Purpose

One of the first tasks in preparing any speech is to select a topic and purpose for speaking that are *appropriate to the audience and occasion.* Even if the topic is assigned, as often happens in the classroom and workplace, you must still adapt it to suit the unique audience and speech situation.

Decide Where to Begin

Selecting a topic, whether for a classroom speech or another venue, can be approached from a variety of angles. You can begin "at the top" by focusing on broad social issues of national or global consequence, or you can investigate grassroots issues of a local nature. You can start even closer to the ground by making an inventory of your own interests and life experiences, from favorite activities and hobbies to deeply held goals and values. Wherever you choose to begin, pick a topic you are drawn to and want to know more about.

IDENTIFYING TOPICS	
PERSONAL INTERESTS	**CURRENT EVENTS AND CONTROVERSIAL ISSUES**
• Volunteer work in a foreign country • Sports and exercise • Fashion • Mentoring teens • Collecting on eBay • Travel • Outdoor life • Service in the armed forces • Home repair • Video games • Cultural and ethnic background	• Pending legislation — crime bills, property taxes, land use • Political races • Abuses of power • National security • Immigration • Banking regulations • Environmental issues • Terrorism
VALUES AND GOALS	**SPECIFIC SUBJECT INTERESTS**
• Spirituality • Community service • Political activism • Attending graduate or professional school • Being fit	• Local history • Ancient history • Health and medicine • Art • Religion • Science
GRASSROOTS ISSUES	**NEW AND UNUSUAL ANGLES**
• Land development vs. conservation • Local organizations • School issues	• Unsolved crimes • Unexplained disappearances • Scandals

Consider the Audience

A good speech topic must pique not only your own curiosity but the audience's. As you explore topics, consider each one's potential appeal to the audience, as well as its appropriateness for the occasion. Will the topic be relevant to your listeners' specific attributes and motivations? Will it meet listeners' expectations of the speech?

Steer Clear of Overused and Trivial Topics

To avoid boring your classmates and instructor, stay away from tired issues, such as drunk driving and gun control, as well as trite topics such as "how to change a tire." Instead, seek out subject matter that yields new insight. As one source of ideas, consider searching your favorite print or online publications. Beware, however, of choosing highly charged topics for which people have deeply held beliefs, such as abortion or prayer in the school. When it comes to core values, people rarely respond to persuasion (see Chapter 24), so speeches on such topics are likely to accomplish little beyond raising tension in the classroom.

Try Brainstorming to Generate Ideas

To generate ideas for topics, try **brainstorming** by word association, topic mapping, or category.

To brainstorm by **word association**, write down a single topic that might interest you and your listeners. Next, write down the first thing that comes to mind. Continue this process until you have a list of fifteen to twenty items. Narrow the list to two or three, and then select the final topic:

health → alternative medicine → naturopathy → homeopathy

QUICK TIP

Explore Topics Using Web Directories

For an electronic version of word association, browse the alphabetized directories of such Internet portals as Yahoo! Directory (dir.yahoo.com) and Open Directory Project (dmoz.org/). On the portal's front page select from among its list of subject categories (e.g., "Society and Culture" or "Health."). Each subject category links to subtopics; each subtopic links to its own subcategories, and so on (see also "Consult Subject [Web] Directories" in Chapter 10, p. 78).

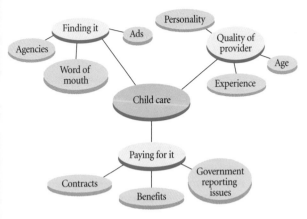

FIGURE 7.1 A Topic Map

To brainstorm by **topic mapping**, put a potential topic in the middle of a piece of paper. As related ideas come to you, write them down, as shown in Figure 7.1.

To narrow your topic, try brainstorming by category. Say your general topic is video games. Categories could include platform (handheld, arcade), type (racing, roleplaying), or operating system (Linux, Macintosh, Windows). As you brainstorm by category, ask yourself: What questions do I have about the topic? What does my audience know about video games and what aspects are they most likely to want to hear about?

Identify the General Purpose of Your Speech

Some of your presentations will have an assigned topic and/or purpose (e.g., "deliver a persuasive speech" about topic X). In others, the choice will be left to you. Even when the topic is specified, you must still refine and adapt the topic to fit the general speech purpose. The **general speech purpose** for any speech answers the question, "Why am I speaking on this topic to this particular audience on this occasion?"

— Are you there to inform listeners about your topic? The general purpose of the informative speech is *to increase the audience's awareness by imparting knowledge.*

— Is your goal to persuade them to accept your views on a topic? The general purpose of the persuasive speech is *to influence the attitudes, beliefs, values, and behaviors of audience members.*

— Are you there to mark a special occasion? The general purpose of the special occasion speech will be variously *to entertain, celebrate, commemorate, inspire, or set a social agenda.*

Narrow the Topic

Once you have identified your topic and general speech purpose, you need to narrow your focus (see Figure 7.1). When you narrow a topic, you focus on specific aspects of it to the exclusion of others. As you do so, carefully evaluate the topic in light of audience interests, knowledge, and needs:

- Consider what your listeners are likely to know about the subject.
- Consider what they are likely to want to learn.
- Consider what aspects of the topic are most relevant to the occasion. Restrict your focus to what you can competently research and then report on in the time you are given to speak.
- Pick a discrete topic category and cover it well.
- Restrict your main points to between two and five.

Form a Specific Speech Purpose

The **specific speech purpose** lays out precisely what you want the audience to get from the speech. To determine the specific purpose, ask yourself: What do you want the audience to learn/do/reconsider/agree with? Be specific about your aim, and then state this aim in action form, as in the following, written for an informative speech:

GENERAL TOPIC:	Consolidating Student Loans
NARROWED TOPIC:	Understanding when and why consolidating student loans makes sense
GENERAL PURPOSE:	To inform
SPECIFIC PURPOSE:	To inform my audience about the factors to consider when deciding whether or not to consolidate student loans

The specific purpose statement is seldom articulated in the speech itself. Nevertheless, it is important to formulate it for yourself in order to implant in your mind exactly what you want your speech to accomplish.

Compose a Thesis Statement

After narrowing your topic and forming your specific purpose, your next step is to formulate a thesis statement. The **thesis statement** (also called central idea) is the theme or central idea of the speech stated in the form of a single, declarative sentence. The thesis statement briefly expresses what you will attempt to demonstrate or prove in your speech. The main points, the supporting material, and the conclusion all relate to the thesis.

The thesis statement and the specific purpose are closely linked. Both state the speech topic, but in different forms. *The specific purpose describes in action form what you want to achieve with the speech; the thesis statement concisely identifies, in a single idea, what the speech is about.* The specific purpose does not have to be stated in the speech itself. The thesis, on the other hand, must be clearly stated because the entire speech rests on it. The difference can be seen in the specific purpose and thesis statement for a persuasive speech on student internships:

SPECIFIC PURPOSE: To convince my audience that internships are beneficial because they link academic studies with future careers.

THESIS STATEMENT: To prepare for a difficult job market and to enhance your résumé, find a student internship that links your academic studies with your future career.

Postpone Development of Main Points

Whether the speech is informative or persuasive, the thesis statement proposes that the statement made is true or is believed. The speech is then developed from this premise; it presents facts and evidence to support the thesis as true. Thus, you should always postpone the development of main points or the consideration of supporting material until you have formulated the speech purpose and thesis (see Chapter 12).

In a persuasive speech, the thesis statement represents what you are going to prove in the address. All the main points in the speech are arguments that develop the thesis:

GENERAL PURPOSE: To persuade

SPECIFIC PURPOSE: To move the audience to raise money on behalf of the Sierra Club

THESIS: A donation to the Sierra Club is the best charitable gift you can give.

Notice that, after you read the thesis, you find yourself asking "Why?" or saying "Prove it!" This will be accomplished by the main points (see Chapter 12).

In informative speaking, the thesis describes what the audience will learn:

GENERAL PURPOSE: To inform

SPECIFIC PURPOSE: To inform my audience of three benefits of keeping a blog

From Source to Speech

Narrowing Your Topic Using a Library Portal

One of several ways to research your topic is to use a library's online portal. This is an especially good approach because using such a tool to generate narrower ideas also guarantees that the new ideas are supported by *credible* sources. For example, to narrow down the topic of smoking in the movies, you could use a library portal to locate relevant books and access online periodical databases that offer full-text articles evaluated for reliability by librarians and other content experts.

Navigating the Library Portal through Basic Searches

To search the portal of the Brooklyn Public Library, you could find sources through links on the home page: "Library Catalog" to find books, and "Articles and Databases" to find full-text articles.

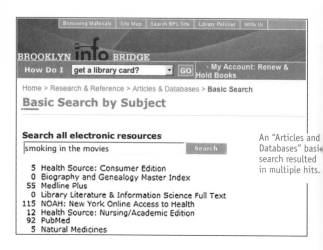

An "Articles and Databases" basic search resulted in multiple hits.

This recent, peer-reviewed psychology journal article would be invisible to general search engines.

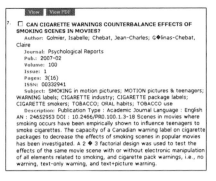

7. ☐ CAN CIGARETTE WARNINGS COUNTERBALANCE EFFECTS OF SMOKING SCENES IN MOVIES?
   Author: Golmier, Isabelle; Chebat, Jean-Charles; G◆linas-Chebat, Claire
   Journal: Psychological Reports
   Pub.: 2007-02
   Volume: 100
   Issue: 1
   Pages: 3(16)
   ISSN: 00332941
   Subject: SMOKING in motion pictures; MOTION pictures & teenagers; WARNING labels; CIGARETTE industry; CIGARETTE package labels; CIGARETTE smokers; TOBACCO; ORAL habits; TOBACCO use
   Description: Publication Type : Academic Journal Language : English AN : 24652953 DOI : 10.2466/PRO.100.1.3-18 Scenes in movies where smoking occurs have been empirically shown to influence teenagers to smoke cigarettes. The capacity of a Canadian warning label on cigarette packages to decrease the effects of smoking scenes in popular movies has been investigated. A 2 ◆ 3 factorial design was used to test the effects of the same movie scene with or without electronic manipulation of all elements related to smoking, and cigarette pack warnings, i.e., no warning, text-only warning, and text+picture warning.

Using Advanced Library Portal Searches

Advanced search allows you to home in on credible sources even more likely to help you. This will help you better distill your specific purpose and develop your thesis statement.

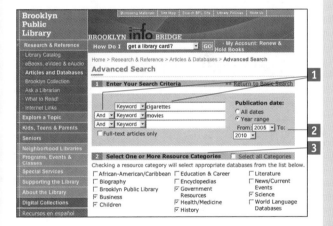

1 Linking search terms *cigarettes* and *movies* by Boolean operator "AND" results only in hits containing both terms.

2 Limiting search from 2005 to 2010 ensures that only published articles in this period appeared.

3 Limiting resource categories eliminates unwanted results by content area.

THESIS: Maintaining a blog lets you sharpen your writing skills, network with persons who share similar interests, and develop basic Web site management skills.

CHECKLIST: Identifying the Speech Topic, Purpose, and Thesis

✓ Have I identified the *general speech purpose* — to inform, persuade, or mark a special occasion?

✓ Is the topic appropriate to the occasion?

✓ Will the topic appeal to my listeners' interests and needs?

✓ Will I be able to offer a fresh perspective on the topic?

✓ Have I identified what the audience is most likely to know about the subject and what they are most likely to want to learn?

✓ Have I considered how much I can competently research and then report on in the time I am given to speak?

✓ Does my thesis statement sum up in a single sentence what my speech is about?

✓ Is it restricted to a single idea?

✓ Does it make the claim I intend to make about my topic?

✓ Is it stated in a way that is relevant to the audience?

Make the Thesis Statement Relevant and Motivating

Try to express the thesis statement in a way that will motivate the audience to listen. In many cases, creating relevant statements can be accomplished by adding a few key words or phrases to the claim. For example, you can preface an informative thesis statement with a phrase such as "Few of us know" or "Contrary to popular belief" or "Have you ever." Thesis statements for persuasive claims can also be adapted to establish relevance for the audience. Phrases such as "As most of you know" or "As informed members of the community" or "As concerned adults" can help gain audience interest and make listeners see the topic's relevance.

Use information about the audience members to make the topic relevant to them. Consider how the following thesis statement has been adapted for an audience living in a troubled community:

SPECIFIC PURPOSE:	To persuade the audience to elect a political candidate
THESIS:	A vote for Politician "X" is a vote for progress.
THESIS WITH RELEVANCE:	Because the time has come for us to deal with the issues in our community, a vote for Politician "X" is a vote for progress.

QUICK TIP

Use the Thesis Statement to Stay Focused
As you develop the speech, use the thesis statement to keep yourself on track. Review your research materials to determine whether they contribute to the thesis or stray from it. When you actually draft your speech, work your thesis statement into it and restate it where appropriate. Doing so will encourage your audience to understand and accept your message.

---

8 | Developing Supporting Material

Good speeches contain accurate, relevant, and interesting **supporting material** in the form of examples, narratives, testimony, facts, and statistics. These "flesh out" the speech—they give substance to the speech's thesis, or central idea. As you research your speech, focus on alternating among several different types of supporting materials.

Offer Examples

Examples illustrate, describe, or represent things. Their purpose is to aid understanding by making ideas, items, or events more concrete. Examples are particularly helpful when they are used to describe or explain things with which the audience is unfamiliar. **Brief examples** offer a single illustration of a point. In a speech titled "The Coming Golden Age of Medicine," Richard F. Corlin offers the following brief example to illustrate what American medicine can do:

> We often hear about the problems of the American health care delivery system, but just think what it can do. My 88-year-old father who needed a hip replacement got it— the week it was discovered that he needed it. That couldn't happen in any other country in the world.[1]

Sometimes it takes more than a brief example to effectively illustrate a point. **Extended examples** offer multifaceted illustrations of the idea, item, or event being described, thereby getting the point across and reiterating it effectively.

Risa Lavizzo-Mourey, M.D., used an extended example to illustrate how physicians could reverse the course of childhood obesity:

> I can think of at least three moments in the past half century that dramatically shifted the course of America's medical and scientific history. The first time came . . . on March 26, 1953 when Jonas Salk . . . announced the discovery of a polio vaccine. The second time, amazingly, came just four weeks later, when Watson and Crick published their discovery of the double helix structure of DNA. The third time was in 1964, when the U.S. surgeon general . . . reported that cigarette smoking does cause cancer and other deadly diseases. For many of you, that was the first day of what turned into a 40-year movement to alter a culture of harm . . . Your science and determination helped America turn the tide against tobacco and smoking—saving the lives of millions.[2]

In some speeches you may need to make a point about something that could happen in the future if certain events were to occur. Since it hasn't happened yet, you'll need a **hypothetical example** of what you believe the outcome might be. Republican Representative Vernon Ehlers of Michigan offered the following hypothetical example when he spoke at a congressional hearing in support of a bill to ban human cloning:

> What if in the cloning process you produce someone with two heads and three arms? Are you simply going to euthanize and dispose of that person? The answer is no. We're talking about human life.[3]

Share Stories

One of the most powerful means of conveying a message is through a **story** (also called **narrative**). Stories help us make sense of our experience.[4] They tell tales, both real and imaginary, about practically anything under the sun. Common to all stories are the essential elements of a plot, characters, setting, and some sort of time line.

Stories can be brief and simple descriptions of short incidents worked into the speech, or relatively drawn-out accounts that constitute most of the presentation. In either case, a successful story will strike a chord and create an emotional connection between speaker and audience members. For example, in 2008, then presidential candidate Barack Obama opened his remarks to members of the Ebeneezer Baptist Church with a parable—a story illustrating a moral or religious lesson—from the Bible:

> The Scripture tells us that when Joshua and the Israelites arrived at the gates of Jericho, they could not enter. The walls of the city were too steep for any one person to climb; too strong to be taken down with brute force. And so they sat for days, unable to pass on through.
> But God had a plan for his people.[5]

Many speakers, whether they're ministers at the Sunday morning pulpit or high-tech entrepreneurs rallying the troops, liberally sprinkle their speeches with **anecdotes**—brief stories of interesting and often humorous incidents based on real life.

QUICK TIP

Give the Story Structure
Speaking expert Earle Gray offers solid storytelling advice: A good story has structure: a blunt beginning that sets the situation ("Let me tell you a story about the importance of higher education . . ."), a rounded middle, and a sharp end. It should be no more than two minutes in a typical talk.[6]

Draw on Testimony

Consider quoting or paraphrasing people who have an intimate knowledge of your topic. **Testimony** is firsthand findings, eyewitness accounts, and people's opinions; **expert testimony** includes findings, eyewitness accounts, or opinions from professionals trained to evaluate a given topic. **Lay testimony**, or testimony by nonexperts such as eyewitnesses, can reveal compelling firsthand information that may be unavailable to others.

Supply the name and qualifications of the person whose testimony you use, and inform listeners when and where the testimony was offered. It isn't always necessary to cite the exact date (though do keep a written record of this); in the oral presentation, terms such as "recently" and "last year" are fine. The following is an example:

> In testimony before the U.S. House Subcommittee on Human Rights and Wellness last week, Derek Ellerman (co-executive director of the Polaris Project) said, "Many people have little understanding of the enormity and the brutality of the sex trafficking industry in the United States. When they think of sex slavery, they think of Thailand or Nepal—not a suburban house in the DC area, with $400,000 homes and manicured lawns . . ."[7]

QUICK TIP

Use a Variety of Supporting Materials

Listeners respond most favorably to a variety of supporting materials derived from multiple sources to illustrate each main point.[8] Alternating among different types of supporting material—moving from a story to a statistic, for example—will make the presentation more interesting and credible while simultaneously appealing to your audience members' different learning styles.

Provide Facts and Statistics

Most people (especially in Western society) require some type of evidence, usually in the form of facts and statistics, before they will accept someone else's claims or position.[9] **Facts** represent documented occurrences, including actual events, dates, times, people, and places. **Statistics** are quantified evidence that summarizes, compares, and predicts things.

Use Statistics Accurately

Statistics add precision to speech claims, *if* you know what the numbers actually mean and use terms that describe them accurately.

> **QUICK TIP**
>
> **Make It Real with Statistics**
> *Used sparingly, statistics can clarify complex information and
> help make abstract concepts or ideas concrete for listeners.
> For example, rather than simply stating, "We are selling
> millions of songs on iTunes," one can say "Steve Jobs, CEO
> of Apple Computer, Inc., described iTune's success this way:
> 'We're selling over five million songs a day now. Isn't that
> unbelievable? That's 58 songs every second of every minute
> of every hour of every day.'"* [10]

Use Frequencies to Indicate Counts

A **frequency** is simply a count of the number of times something occurs:

> "On the midterm exam there were 8 A's, 15 B's, 7 C's, 2 D's, and 1 F."

Frequencies can help listeners understand comparisons between two or more categories, indicate size, or describe trends:

- According to *Census 2000,* the total population of the State of Colorado was comprised of 2,165,983 males and 2,135,278 females.[11] *(compares two categories)*
- Inside the cabin, the Airbus A380 has room for at least 550 passengers—and as many as 1,000.[12] *(shows size)*
- According to the CDC, the birthrate among young adolescents aged 10 to 14 has declined steadily from a peak of 12,901 in 1994 to the current low of 7,315.[13] *(describes a trend)*

Use Percentages to Express Proportion

A **percentage** is the quantified portion of a whole. Describing the frequencies of males and females in the 2000 Colorado population in percentages shows even more clearly how similar the two amounts are: 50.36% male and 49.64% female. (Common practice in speeches permits us to round off figures, using such terms as "roughly.")

Percentages are especially useful when comparing categories of something, as, for example, in the reasons for delays of domestic flights:

- Nearly 8 percent of April 2007 flights were delayed by aviation system delays; over 7 percent by late-arriving aircraft; over 6 percent by factors within the airline's control, such as maintenance or crew problems; 0.70 percent by extreme weather; and 0.06 percent for security reasons.[14]

Use Averages to Describe Typical Characteristics

An **average** describes information according to its typical characteristics. Usually we think of the average as the sum of the scores divided by the number of scores. This is the *mean,* the arithmetic average. But there are two other kinds of averages—the *median* and the *mode.*

Consider a teacher, whose nine students scored 5, 19, 22, 23, 24, 26, 28, 28, and 30, with 30 points being the highest possible grade. The following illustrates how she would calculate the three types of averages:

- The **mean** score is 22.8, the *arithmetic average,* the sum of the scores divided by 9.

- The **median** score is 24, *the center-most score in a distribution* or the point above and below which 50% of the nine scores fall.

- The **mode** score is 28, the *most frequently occurring score* in the distribution.

The following speaker, claiming that a rival organization misrepresented the "average" tax rate, illustrates how the inaccurate use of averages can distort reality:

The Tax Foundation determines an *average* [*mean*] tax rate for American families simply by dividing all taxes paid by the total of everyone's income. For example, if four middle-income families pay $3,000, $4,000, $5,000, and $6,000, respectively, in taxes, and one very wealthy family pays $82,000 in taxes, the *average* [*mean*] tax paid by these five families is $20,000 ($100,000 in total taxes divided by five families). But four of the five families [actually] have a tax bill equaling $6,000 or less. . . . [Many] analysts would define a *median* income family—a family for whom half of all families have higher income and half have lower income—to be the "typical family" and describe the taxes paid by such a median-income family as the taxes that typical middle-class families owe.[15]

Present Statistics Ethically

Offering listeners inaccurate statistics is unethical. Following are steps you can take to reduce the likelihood of using false or misleading statistics:

Use only reliable statistics. Include statistics from the most authoritative source you can locate, and evaluate the methods used to generate the data. The more information that is available about how the statistics came about, the more reliable the source is likely to be.

Present statistics in context. Inform listeners of when the data were collected, the method used to collect the data, and the scope of the research:

> These figures represent data collected during 2008 from questionnaires distributed to all public and private schools in the U.S. with students in at least one of grades 9–12 in the 50 states and the District of Columbia.

Avoid confusing statistics with "absolute truth." Even the most recent data available will change the next time data are collected. Nor are statistics necessarily any more accurate than the human who collected them. Offer data as they appropriately represent your point, but refrain from declaring that these data are definitive.

QUICK TIP

Avoid Cherry-Picking
*When you search for statistics to confirm an opinion or belief you already hold, you are probably **cherry-picking**— selectively presenting only those statistics that buttress your point of view while ignoring competing data.[16] Locating statistical support material is not a trip through a buffet line to select what looks good and discard what doesn't. Present statistics in context or not at all.*

Refer Orally to Your Sources

Clearly identify the source of your information and provide enough context (including approximate date of publication) to accurately interpret it. For guidelines on orally citing your sources, see Chapter 11, "Citing Sources in Your Speech."

CHECKLIST: Evaluating Your Research Needs

Do you need . . .

✓ Examples to illustrate, describe, or represent your ideas?

✓ A story or anecdote to drive your point home?

✓ Firsthand findings, in the form of testimony, to illustrate your points or strengthen your argument?

✓ Relevant facts, or documented occurrences, to substantiate your statements?

✓ Statistics to demonstrate relationships?

9 Locating Supporting Material

Finding the right mix of supporting material (e.g., examples, facts, statistics, opinions, stories, and testimony) for your speech requires that you conduct primary research, secondary research, or, perhaps most beneficially, a combination of both. **Primary research** is original or firsthand research such as interviews and surveys (see Chapter 6). **Secondary research**, the focus here, includes information produced by others.

QUICK TIP

Assess Your Primary and Secondary Research Needs
Before beginning your search, review your thesis statement. What do you need to elaborate upon, explain, demonstrate, or prove? Different topics suggest varying amounts of primary and secondary research. A speech on drinking habits on campus, delivered to classmates in a beginning speech course, suggests at least some primary research in the form of interviews, surveys, or personal observations. Nearly all topics benefit from a mix of both primary and secondary research.

Locate Secondary Sources

The most likely sources of secondary research include books, newspapers, periodicals, government publications, blogs, and reference works such as encyclopedias, almanacs, books of quotations, and atlases. As you gather these materials, consider how you can use them to generate interest, illustrate meaning, and add solid evidence to assertions.

Books

Books explore topics in depth. A well-written book provides detail and perspective and can serve as an excellent source of supporting examples, stories, facts, and statistics. To locate a book in your library's holdings, refer to the library's online catalog. To search the titles of all books currently in print in the United States, refer to *Books in Print* at www.booksinprint .com. Alternatively, log on to Amazon.com, BarnesandNoble .com, the Library of Congress Online Catalog (www.loc.gov), or an online bookseller and key in your topic.

Newspapers and Periodicals

In addition to reports on the major issues and events of the day, many newspaper stories include detailed background or historic information. Several Web sites devoted to newspapers include newspaper archives (e.g., www.newspaperarchive .com), U.S. newspapers (www.newsvoyager.com), and online world newspapers (world-newspapers.com).

A **periodical** is a regularly published magazine or journal. Periodicals can be excellent sources because they generally include all types of supporting material, as discussed in Chapter 8. Periodicals include general-interest magazines such as *Time* and *Newsweek*, as well as the thousands of specialized magazines, newsletters, and refereed journals. Articles in *refereed journals* are evaluated by experts before being published and supply sources for the information they contain. Articles in *general-interest magazines* rarely contain citations and may or may not be written by experts on the topic.

Most general-interest magazines are available in *Infotrac Online.* Many libraries offer access to *Academic Search Premier* and *EBSCO Academic Search Elite*, both of which offer general periodicals and more specialized scholarly journals. There is also an ever-increasing array of databases devoted to individual disciplines such as business, health, education, and psychology.

Government Publications

Nearly all the information contained in government documents comes from primary sources and is therefore highly credible. Get started by logging on to FirstGov.gov, the official portal to all government information and services, with links to millions of Web pages from federal, local, and tribal governments as well as to nations around the world. The site also includes links to reliable statistics of every kind. The University of Michigan's Documents Center (www.lib.umich.edu/govdocs/) is another excellent starting point.

Reference Works

Reference works include, but are not limited to, encyclopedias, almanacs, biographical resources, books of quotations, poetry collections, and atlases.

ENCYCLOPEDIAS **Encyclopedias** summarize knowledge that is found in original form elsewhere. Their usefulness lies in providing an overview of subjects. *General encyclopedias* attempt to cover all important subject areas of knowledge. *Specialized encyclopedias* delve deeply into one subject area, such as religion, science, art, sports, or engineering. The most comprehensive of the general encyclopedias is the *Encyclopaedia Britannica.*

For a more in-depth look at a topic, specialized encyclopedias of all types range from the *Oxford Encyclopedia of Latinos & Latinas in the United States* to the *Encyclopedia of Physical Education, Fitness, and Sports.*

ALMANACS **Almanacs** and **fact books** contain facts and statistics on many subject areas and are published annually. As with encyclopedias, there are both general and specialized almanacs. In the general category are the *World Almanac and Book of Facts, The Information Please Almanac,* and *The People's Almanac.* One of the better-known specialized almanacs is *The Guinness Book of World Records.*

BIOGRAPHICAL RESOURCES For information about famous or noteworthy people, the *Biography & Genealogy Master Index* is an excellent starting point. Fully one-third of the *Encyclopaedia Britannica* is devoted to biographies. For analyses and criticism of the published works of, individuals you may be speaking about, see *Current Biography* or *Dictionary of American Biography.* Countless *specialized biographies* feature everything from *African American Inventors* to *Famous Hispanics in the World and in History* (access is free at coloquio.com/famosos/alpha.htm).

BOOKS OF QUOTATIONS Quotations frequently appear in speech introductions and conclusions; they are also liberally sprinkled throughout examples, narratives, and testimony. *Bartlett's Familiar Quotations* contains passages, phrases, and proverbs traced to their sources. Many collections are targeted directly to public speakers, including *Quotations for Public Speakers: A Historical, Literary, and Political Anthology*, by Robert G. Torricelli,[1] and *Nelson's Complete Book of Stories, Illustrations, and Quotes* by Robert J. Morgan.[2] Depending on your topic, consult specialized books of quotations, from business to baseball.

POETRY COLLECTIONS   Speakers often use lines of poetry or entire poems both to introduce and conclude speeches and to illustrate points in the speech body. Every library has a collection of poetry anthologies as well as the collected works of individual poets. The *Columbia Granger's World of Poetry* indexes poems by author, title, and first line. Online, search for poetry on poetryarchive.org (www.poetryarchive.org/poetryarchive/home.do).

ATLASES   An **atlas** is a collection of maps, text, and accompanying charts and tables. As well as serving to locate a particular locale and learn about its terrain and demographics, many atlases use maps to explore art history, human anatomy, and many other subjects. For straightforward geographic atlases in print, consult *National Geographic Atlas of the World* and the *Rand McNally Commercial Atlas and Guide*. Online, go to the National Geographic Web site. To learn about what atlases offer beyond geography, conduct a search of atlases related to your topic, e.g., "art AND atlas."

CHECKLIST: Finding Speeches Online

Online, you can find numerous video and audio files of speeches. These can be useful as research and as models of speeches.

✓ *American Rhetoric* (www.americanrhetoric.com/) contains 5000+ speeches.

✓ *Gifts of Speech* (http://gos.sbc.edu/) features speeches by women from around the world.

✓ The Wake Forest University's Political Speeches gateway (www.wfu.edu/~louden/Political%20Communication/Class %20Information/SPEECHES.html) offers links to collections of political speeches.

✓ The United States Senate (www.senate.gov) includes speeches by U.S. Senators.

✓ Vital Speeches of the Day (www04.mcmurry.com/product/VITAL), published twelve times annually, features current speeches delivered in the United States.

From Source to Speech

Recording and Citing Books

When using a book as a source, locate and record the
following citation elements:

1 Title

2 Author

3 Publisher

4 City of Publication

5 Year of Publication

6 Page Number

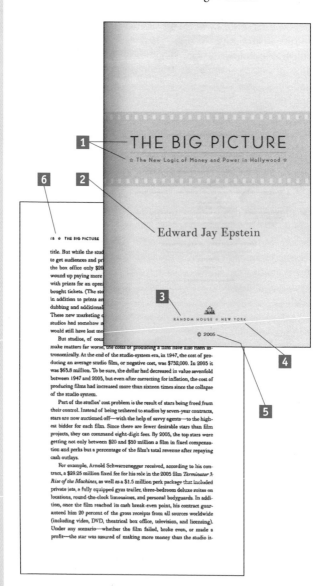

Record Notes

When taking notes, create a separate heading for each idea and record each of the citation elements (author, title, and so forth). Indicate whether the material is a *direct quotation* (statements made word-for-word); a *paraphrase* (restatement of someone else's ideas); or a *summary* (brief overview of someone else's ideas) of the information (for more on these, see Chapter 4).

Following is a sample note for a summary (see also sample notes for paraphrases, p. 71, and quotations, p. 81).

NOTES FOR A SUMMARY:

Subject   Source

Increasing cost of producing movies
Edward Jay Epstein, The Big Picture: The New Logic of Money and Power in Hollywood (New York: Random House, 2005).

Studios' increasing production costs are in part due to the extremely high fees that movie stars can demand for their work on a single film, since actors are no longer tied by contract to specific studios. (p. 18)
(Summary)

Summary

Orally Cite Sources in Your Speech

In your speech, alert the audience to the source of any ideas not your own:

SPEECH EXCERPT INDICATING A SUMMARY:

> **According to Edward Jay Epstein in *The Big Picture: The New Logic of Money and Power in Hollywood*,** studios' increasing production costs are in part due to the extremely high fees that today's stars can demand. No longer tied by contracts to studios, stars' salaries are now settled by bidding wars.

You can find more information on oral citation in Chapter 11.

For guidelines on various citation styles including *Chicago*, APA, MLA, CSE, and IEEE see Appendix A.

From Source to Speech

Recording and Citing Articles from Periodicals

When using an article as a source, locate and record the following citation elements:

1 Author   **4** Date of Publication

2 Article Title   **5** Page Number

3 Periodical Title

2

How to Fix School Lunch

Celebrity chefs, politicians and concerned parents are joining forces to improve the meals kids eat every day.

1

BY PEG TYRE AND
SARAH STAVELEY-O'CARROLL

OR JORGE COLLAZO, EXECUTIVE chef for the New York City public schools, coming up with the perfect jerk sauce is yet another step toward making the 1.1 million schoolkids he serves healthier. In a little more than a year, he's introduced salad bars and replaced whole milk with skim. Beef patties are now served on whole-wheat buns. Until recently, "every piece of chicken the manufacturers sent us was either breaded or covered in a glaze," says Collazo. Brandishing the might of his $125 million annual food budget, he switched to plain cutlets and asked suppliers to come up with something healthy—and appealing—to put on top. Collazo tastes the latest offering. The jerk sauce isn't overly processed and doesn't have trans fats. "Too salty," he says with a grimace. Within minutes, the supplier is hard at work on a lower-sodium version.

A cramped public-school test kitchen might seem an unlikely outpost for a food revolution. But Collazo and scores of others across the country—celebrity chefs and lunch ladies, district superintendents and politicians—say they're determined to improve what kids eat in school. Nearly everyone agrees something must be done. Most school cafeterias are staffed by poorly trained, badly equipped workers who churn out 4.8 billion hot lunches a year. Often the meals, produced for about $1 each, consist of breaded meat patties, french fries and overcooked vegetables. So the kids buy muffins, cookies and ice cream instead—or they feast on fast food from McDonald's, Pizza Hut and Taco Bell, which is available in more than half the schools in the nation.

Vending machines packed with sodas and candy line the hallways. "We're killing our kids" with the food we serve, says Texas Education Commissioner Susan Combs.

As rates of childhood obesity and diabetes skyrocket, public-health officials say schools need to change the way kids eat. It won't be easy. Some kids and their parents don't know better. Home cooking is becoming a forgotten art. And fast-food companies now spend $3 billion a year on television ads aimed at children. Along with reading and writing, schools need to teach kids what to eat to stay healthy, says culinary innovator Alice Waters, who is introducing gardening and fresh produce to 16 schools in California. It's a golden opportunity, she says, "to affect the way children eat for the rest of their lives." Last year star English chef Jamie Oliver took over a school cafeteria in a working-class suburb of London. A documentary about his work shamed the British government into spending $500 million to revamp the nation's school-food program. Oliver says it's the United States' turn now. "If you can put a man on the moon," he says, "you can give kids the food they need to make them lighter, fitter and live longer."

Changing school food takes time. More than a decade ago, when local restaurateur Lynn Walters lobbied school-board members in Santa Fe, N.M., to provide kids with

3

4

5

OR JORGE COLLAZO, EXECUTIVE chef for the New York City public schools, coming up with the perfect jerk sauce is yet another step toward making the 1.1 million schoolkids he serves healthier. In a little more than a year, he's introduced salad bars and replaced whole milk with skim. Beef patties are now served on whole-wheat buns. Until recently, "every piece of chicken the manufacturers sent us was either breaded or covered in a glaze," says Collazo.

Record Notes

When taking notes, create a separate heading for each idea and record each of the citation elements (author, title, and so forth). Indicate whether the material is a direct quotation, a paraphrase, or a summary of the information. Following is a sample note for a paraphrase (see also sample notes for summaries, p. 69, and quotations, p. 81).

NOTES FOR A PARAPHRASE:

Subject   Source

Problems with cafeteria food
Peg Tyre and Sarah Staveley-O'Carroll, "How to Fix School
Lunch: Celebrity Chefs, Politicians, and Concerned Parents
Are Joining Forces to Improve the Meals Kids Eat Every Day,"
Newsweek, 8 August 2005, 50-51.

Jorge Collazo, executive chef for the New York City Public
Schools, says that until recently the schools served breaded
foods, whole milk, and white-floured breads. (p. 50)
(Paraphrase)

Paraphrase

Orally Cite Sources in Your Speech

In your speech, alert the audience to the source of any ideas not your own:

SPEECH EXCERPT INDICATING A PARAPHRASE:

> **As reported in the August 8th, 2005, edition of
> *Newsweek,* executive chef Jorge Collazo of the
> New York City public schools claimed** that
> until recently, virtually every piece of chicken
> that was served was breaded or glazed; students
> drank whole rather than skim milk, and ate
> white rather than whole-wheat bread.

You can find more information on oral citation in Chapter 11.

For guidelines on various citation styles including *Chicago,* APA, MLA, CSE, and IEEE see Appendix A.

WEBLOGS AND SOCIAL NEWS SITES   Blogs and social news sites can provide up-to-the-minute information and opinions on certain speech topics, *if the source is reputable.* A **blog** is a site maintained by individuals or groups containing journal-type entries. Newest entries appear first. A **social news site** allows users to submit news stories, articles, and videos, to share with other users of the site. The most popular items win more visibility.

Use these sources of supporting material with extreme care, referencing only those that are affiliated with reputable (local, regional, or national) news agencies and media outlets, or by well-known bloggers. See Chapter 10, "Doing Effective Internet Research," for information on locating blogs and news sites.

Critically Evaluate Your Sources

Whether you are reviewing a book, a newspaper article, or any other source, consider the following:

- What is the author's background—experience, training, and reputation—in the field of study?

- How credible is the publication? Who is the publisher? Is the person or organization reputable? What other publications has the author or organization published?

- How reliable are the data, especially the statistical information? Generally, statistics drawn from government documents and scientific and academic journals are more reliable than those reported in the popular press (e.g., general-interest magazines).

- How recent is the reference? As a rule, it is best to be familiar with the most recent source you can find, even when the topic is historical. (See Chapter 11 for directions on how to orally credit sources in your speech.)

Record References as You Go

To avoid losing track of sources, maintain a **working bibliography** as you conduct your research. For visual guidelines on keeping track of sources, see the "From Source to Speech" sections on citing books (p. 68), periodicals (p. 70) and Web sources (p. 80). See Appendix A for guidance on preparing an end-of-speech bibliography.

10 Doing Effective Internet Research

As with conducting research in a library, the key to a productive search on the Internet lies in a well-thought-out research strategy, an understanding of the kinds of information that are available, and a grasp of how to use search tools effectively.

Find Print and Online Sources Using a Library Portal

As you search for speech materials, easy access to the Internet may lead you to rely heavily or even exclusively on popular search engines such as Google or Yahoo! In doing so, however, you risk finding false and/or biased information *and* overlooking key sources. For these reasons, when researching your speech online it is a good idea to begin your search at your school's **library portal**, or electronic entry point into its holdings (e.g., the library's home page). The databases and other resources on a library's portal are as much a part of its holdings as are its shelved materials. (For details on how to narrow your speech topic using a library portal, see "From Source to Speech" in Chapter 7, p. 54.)

Library holdings are built through careful and deliberate selection processes by trained professionals.[1] When you select a speech source from a library's print or electronic resources, be it a quotation from an e-journal article or a statistic from a government Web site, you can be assured that an information specialist has vetted that source for reliability and credibility. No such standards exist for popular Web search engines.

TABLE 10.1 • TYPICAL RESOURCES FOUND ON LIBRARY PORTALS

- Full-text databases (newspapers, periodicals, journals)
- Reference works (dictionaries, encyclopedias, quotation resources, fact books, directories)
- Books and monographs
- Statistical resources (e.g., FedStats.gov and *Statistical Abstract*)
- Journals
- Digitized texts (primary documents; digitized books)
- Digitized image collections (e.g., ARTstor Digital Library and Internet Archive)
- Video collections

Access the Invisible Web

In addition to the online collections of actual libraries, a host of **virtual libraries** existing only in the electronic environment often take you to links that do not readily appear in general search engines such as Google. They are considered part of the **invisible Web**—the large portion of the Web that general search engines often fail to find. Countless documents and Web sites form part of the invisible Web; this is yet another reason why you should not rely solely on popular search engines for your speech sources.

TABLE 10.2 • SELECTED VIRTUAL LIBRARIES

- **WWW Virtual Library:** vlib.org
- **Librarians' Index to the Internet:** lii.org/search
- **Internet Public Library (IPL):** www.ipl.org
- **Academic Info:** www.academicinfo.net
- **Digital Librarian:** www.digital-librarian.com
- **The Library of Congress:** www.loc.gov/rr/index.html
- **Infomine:** infomine.ucr.edu

Be a Critical Consumer of Information

Apart from using a library's electronic resources section, how can you distinguish between information on the Internet that is credible and information that is untrustworthy? Search engines such as Google cannot discern the quality of information; only a human editor can do this. Each time you examine a document, especially one that has not been evaluated, ask yourself, "When was the information posted, and is it timely? Where is similar information found?" (See the following "From Source to Speech: Evaluating Web Sources.") If you doubt whether the document has been rated by credible editors, ask, "Who put this information here? Why did they do so? Will these sources be accepted by my audience as credible?" (See "From Source to Speech: Demonstrating Your Sources' Reliability and Credibility," p. 86.)

Distinguish among Information, Propaganda, Misinformation, and Disinformation

Be alert to the quality of the information you examine. Is it reliable *information,* or is it *propaganda, misinformation,* or *disinformation?*[2]

- **Information** is data that are understandable and have the potential to become knowledge when viewed critically and added to what we already know. "Eight million" and "nine percent" are bits of data. However, "The population of New York City in 2000 was reported to top 8,000,000 persons, a growth of 9 percent since 1990" is information because it puts the data in context.

- **Propaganda** is information represented in such a way as to provoke a desired response. The purpose of propaganda is to instill a particular attitude—to encourage you to think a particular way. Military posters that encourage you to enlist are an example of propaganda.

- **Misinformation** always refers to something that is not true. One common form of misinformation on the Internet is the *urban legend*—a fabricated story passed along by unsuspecting people.

- **Disinformation** is the deliberate falsification of information. Doctored photographs and falsified profit-and-loss statements are examples of disinformation in action. The Internet is widely used for disinformation.

Make the Most of Internet Search Tools

To locate information on the Internet efficiently and find the best sources for your speech, you must be familiar with the function of search engines and subject (Web) directories.

Distinguish among Types of Search Engines

Search engines index the contents of the Web, "crawling" the Web, automatically scanning up to billions of documents that contain the keywords and phrases you command them to search. Results are generally ranked from most to least relevant, though criteria for relevance vary.

Individual search engines (such as Google, Yahoo!, and MSN Search) compile their own databases of Web pages. **Meta-search engines** (such as Ixquick, MetaCrawler, and Dogpile) scan a variety of individual search engines simultaneously. (Note that increasingly, librarians discourage the use of meta-search engines because so many return only the top listings from each search engine and include far too many paid listings.)[3] **Specialized search engines** let you conduct narrower but deeper searches into a particular field. Examples of these include Scirus Science Search; Bioethics.gov, sponsored by the President's Council on Bioethics; and

From Source to Speech

Evaluating Web Sources

Check the Most Authoritative Web Sites First

Seek out the most authoritative Web sites on your topic. If your speech explores the NBA draft, investigate the NBA's official Web site first. Check government-sponsored sites such as www.usgov.gov. Government-sponsored sites are free of commercial taint and contain highly credible primary materials.

Evaluate Authorship and Sponsorship

1 *Examine the* **domain** *in the Web address*—the suffix at the end of the address that tells you the nature of the site: educational (".edu"), government (".gov"), military (".mil"), nonprofit organization (".org"), business/commercial (".com"), and network (".net"). A tilde (~) in the address usually indicates that it is a personal page rather than part of an institutional Web site. Make sure to assess the credibility of each site, whether it is operated by an individual, a company, a governmental agency, or a nonprofit group.

2 *Look for an "About" link that describes the organization or a link to a page that gives more information.* These sections can tell a great deal about the nature of a site's content. Be wary of sites that do not include such a link.

3 *Identify the creator of the information.* If an individual operates the site, does the document provide relevant biographical information, such as links to a résumé or a listing of the author's credentials? Look for contact information. A source that doesn't want to be found, at least by e-mail, is not a good source to cite.

Check for Currency

4 *Check for a date that indicates when the page was placed on the Web and when it was last updated.* Is the date current? Web sites that do not have this information may contain outdated or inaccurate information.

Check That the Site Credits Its Sources and That Sources Are Trustworthy

5 *Check that the Web site documents its sources.* Reputable Web sites document the sources they use. Follow any links to these sources, and apply the same criteria to them that you did to the original source document. Verify the information you find with two other independent and reputable sources.

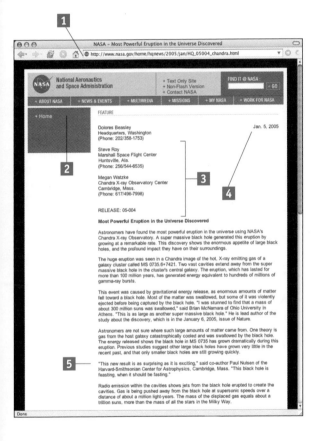

Google Scholar, which searches scholarly literature, including peer-reviewed papers, theses, books, abstracts, and technical reports. New specialized search engines emerge continually.

QUICK TIP

Find a Specialized Search Engine on Your Topic
To find a search engine geared specifically to your topic, type in the topic term with the keywords "search engine." For example, a search for "global warming" AND "search engine" will lead you to many dedicated sites, including Climate Ark (climateark.org) and Redd and Climate Search (forestclimate.net).

Consult Subject (Web) Directories

A **subject (Web) directory** is a catalog of Web sites, organized by a human editor, into subject categories such as "Science," "Reference," or "Arts and Humanities." Subject directories allow you to progressively narrow your searches (see Figure 10.1). If your speech is on some aspect of baseball teams, for example, you would follow these links until you find what you want:

sports→baseball→amateur→leagues→teams

Three of the most reliable general subject directories include Infomine (infomine.ucr.edu), Librarians' Internet Index (www.lii.org), and Yahoo! Directory (Dir.yahoo.com).

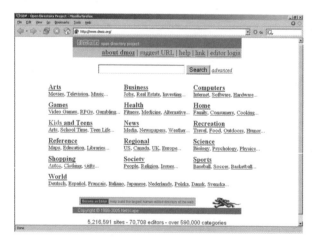

FIGURE 10.1 Home Page for the Open Directory Project (DMOZ)

Locating Blogs and Social News Sites

To find blogs, use a blog-only search engine such as Technorati (www.technorati.com). Review its list of the Top 100 blogs and use its engine to search for blogs on your topic. To locate information on social news sites, visit Digg or Reddit, or conduct a search for your topic (e.g., "environment") AND "social news."

CHECKLIST: Choosing between a Subject Directory and a Search Engine

✓ If you are looking for a list of reputable sites on the same subject, use a subject directory.

✓ If you are looking for a specific page within a site, use a search engine.

✓ If you need to find specific terms, facts, figures, or quotations that may be buried within documents, use a search engine.

✓ If you want to locate a wide variety of materials related to your search, use a subject directory first and then use a search engine.

Beware of Commercial Factors

When researching your topic outside of a library portal or a virtual library, you will want to be alert to unwanted commercial influences on your search results—specifically, whether a listing appears merely because an advertiser has paid to put it there.

Some engines and directories accept fees from companies in exchange for a guaranteed higher ranking within results (called **paid placement**). Others accept fees to include companies in the full index of possible results, without a guarantee of ranking (called **paid inclusion**).[4] You can identify obvious paid-placement listings by looking for a heading labeled "sponsored links" or "sponsored results" at the top, side, or bottom of the main page. It can be much harder to identify paid-inclusion results, however. See Consumerwebwatch.org for helpful tips.

From Source to Speech

Recording and Citing Web Sources

When using a Web document as a source, locate and record the following citation elements:

1 Author of the Work

2 Title of the Work

3 Title of the Web Site

4 Date of Publication/ Last Update

5 Site Address (URL) and Date Accessed

5

http://nobelprize.org/nobel_prizes/literature/articles/cullhed/index.html

Nobel Foundation | Nobel Media | Nobel Museum | Nobel Peace Center | Nobel Web   HOME | CONTACT US | SEARCH

Nobelprize.org **3**

NOBEL PRIZES | ALFRED NOBEL | PRIZE AWARDERS | NOMINATION | PRIZE ANNOUNCEMENTS | AWARD CEREMONIES | EDUCATIONAL GAMES

By Year | Nobel Prize in Physics | Nobel Prize in Chemistry | Nobel Prize in Medicine | **Nobel Prize in Literature** | Nobel Peace Prize | Prize in Economics

Nobel Prize Authors on Time — **2**

1 by Anders Cullhed
August 28, 2001

4

What is Time?

Time is one of the main problems of Western philosophy and literature. Ever since the thinkers of classical Greece tried to understand the swiftness of our seconds, minutes and hours - the impossibility of stepping into the same river twice - the problem of time has haunted our imagination. It is even more than a problem, it is a mystery.

"What is time? It is a secret - lacking in substance and yet almighty." Those are the words of the German Nobel Prize winner in Literature, Thomas Mann, in his great novel *The Magic Mountain* (1924). Mann was a very modern writer, and yet his definition of time was more or less the same as the one provided by the Roman Church Father Saint Augustine in his famous autobiography, *Confessions*, more than fifteen hundred years earlier:

> What, then, is time? I know well enough what it is, provided that nobody asks me; but if I am asked what it is and try to explain, I am baffled.

In ancient Greece, people generally conceived of time as a circle. Hesiod, the famous Greek historian from the 8th century B.C., described five ages of mankind, beginning with the golden age in a remote past, where human beings lived in peace with each other and in harmony with nature, down to the miserable contemporary age of iron, characterized by dispute and warfare.

Two hundred years later, the Pre-Socratic philosopher Pythagoras depicted history as one Great Year (in Latin: Magnus Annus). When such a world historical cycle came to an end, the sun, the moon and all other planets would return to their original positions. Exactly the same people would return to earth, all that had happened would happen once again. These so called eternal recurrences have been of great interest to modern writers, such as the German philosopher Friedrich Nietzsche, and they have inspired the Irish

Done

Record Notes

When taking notes, create a separate heading for each idea and record the citation elements from your sources. Indicate whether the material is a direct quotation, a paraphrase, or a summary of the information. Following is a sample note for a quotation (see also sample notes for summaries, p. 69, and paraphrases, p. 71).

NOTES FOR A QUOTATION:

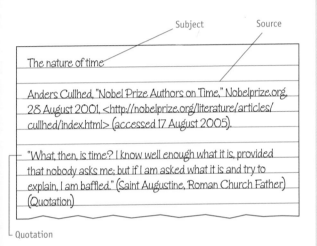

Subject   Source

The nature of time

Anders Cullhed, "Nobel Prize Authors on Time," Nobelprize.org, 28 August 2001, <http://nobelprize.org/literature/articles/cullhed/index.html> (accessed 17 August 2005).

"What, then, is time? I know well enough what it is, provided that nobody asks me; but if I am asked what it is and try to explain, I am baffled." (Saint Augustine, Roman Church Father) (Quotation)

Quotation

Orally Cite Sources in Your Speech

In your speech, alert the audience to the source of any ideas not your own:

QUOTATION:

> **In an article on the nature of time posted on the Web site Nobelprize.org, professor of comparative literature Anders Cullhed notes** how difficult it is to understand the nature of time. For example, **he quotes Saint Augustine, who said,** "What, then, is time? I know well enough what it is, provided that nobody asks me; but if I am asked what it is and try to explain, I am baffled."

You can find more information about oral citation in Chapter 11.

For guidelines on various citation styles including *Chicago*, APA, MLA, CSE, and IEEE see Appendix A.

CHECKLIST: Identifying Paid Listings in Search Results

✓ Look for a heading labeled "Sponsored Links" or "Sponsored Results" at the top, side, or bottom of the main page. This indicates a paid-placement listing.

✓ Use multiple search engines and compare the results.

✓ Beware of meta-search engines, which often include many paid-inclusion listings.

✓ Click beyond the first page of your search results to find relevant sites.

✓ Read the fine print on a search engine's disclosure pages to find its policy on paid inclusion.

Conduct Smart Searches

Familiarize yourself with the features of the search tools you select. Most are programmed to respond to such basic commands as *quotation marks* (" ")—used to find exact phrases (e.g., "white wine")—and *Boolean operators*—words placed between keywords in a search to specify how keywords are related (e.g., AND, OR, NOT, +/−).

Advanced searching (also called field searching) goes beyond the basic search commands to narrow results even more (see Figure 10.2).

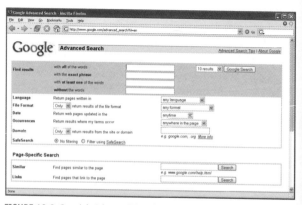

FIGURE 10.2 Google's Advanced Search Page for Conducting Field Searches

An advanced search option includes (at least) the following fields:

- *Keywords.* "All," "exact phrase," "at least one," and "without" filter results for keywords in much the same way as basic search commands.
- *Language* includes search results in the specified language.
- *Country* searches results originating in the specified country.
- *File format* returns results in document formats such as Microsoft Word (.doc), Adobe Acrobat (.pdf), PowerPoint (.ppt), and Excel (.xls).
- *Domain* limits results to specified Internet domains (e.g., .com, .edu, .gov, .org, etc.).
- *Date* searches focus on a specified range of time.

Record Internet Sources

Because Internet sites often change, be sure to keep track of your speech sources. Record source information as you use it, either by creating footnotes with your word-processing program or with citation tools such as EndNote or RefWorks. Refer to the "From Source to Speech" visual guides on citing books (p. 68), periodicals (p. 70), and Web sources (this chapter) for help with keeping track of your speech sources. Also see Appendix A for instructions on maintaining a working bibliography.

11 Citing Sources in Your Speech

Acknowledging sources is a critical aspect of delivering a speech or presentation. When you credit speech sources, you:

- Demonstrate the quality and range of your research to audience members.
- Avoid plagiarism and gain credibility as an ethical speaker who acknowledges the work of others.
- Enhance your own authority and win more support for your point of view.
- Enable listeners to locate your sources and pursue their own research on the topic.

As described in Chapter 4 (pp. 23–30), ethically you are bound to attribute any information drawn from other people's ideas, opinions, and theories, as well as any facts and statistics gathered by others to their original sources. Remember, you need not credit sources for ideas that are *common knowledge*— established information likely to be known by many people and described in multiple places (see p. 29).

Alert Listeners to Key Source Information

For each source, plan on briefly alerting the audience to the following:

1. The *author* or *origin of the source* ("documentary film-maker *Ken Burns . . .*"; or "On the *National Science Foundation Web site . . .*")

2. The *type of source* (magazine, book, personal interview, Web site, blog, online video, etc.)

3. The *title* or a *description of the source* ("In the book *Endangered Minds. . .*"; or "In *an article on sharks . . .*")

4. The *date of the source* ("The article, published in the *October 10th, 2010,* issue . . ." or "On their Web page, *last updated March 8, 2010 . . .*")

Oral presentations need not include the complete biblio-graphic reference (full names, dates, titles, volume, and page numbers). However, keep a running list of source details for a bibliography to appear at the end of your speech draft or outline. (For guidelines on creating a written bibliography for your speeches, see Appendix A.)

Establish the Source's Trustworthiness

Too often, inexperienced speakers credit their sources in bare-bones fashion, offering a rote recitation of citation ele-ments. For example, they might cite the publication name and date but leave out key details that could convince the audience to accept the source as reliable and its conclusions as true. But discerning listeners will accept as legitimate the supporting materials you offer for your claims—examples, stories, testimony, facts, and statistics (see Chapter 8)—only if they believe that the sources are reliable and accurate.

Source reliability refers to our level of trust in a source's credentials and track record for providing accurate infor-mation. If you support a scientific claim by crediting it to an unknown 14-year-old's personal blog, for example, most listeners won't find it as reliable as if you credited it to a scientist affiliated with a reputable institution.

While a source that is reliable is usually accurate, this is not always so.[1] Sometimes we have information that contradicts what we are told by a reliable source. For example, a soldier based in Iraq might read a news article in the *Wall Street Journal* about a battle in which he or she participated. The soldier knows the story contains inaccuracies because the soldier was there. In general, however, the soldier finds the *Wall Street Journal* a reliable source. Since even the most reliable source can sometimes be wrong, *it is always better to offer a variety of sources, rather than a single source, to support a major point.* This is especially the case when your claims are controversial.

To demonstrate a source's trustworthiness, briefly describe the source's qualifications to report on the information, mentioning relevant affiliations and credentials. The "From Source to Speech" guide on p. 86 illustrates how you can orally cite your sources in a way that listeners will accept them.

QUICK TIP

Consider Audience Perception of Sources

Not every trustworthy source is necessarily appropriate for every audience. For example, a politically conservative audience may reject information from a liberal publication. Thus audience analysis should factor in your choice of sources. In addition to checking that your sources are reliable, consider whether they will be seen as credible by your particular audience.[2]

Avoid a Mechanical Delivery

Acknowledging sources need not interrupt the flow of your speech. On the contrary, audience members will welcome information that adds backing to your assertions. The key is to avoid a formulaic, or mechanical, delivery. You can do this by varying your wording. For example, if you introduce one source with the phrase, "According to . . .," switch to another construction, "As reported by . . ." for the next.

From Source to Speech
Demonstrating Your Sources' Reliability and Credibility

How Can I Lead the Audience to Accept My Sources as Reliable and Credible?

- If the source is affiliated with a respected institution, identify that affiliation.
- If citing a study linked to a reputable institution, identify the institution.
- If a source has relevant credentials, note the credentials.
- If the source has relevant real-life experience, mention that experience.

In the following excerpt from a speech about emergency room care in the United States, the speaker omits information about her key sources that would help convince the audience that her evidence and sources are trustworthy:

> According to a series of three reports by the Institute of Medicine on the breakdown of our emergency room system, the need for emergency rooms has increased by 26% since 1993. Today, we'll uncover the catastrophic conditions existing in America's emergency rooms, discover what is causing these conditions, and look at how to restore faith in a system that has — to quote from a New York editorial — "reached a breaking point."

Below we see a much more convincing use of the same sources.

1   **2**   **3**

> According to a **landmark** series of three reports on the breakdown of our emergency room system conducted by the **Institute of Medicine, a unit of the National Academy of Sciences**, the need for emergency rooms has increased by 26% since 1993.
>
> ... Today, we'll uncover the catastrophic conditions existing in America's emergency rooms, discover what is causing these conditions, and look at how to restore our faith in a system that has — to quote from an editorial in the **June 21st, 2006, edition of the New York Times** — "reached a breaking point."

4

1 The speaker wisely includes the adjective "landmark" to signal credibility for her evidence.

2 The speaker communicates relevant affiliations, connecting the source to an entity that raises audience's confidence level.

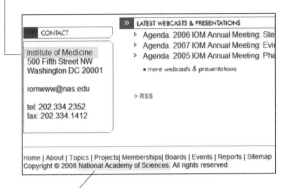

3 The speaker identifies the source as a respected government agency. Listeners are more likely to trust the source if it is connected to a trusted entity.

4 The speaker supports her thesis that a crisis exists with a quotation from a notable source: the *New York Times*, a well-known, well-respected national paper.

> Crisis of care in ERs
>
> Editorial, "Emergency in the Emergency Rooms," NYTimes.com, June 21, 2006, http://www.nytimes.com/2006/06/21/opinion/21Wed4 .html?_r=1 (accessed June 26, 2006).
>
> "The nation's emergency rooms have been stretched thin for at least a decade or more, but a new analysis suggest that they have reached a breaking point." (New York Times Editorial, Quotation)

Overview of Source Types with Sample Oral Citations

Following is an overview of common types of sources cited in a speech, the specific citation elements to mention, and examples of how you might refer to these elements in a presentation. Note that each example includes a **source qualifier**, or brief description of the source's qualifications to address the topic ("Pulitzer-Prize winning author," "researcher at the Mayo Clinic"). Including a source qualifier in your presentation can make the difference between winning or losing acceptance for your supporting material.

BOOK

Citation Elements to Mention: If *two* or *fewer* authors, state first and last names, source qualifier, title, and date of publication. If *three* or *more authors*, state first and last name of first author and "coauthors."

Example: In the book *1948: The First Arab-Israeli War*, published in *2008*, noted *Israeli historian* Benny Morris claims that . . .

Example: In *Paid to Play: An Insider's Guide to Video Game Careers*, published in 2006, career counselor *Alice Rush* and her *two coauthors, both professional game writers*, wrote that . . .

PRINT ARTICLE

Citation Elements to Mention: Same as for "Book."

Example: In an article on honey bees published in the December 2008 edition of *World Watch Magazine, science writer* Sarah DeWeerdt, *who specializes in biology and the environment*, claims that . . .

ONLINE-ONLY MAGAZINE

Citation Elements to Mention: See "Book" and identify publication as "online magazine."

Example: *Columnist* Jacob Liebenluft, writing on laptops and battery conservation in the *December 2, 2008*, edition of the *online magazine* Slate, *which is owned by the* Washington Post . . .

WEB SITE

Citation Elements to Mention: Name the Web site, source qualifier, section of Web site cited (if applicable), and last update.

Example: On its Web site, *last updated September 10, 2006*, the *Society of Interventional Radiology* explains that radio waves are harmless to healthy cells . . .

WEBLOG

Citation Elements to Mention: Name the blogger, source qualifier, affiliated Web site (if applicable), and date of posting.

Example: In a *December 18, 2008*, blog posting on *TechPresident.com*, a group blog that investigates how political candidates use the Web for campaigning, *Patrick Ruffini, former eCampaign Director of the RNC* notes that . . .

TELEVISION OR RADIO PROGRAM

Citation Elements to Mention: Name the program, segment, reporter, source qualifier, and date aired.

Example: Jim Lehrer, *National Public Television's* Newshour host, described in a segment on the auto industry *aired on June 2, 2010* . . .

ONLINE VIDEO

Citation Elements to Mention: Name the online video source, program, segment, source qualifier, and date aired (if applicable).

Example: In a session on mindfulness delivered on the Google campus on *November 12, 2007*, and *broadcast on YouTube*, Jon Kabat-Zinn, *scientist, author, and founding director of the Stress Reduction Clinic* . . .

TESTIMONY (LAY OR EXPERT)

Citation Elements to Mention: Name the person, source qualifier, context in which information was offered, and date information was offered.

Example: On *July 8, 2004*, in *Congressional* testimony before the *U.S. House Subcommittee* on Human Rights and Wellness, *Derek Ellerman* (*co-executive director of the Polaris Project*) said . . ."

PERSONAL INTERVIEW

Citation Elements to Mention: Name the person, source qualifier, and date of interview.

Example: In an interview I conducted *last week, Tim Zeutenhorst, Chairman* of the *Orange City Area Health System Board*, at Orange City Hospital in Iowa, said . . .

Properly Citing Facts and Statistics

Some facts (documented occurrences, including actual
events, dates, times, people, and places; see Chapter 8) are
common knowledge—for example, that the earth revolves
around the sun. Facts that are widely disseminated and commonly known require no attribution. Otherwise, credit the
source of the fact in your speech:

> *According to the Galileo Project Web site* (name), *a project
> supported by Rice University* (source qualifier), *Galileo was
> appointed professor of mathematics at the University of Padua
> in 1592* (fact).

TABLE 11.1 • TYPES OF SUPPORTING MATERIALS AND SAMPLE ORAL CITATION	
TYPE OF SUPPORTING MATERIAL	**SAMPLE ORAL CITATION**
EXAMPLES (real or hypothetical)	"One example of a fiscally effective charity is Lance Armstrong's Livestrong Foundation. According to the Foundation's Annual Report, in 2007 the Livestrong Challenge events raised $78,500 in donations . . ."
STORIES (extended or anecdotal)	"In J.R.R. Tolkien's classic trilogy, *The Lord of the Rings*, a young Hobbit boy named Frodo . . ."
TESTIMONY (expert or lay)	"Dr. Mary Klein, a stem-cell researcher from the Brown University School of Medicine, echoed this sentiment when she spoke last Monday at the Public Health Committee meeting . . ."
FACTS	"According to the *Farmer's Almanac*, published every year since 1818, originally the phrase 'blue moon' referred to the second of two full moons appearing in a single month."
STATISTICS	"Data from the *U.S. Census Bureau*, which produces national population estimates annually using the latest available data on births, deaths, and international migration, indicates that in 2009, there was one birth every eight seconds and one death every twelve seconds in the United States."

Used sparingly, statistics (quantified evidence) add credibility to speech claims, *if* you tell listeners what the numbers actually mean, use terms that describe them accurately, and reveal the methods and scope of the research:

> *According to a landmark series of three reports* (methods and scope of research) on the breakdown of our emergency room system *conducted by the Institute of Medicine* (source qualifier), *the need for emergency rooms has increased by 26 percent since 1993; during the same period, 425 emergency departments closed their doors* (what the numbers actually mean).

Data changes over time, so rather than using phrases such as "this number proves," which represents the statistics as absolute truth, use conditional language such as "these numbers suggest/imply. . . ." For more detailed guidelines on citing statistics see Chapter 8, p. 60.

Properly Citing Summarized, Paraphrased, and Quoted Information

As discussed in Chapter 4, information not your own may be cited in the form of a *summary* (a brief overview of someone else's ideas, opinions, or theories), *paraphrase* (a restatement of someone else's ideas, opinions, or theories in the speaker's own words), or *direct quotation* (statements made verbatim by someone else).

For examples of how to cite quotations, paraphrases, and summaries, see Chapter 4, pp. 27–29, and Visual Guides on pp. 68–69, 70–71, and 80–81.

Part 3
Organization

12 Organizing the Speech

A speech structure is simple, composed of just three general parts: an introduction, a body, and a conclusion. The **introduction** establishes the purpose of the speech and shows its relevance to the audience. The **body** of the speech presents main points that are intended to fulfill the speech purpose. Main points are developed with supporting material to fulfill this purpose. The **conclusion** brings closure to the speech by restating the purpose, summarizing main points, and reiterating why the thesis is relevant to the audience. In essence, the introduction of a speech tells listeners where they are going, the body takes them there, and the conclusion lets them know they have arrived.

Chapter 15 focuses on how to create effective introductions and conclusions. In this chapter we explore the body of the speech. It consists of three elements: *main points, supporting points*, and *transitions*.

Use Main Points to Make Your Claims

Main points express the key ideas of the speech. Their function is to represent each of the main elements or claims being made in support of the speech thesis. To create main points, identify the central ideas and themes of the speech. What are the most important ideas you want to convey? What is the thesis? What key ideas emerge from your research? Each of these ideas or claims should be expressed as a main point.

Use the Purpose and Thesis Statements as Guides

Main points should flow directly from the speech goal and thesis, as in the following example:

SPECIFIC PURPOSE:	(the goal of the speech): To show my audience, through a series of easy steps, how to meditate.
THESIS:	(the central idea of the speech): When performed correctly, meditation is an effective and easy way to reduce stress.
MAIN POINTS:	I. The first step of meditation is the "Positioning."
	II. The second step of meditation is "Breathing."
	III. The third step of meditation is "Relaxation."

93

Restrict the Number of Main Points

Research has shown that audiences can comfortably take in only between two and seven main points.[1] For most speeches, and especially those delivered in the classroom, between two and five main points should be sufficient. If you have too many main points, further narrow your topic or check the points for proper subordination (see p. 97).

Restrict Each Main Point to a Single Idea

A main point should not introduce more than one idea. If it does, split it into two (or more) main points:

INCORRECT:	I. West Texas has its own Grand Canyon, and South Texas has its own desert.
CORRECT:	I. West Texas boasts its own Grand Canyon.
	II. South Texas boasts its own desert.

Each main point should be mutually exclusive of one another. If they are not, consider whether a main point more properly serves as a subpoint.

Express each main point as a *declarative sentence* (one that states a fact or argument). This emphasizes the point and alerts audience members to the main thrusts of your speech. For example, if one of your main points is that children need more vitamin D, you should clearly state, "According to the nation's leading pediatricians, children from infants to teens should double the recommended amount of vitamin D." As shown in the example about West Texas and South Texas, when possible state your main points (and supporting points; see below) in **parallel form** — that is, in similar grammatical form and style. This helps listeners understand and retain the points, and it lends power and elegance to your words.

QUICK TIP

Save the Best for Last — or First

Listeners have the best recall of speech points made at the beginning and the end of a presentation. If it is especially important that listeners remember certain ideas, introduce the points near the beginning of the speech and reiterate them at the conclusion.

Use Supporting Points to Prove Your Claims

Supporting points represent the supporting material or evidence you have gathered to justify the main points. Use them to substantiate or prove your thesis with the material you've gathered in your research — examples, narratives, testimony, facts, and statistics (see Chapter 8).

QUICK TIP

Tailor Support to the General Speech Goal
To guide the creation of your supporting points, focus on the general speech goal. If your goal is to inform, include details that help listeners grasp the topic. If it is to persuade, subpoints should include compelling reasons, causes, and facts that help convince listeners to agree with you. If your goal is to entertain, appeal to humor or goodwill.

Use Indentation to Arrange Supporting Points

In an outline, supporting points appear in a subordinate position to main points. This is indicated by **indentation**. As with main points, supporting points should be arranged in order of their importance or relevance to the main point. The most common format is the **roman numeral outline**. Main points are enumerated with uppercase roman numerals (I, II, III . . .), while supporting points are enumerated with capital letters (A, B, C . . .), Arabic numerals (1, 2, 3 . . .), and lowercase letters (a, b, c . . .), as seen in the following:

I. Main point
   A. Supporting point
      1. Sub-supporting point
         a. Sub-sub-supporting point

Here is an example (in phrase outline form; see p. 11) from a speech about using effective subject lines in business-related e-mails:

I. Subject line most important, yet neglected part of e-mail.
   A. Determines if recipient reads message
      1. Needs to specify point of message
      2. Needs to distinguish from spam

    B. Determines if recipient ignores message
       1. May ignore e-mail with missing subject line
       2. May ignore e-mail with unclear subject line

II. Use proven techniques for effective subject lines
    A. Make them informative
       1. Give specific details
       2. Match central idea of e-mail
       3. Be current
    B. Check for sense
       1. Convey correct meaning
       2. Reflect content of message
    C. Avoid continuing subject line in text
       1. May annoy the reader
       2. May be unclear
          a. Could be confused with spam
          b. Could be misinterpreted

QUICK TIP

Spend Time Organizing Speech Points

*Don't skimp on organizing speech points. Listeners'
understanding of a speech is directly linked to how well it is
organized;[2] audience attitudes plummet when the speech is
disorganized.[3] Listeners also find speakers whose speeches are
well organized more believable than those who present poorly
organized ones.[4]*

Principles of Organizing Main and Supporting Points

A well-organized speech is characterized by unity, coherence,
and balance. Try to adhere to these principles as you arrange
your speech points.

Unity

A speech exhibits *unity* when it contains only those points
implied by the purpose and thesis statements. Each main
point supports the thesis, and each supporting point provides evidence for the main points. Each sub-supporting
point supports each supporting point. Finally, each point
should focus on a single idea.

Coherence

A speech exhibits *coherence* when it is organized clearly and logically. The speech body should follow logically from the introduction, and the conclusion should follow logically from the body. Within the body of the speech itself, main points should follow logically from the thesis statement, and supporting points should follow logically from the main points. Transitions serve as logical bridges that help establish coherence.

To ensure coherence, adhere to the principle of **co-ordination and subordination** — the logical placement of ideas relative to their importance to one another. Ideas that are coordinate are given equal weight. An idea that is subordinate to another is given relatively less weight. In outlines, **coordinate points** are indicated by their parallel alignment and **subordinate points** are indicated by their indentation below the more important points. For an example, see the outline shown earlier on using effective subject lines in business-related e-mails: Coordinate points are aligned with one another, while subordinate points are indented below the points that they substantiate. Thus Main Point II is coordinate with Main Point I, Subpoint A is subordinate to Main Point I, Subpoint B is coordinate with Subpoint A, and so forth.

Balance

The principle of *balance* suggests that appropriate emphasis or weight be given to each part of the speech relative to the other parts and to the theme. The body of a speech should always be the longest part, and the introduction and conclusion should be of roughly the same length. Stating the main points in parallel form is one aspect of balance. Assigning each main point at least two supporting points is another.

QUICK TIP

Create at Least Two Subpoints . . . or None
If you have only one subpoint, consider how you might incorporate it into the superior point. Think of a main point as a body and supporting points as legs; without at least two legs, the body cannot stand.

Use Transitions to Give Direction to the Speech

Transitions are words, phrases, or sentences that tie the speech ideas together, enabling the speaker to move smoothly from one point to the next. Transitions can be considered the "neurosystem" of speeches: They provide consistency of movement from one point to the next and cue the audience that a new point will be made. Transitions can take the form of full sentences, phrases, or single words.

Use Transitions between Main Points

When moving from one main point to another, **full-sentence transitions** are especially effective. For example, to move from Main Point I in a speech about sales contests (*Top management should sponsor sales contests to halt the decline in sales over the past two years*) to Main Point II (*Sales contests will lead to better sales presentations*), the speaker might use the following transition:

> Next, let's look at exactly what sales contests can do for us.

CHECKLIST: Reviewing Main and Supporting Points

✓ Do the main points express the key points of the speech?

✓ Is each main point truly a main point or a subpoint of another main point?

✓ Is each main point substantiated by at least two supporting points — or none?

✓ Do you spend roughly the same amount of time on each main point?

✓ Are the supporting points truly subordinate to the main points?

✓ Does each main point and supporting point focus on a single idea?

✓ Are your main and supporting points stated in parallel form?

Use Transitions between Supporting Points

Transitions between supporting points can also be handled with full sentences. For example, to move from Supporting Point A (*Sales personnel will be motivated by competition*) to

Supporting Point B (*Contests are relatively inexpensive*), the speaker might use the following transition:

Another way that sales competitions will benefit us is by their relative cost effectiveness.

Conjunctions or phrases (also called **signposts**) such as the following can be just as effective:

Next . . .

First . . . (second, third, and so forth)

We now turn . . .

Finally, let's consider . . .

If you think that's shocking . . .

Similarly . . .

TRANSITIONAL WORDS AND PHRASES
To show comparisons: Similarly; In the same way; Likewise; Just as
To contrast ideas: On the other hand; And yet; At the same time; In spite of; However; In contrast
To illustrate cause and effect: As a result; Hence; Because; Thus; Consequently
To illustrate sequence of time or events: First, second, third . . . ; Following this; Later; Earlier; At present; In the past
To indicate explanation: For example; To illustrate; In other words; To simplify; To clarify
To indicate additional examples: Not only; In addition to; Let's look at
To emphasize significance: Most importantly; Above all; Remember; Keep in mind
To summarize: In conclusion; In summary; Finally; Let me conclude by saying

Sample Techniques for Posing Transitions

Transitions are often posed in **restate-forecast form,** restating the point just covered and previewing the point to be covered next:

Now that we've established a need for sales contests (*restatement*), let's look at what sales contests can do for us (*forecast*).

Transitions can also be stated as *rhetorical questions,* or questions that do not invite actual responses. Instead, they

From Point to Point

Using Transitions to Guide Your Listeners

Transitions direct your listeners from one point to another in your speech. At a bare minimum, plan on using transitions to move between:

- The introduction and the body of the speech
- The main points
- Key subpoints
- The body of the speech and the conclusion

Introduction

I. Today I'll explore the steps you can take to create a greener campus...

(**Transition:** Let's begin by considering what "going green" actually means.)

Body

I. "Going green" means taking action to promote and maintain a healthy environment.

    (**Transition:** So how do you go green?)

    A. Get informed—understand what is physically happening to the planet

(**Transition:** Understanding the issues is only part of going green, however. Perhaps most importantly....)

    B. Recognize that change starts here, on campus, with you....

While transitions help guide your listeners from point to point, they can also do a lot more, including:

- Signal explanations and examples
- Emphasize, repeat, compare, or contrast ideas
- Introduce propositions (major speech points)
- Illustrate cause and effect
- Summarize and preview information
- Suggest conclusions from evidence

Following is an excerpt from a working outline on a speech about campuses going green. Note how the student edits himself to ensure that he (1) uses transitions to help listeners follow along and retain his speech points and (2) uses transitions strategically to achieve his goal of persuading the audience.

1 — (**Transition:** Why are environmentalists targeting college campuses?)

I. College campuses generate the waste equivalent of many large towns...

2 — (**Transition:** As a result...)

    A. Colleges face disposal issues, especially of electronics...

    B. Administrators face decisions about mounting energy costs...

3 — (**Transition:** Following are some ideas to create a greener campus. First...)

II. Promote a campus-wide recycling program

4 — (**Transition:** For example...)

    A. Decrease the availability of bottled water and disposable...

    B. Insist on recycling bins at all residence hall...

    C. Encourage computer centers to recycle...

5 — (**Transition:** Recycling is a critical part of going green. Decreasing the consumption of plastic and paper, installing recycling bins, and responsibly disposing of print cartridges will make a huge difference. Another aspect of going green is using sustainable energy...)

III. Lobby administrators to investigate solar, wind, and geothermal...

    A. Make an argument for "eco-dorms..."

    B. Explore alternative heating....

6 — (**Transition:** So far, we've talked about practical actions we can take to encourage a greener lifestyle on campus, but what about beyond the campus?)

IV. Get involved at the town government level

    A. Town-grown committees...

    B. Speak up and voice your concerns...

7 — (**Transition:** As you can see, we have work to do...)

Conclusion

I. If we want our children and our children's children to live to see a healthy earth, we must take action now...

1 Student inserts a transition (**rhetorical question**) to introduce a new proposition (e.g., main point).

2 Student realizes he needs to insert this transitional phrase to signal a **cause-effect relationship**.

3 Student uses a transition to **move to the next proposition**.

4 This transitional phrase **introduces additional examples**.

5 Student inserts an **internal summary** to help listeners retain information and transition to the next main point.

6 Student inserts an **internal summary** to move to the next main point.

7 Student inserts a transition to signal a **shift to his concluding point**.

101

stimulate listeners to anticipate probable answers, alerting them to the forthcoming point (see Chapter 15).

> Will contests be too expensive? Well, actually . . .

Use Previews and Summaries as Transitions

Previews are transitions that tell the audience what to expect next. In speech introductions a **preview statement** briefly introduces the main points of the speech (see Chapter 15). Within the body itself, **internal previews** can be used to alert audience members to a shift from one main point or idea to another:

> Victoria Woodhull was a pioneer in many respects. Not only was she the first woman to run her own brokerage firm; she was also the first to run for the presidency of the United States, though few people know this. Let's see how she accomplished these feats.

Similar to the internal preview, the **internal summary** draws together important ideas before the speaker proceeds to another speech point. Internal summaries help listeners review and evaluate the thread of the theme thus far:

> It should be clear that the kind of violence we've witnessed in the schools and in our communities has a deeper root cause than the availability of handguns. Our young children are crying out for a sense of community, of relatedness and meaning, that they just aren't finding in the institutions that are meant to serve them.

See Chapter 14, "Outlining the Speech," to learn how to include transitions in the outline of your speech.

CHECKLIST: Reviewing Transitions

✓ Do you include enough transitions to adequately guide listeners through your speech?

✓ Do you use transitions to move from one main point to another and one subpoint to the next?

✓ Do you use internal previews and summaries where appropriate?

✓ Do you use transitions between the introduction and the body and between the body and the conclusion?

13 Selecting an Organizational Pattern

Once you have selected the main points for your speech, you must decide on the type of organizational arrangement (or combination of arrangements) for them. You can then proceed to flesh out the points with subordinate ideas. Speeches make use of at least a dozen different arrangements of main and supporting points. Here we look at seven commonly used patterns for all forms of speeches: chronological, spatial, causal (cause-effect), problem-solution, topical, narrative, and circular. These patterns offer an organized way to link points together to maximum effect. In Chapter 24, you will find three additional patterns of organization designed specifically for persuasive speeches: *Monroe's motivated sequence, refutation,* and *comparative advantage.*

Arranging Speech Points Chronologically

Topics that describe a series of events in time or that develop in line with a set pattern of actions or tasks lend themselves to the arrangement of main points according to their occurrence in time relative to one another. A **chronological pattern of arrangement** (also called a *temporal pattern*) follows the natural sequential order of the main points. A speaker might describe events leading to the adoption of a peace plan, for example, or describe how to build a model car. A speech describing the development of the World Wide Web, for example, calls for a chronological, or time-ordered, sequence of main points:

THESIS STATEMENT:	The Internet evolved from a small network designed for military and academic scientists into a vast array of networks used by billions of people around the globe.
MAIN POINTS:	I. The Internet was first conceived in 1962 as the ARPANET to promote the sharing of research among scientists in the United States.
	II. In the 1980s, a team created TCP/IP, a language that could link networks, and the Internet as we know it was born.
	III. At the end of the Cold War, the ARPANET was decommissioned, and the World Wide Web constituted the bulk of Internet traffic.[1]

QUICK TIP

Blend Organizational Patterns

The pattern of organization for your subpoints need not always follow the pattern you select for your main points. Do keep your main points in one pattern, but feel free to use other patterns for subpoints when it makes sense to do so. For instance, for a speech about the history of tattooing in the United States, you may choose a chronological pattern to organize the main points but use a cause-effect arrangement for some of your subpoints regarding why tattooing is on the rise today. Organization, whether of main points or subpoints, should be driven by the demands of the content.

Arranging Speech Points Using a Spatial Pattern

When describing or explaining the physical arrangement of a place, a scene, or an object, logic suggests that the main points can be arranged in order of their physical proximity or direction relative to one another. This calls for a **spatial pattern of arrangement**. For example, you can select a spatial arrangement when your speech provides the audience with a "tour" of a particular place:

THESIS STATEMENT: El Morro National Monument in New Mexico is captivating for its variety of natural and historical landmarks.

MAIN POINTS: I.   Visitors first encounter an abundant variety of plant life native to the high-country desert.

II. Soon visitors come upon an age-old watering hole that has receded beneath the 200-foot cliffs.

III. Beyond are the famous cliff carvings made by hundreds of travelers over several centuries of exploration in the Southwest.

In a speech describing a computer company's market growth across regions of the country, a speaker might use the spatial arrangement as follows:

THESIS STATEMENT: Sales of Digi-Tel Computers have grown in every region of the country.

MAIN POINTS: I.   Sales are strongest in the Eastern Zone.

II. Sales are growing at a rate of 10 percent quarterly in the Central Zone.

III. Sales are up slightly in the Mountain Zone.

Arranging Speech Points Using a Causal (Cause-Effect) Pattern

Some speech topics represent cause-effect relationships. Examples include (1) events leading to higher interest rates, (2) reasons students drop out of college, and (3) causes of spousal abuse. The main points in a **causal (cause-effect) pattern of arrangement** usually take the following form:

I. Cause

II. Effect

Sometimes a topic can be discussed in terms of multiple causes for a single effect, or a single cause for multiple effects:

MULTIPLE CAUSES FOR A SINGLE EFFECT: REASONS STUDENTS DROP OUT OF COLLEGE	SINGLE CAUSE FOR MULTIPLE EFFECTS: RESULTS OF DROPPING OUT OF COLLEGE
I. Cause 1 (lack of funds)	I. Cause (lack of funds)
II. Cause 2 (unsatisfactory social life)	II. Effect 1 (lowered earnings over lifetime)
III. Cause 3 (unsatisfactory academic performance)	III. Effect 2 (decreased job satisfaction over lifetime)
IV. Effect (drop out of college)	IV. Effect 3 (increased stress level over lifetime)

Some topics are best understood by presenting listeners with the effect(s) first and the cause or causes subsequently. For example, in an informative speech on the 1988 explosion of Pan Am Flight 103 over Lockerbie, Scotland, a student speaker arranges his main points as follows:

THESIS STATEMENT: The explosion of Pan Am Flight 103 over Lockerbie, Scotland, killed 270 people and resulted in the longest-running aviation investigation in history.

MAIN POINTS: I.   (Effect) Two hundred and fifty-nine passengers and crew members died; an additional eleven people on the ground perished.

MAIN POINTS: II.   (Effect) Longest-running aviation investigation in history.

III.   (Cause) Court found cause of explosion was a terrorist act, a bomb planted by Libyan citizen Al Megrahi.

IV.   (Cause) Many people believe that Megrahi did not act alone, if he acted at all.

Arranging Speech Points Using a Problem-Solution Pattern

The **problem-solution pattern of arrangement** organizes main points to demonstrate the nature and significance of a problem and to provide justification for a proposed solution. This type of arrangement can be as general as two main points:

I.   Problem (define what it is)

II.   Solution (offer a way to overcome the problem)

But many problem-solution speeches require more than two points to adequately explain the problem and to substantiate the recommended solution:

I.   The nature of the problem (identify its causes, incidence, etc.)

II.   Effects of the problem (explain why it's a problem, for whom, etc.)

III.   Unsatisfactory solutions (discuss those that have not worked)

IV.   Proposed solution (explain why it's expected to work)

The following is a partial outline of a persuasive speech about online bullying arranged in a problem-solution format as illustrated above (for more on the problem-solution pattern, see Chapter 24).

THESIS STATEMENT: To combat Internet ("cyber") bullying, we need to educate others about it, report it when it happens, and punish the offenders.

MAIN POINT: I.   Nature of online bullying

A.   Types of activities involved

1.   Name-calling, insults

            2. Circulation of embarrassing
               pictures

            3. Sharing private information

            4. Threats

         B. Incidence of bullying

         C. Profile of offenders

MAIN POINT: II. Effects of online bullying on victims

         A. Acting out in school

         B. Feeling unsafe in school

         C. Skipping school

         D. Experiencing depression

MAIN POINT: III. Unsuccessful attempts at solving
              online bullying

         A. Letting offenders and victims
            work it out on their own

         B. Ignoring problem, assuming it
            will go away

MAIN POINT: IV. Ways to solve online bullying

         A. Educate in schools

         B. Report incidents to authorities

         C. Suspend or expel offenders

Arranging Speech Points Topically

When each of the main points is a subtopic or category of the
speech topic, try the **topical pattern of arrangement** (also
called *categorical pattern*). Consider an informative speech
about choosing Chicago as a place to establish a career. You
plan to emphasize three reasons for choosing Chicago: the
strong economic climate of the city, its cultural variety, and
its accessible public transportation. Since these three points
are of relatively equal importance, they can be arranged in
any order without affecting one another or the speech purpose negatively. For example:

THESIS STATEMENT: Chicago is an excellent place to establish
                   a career.

MAIN POINTS: I.   Accessible transportation

         II. Cultural variety

         III. Economic stability

This is not to say that, when using a topical arrangement,
you should arrange the main points without careful

consideration. You may decide to arrange the points in order of the audience's most immediate needs and interests:

I. Economic stability

II. Cultural variety

III. Accessible transportation

QUICK TIP

Find Freedom with the Topical Pattern

Topical arrangements give you the greatest freedom to structure main points according to the way you wish to present your topic. You can approach a topic by dividing it into two or more categories, for example. You can lead with your strongest evidence or leave your most compelling points until you near the conclusion. If your topic does not call out for one of the other patterns described in this chapter, be sure to experiment with the topical pattern.

Arranging Speech Points Using the Narrative Pattern

Storytelling is often a natural and effective way to get your message across. In the **narrative organizational pattern**, the speech consists of a story or series of short stories, replete with character, settings, plot, and vivid imagery.

In practice, a speech built largely upon a story (or series of stories) is likely to incorporate elements of other designs. For example, you might organize the main points of the story in an effect-cause design, in which you first reveal why something happened (such as a drunken driving accident) and then describe the events that led up to the accident (the causes).

Whatever the structure, simply telling a story is no guarantee of giving a good speech. Any speech should include a clear thesis, a preview, well-organized main points, and transitions. For example, in a speech entitled "Tales of the Grandmothers," Anita Taylor[2] who uses the real-life history of her grandmother to illustrate how women in the United States have always worked, even if they were unpaid, frequently leaves off and picks up the story's thread in order to orient her listeners and drive home her theme. In addition to explicitly stating her thesis, Taylor pauses to preview main points:

> "My grandmothers illustrate the points I want to make . . ."

Taylor also makes frequent use of transitions, including internal previews, summaries, and simple signposts, to help her listeners stay on track:

"But, let's go on with Luna Puffer Squire Nairn's story."

Taylor also pauses in her story to signal the conclusion:

"So here we are today . . . And finally . . ."

Arranging Speech Points in a Circular Pattern

A pattern that is particularly useful when you want listeners to follow a line of reasoning is the *circular organizational pattern.* Here, you develop one idea, which leads to another, which leads to a third, and so forth, until you arrive back at the speech thesis.[3] In a speech on the role friendship plays in physical and mental well-being, a student speaker showed how acts of consideration and kindness lead to more friendships, which in turn lead to more social support, which then results in improved mental and physical health. Each main point leads directly to another main point, with the final main point leading back to the thesis.

CHECKLIST: Choosing an Organizational Pattern

Does your speech . . .

✓ Describe a series of developments in time or a set of actions that occur sequentially? Use the *chronological pattern of organization.*

✓ Describe or explain the physical arrangement of a place, a scene, or an object? Use the *spatial pattern of organization.*

✓ Explain or demonstrate a topic in terms of its underlying causes or effects? Use the *causal (cause-effect) pattern of organization.*

✓ Demonstrate the nature and significance of a problem and justify a proposed solution? Use the *problem-solution pattern of arrangement.*

✓ Stress natural divisions in a topic, in which points can be moved to emphasize audience needs and interests? Use a *topical pattern of arrangement.*

✓ Convey ideas through a story, using character, plot, and settings? Use a *narrative pattern of arrangement,* perhaps in combination with another pattern.

✓ Stress a particular line of reasoning that leads from one point to another, and then back to the thesis? Use a *circular pattern of arrangement.*

14 Outlining the Speech

Once you've selected a pattern for organizing your main points, the next step is to outline the speech. Outlines are critical to organizing a speech, revealing any weaknesses in the logical ordering of points and providing a blueprint for presentation.

Plan on Creating Two Outlines

As you develop a speech, you will actually create two outlines: a working outline (also called *preparation* or *rough outline*) and a speaking, or delivery, outline. The purpose of the **working outline** is to organize and firm up main points and, using the evidence you've collected, to develop supporting points to substantiate them. Completed, the working outline will contain your entire speech, organized and supported to your satisfaction.

The **speaking outline** (also called a *delivery* outline) is the one you will use when you are practicing and actually presenting the speech. Speaking outlines, which contain your ideas in condensed form, are much briefer than working outlines. Figure 14.1 provides an overview of the steps involved in organizing and outlining a speech.

Use Sentences, Phrases, or Key Words

Speech outlines can be created using complete sentences, phrases, or key words. Working outlines typically contain full sentences, reflecting much of the text of the speech; speaking outlines use phrases or key words.

In a **sentence outline**, each main and supporting point is stated in sentence form as a declarative sentence (one that makes an assertion about a subject). So too are the introduction and conclusion. Often, these sentences are stated in much the same way the speaker wants to express the idea.

The following is an excerpt of a working outline in sentence format from a speech by Mark B. McClellan[1] on keeping prescription drugs safe:

I. The prescription drug supply is under unprecedented attack from a variety of increasingly sophisticated threats.

   A. Technologies for counterfeiting, ranging from pill molding to dyes, have improved across the board.

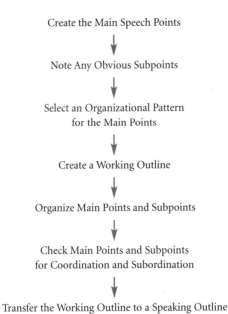

Create the Main Speech Points

↓

Note Any Obvious Subpoints

↓

Select an Organizational Pattern
for the Main Points

↓

Create a Working Outline

↓

Organize Main Points and Subpoints

↓

Check Main Points and Subpoints
for Coordination and Subordination

↓

Transfer the Working Outline to a Speaking Outline

FIGURE 14.1 Steps in Organizing and Outlining the Speech

   B. Inadequately regulated Internet sites have become
      major portals for unsafe and illegal drugs.

Once you've completed the working outline, transfer its
ideas to a speaking outline that uses phrases or key words. An
outline that uses full sentences is not recommended because
it restricts eye contact and forces the speaker to focus more
on reading verbatim from the outline than on actually delivering the speech.

A **phrase outline** uses partial construction of the
sentence form of each point. Phrase outlines encourage you
to become so familiar with your speech points that a glance
at a few words is enough to remind you of exactly what to
say. A section of McClellan's sentence outline would appear
as follows:

I. Drug supply under attack

   A. Counterfeiting technologies more sophisticated

   B. Unregulated Internet sites

The **key-word outline** uses the smallest possible units of understanding to outline the main and supporting points.

I. Threats

   A. Counterfeiting

   B. Internet

Many speaking experts recommend using the key-word format for delivery, suggesting that less reliance on outline notes allows you increased eye contact with the audience and greater freedom of movement. This format also ensures that you are prepared and in better control of your thoughts and actions. With sufficient practice, the key words will jog your memory so that the delivery of your ideas becomes more natural.

QUICK TIP

Use Outlining to Sharpen Your Thinking
Skill in outlining serves you well in school, on the job, and in the community. Many classroom speaking and writing assignments require that you demonstrate your thoughts in organized fashion. On the job, employers hire people who can communicate ideas logically and convincingly, both orally and in writing. You will also make a greater impact in the community when your ideas are convincingly and compellingly arranged. No better tool exists for ensuring the logical flow of ideas in each of these arenas than that of outlining.

Create a Working Outline First

Begin with a working outline (many experts and instructors suggest using full sentences) before you prepare the actual speaking outline; doing so will give you confidence that you've satisfactorily fleshed out your speech points and that they follow in a logical and compelling progression. Rather than writing out the speech word for word, however, focus on charting a coherent and well-supported course:

• Prepare the body of the speech before the introduction or conclusion, keeping the introduction and conclusion *separate from* the main points.

CHECKLIST: Steps in Creating a Working Outline

✓ Write out your topic, general purpose, specific speech purpose, and thesis.

✓ Establish your main points (optimally two to five).

✓ Flesh out supporting points.

✓ Check for correct subordination and coordination.

✓ Label each speech part (i.e., "Introduction," "Body," and "Conclusion").

✓ Write out each speech point in sentence format.

✓ Label and write out transitions.

✓ Note sources in parentheses.

✓ Add a list of references to the outline.

✓ Assign the speech a title.

- Clearly mark where speech points require source credit. Once you complete the outline, prepare a bibliography. For guidelines on what to include in a source note, see "From Source to Speech" guides in Chapters 9, 10, and 11, and Appendix A for individual citation styles.

- Assign the speech a title, one that informs people of its subject in a way that invites them to listen to or read it.

SAMPLE WORKING OUTLINE

The following outline is from a speech delivered by John Coulter at Salt Lake Community College. It uses the sentence format and includes labeled transitions.

Staying ahead of Spyware

JOHN COULTER
Salt Lake Community College

TOPIC: Problems and solutions associated with spyware

SPECIFIC PURPOSE: To inform my audience of the dangers of spyware so that they may take steps to prevent infection

THESIS STATEMENT: Computer users must understand the nature of spyware and how it works in order to take the necessary steps to protect themselves.

INTRODUCTION

I. Imagine how you would feel if someone were tracking everything you did on the Internet, including recording your passwords and credit card numbers. *(Attention getter)*

II. A type of software known as spyware can install itself on your computer without your knowledge and harvest this sensitive information.

III. To protect yourself, you need to understand how spyware works. (*Thesis*)

IV. Today, I'll talk about what spyware is, the harm it causes, who it affects, and how to keep your computer from becoming infected. (*Preview*)

TRANSITION: So, what exactly is spyware?

BODY

I. Spyware is about a decade old and appears in many guises.

    A. Until the year 2000, "spyware" referred to monitoring devices on cameras. (FTC, March 2005 Report)

        1. Its first link to software apparently was in connection with the *Zone Alarm* security program.

        2. Today, the Federal Trade Commission defines spyware as any computer code that installs in your computer, gathers data from it, and sends the information back to a remote computer without your consent. (FTC, *Consumer Alert*)

           (a) Spyware includes software that will advertise on your computer.

           (b) It also includes software that collects personal information.

TRANSITION: You may be wondering how spyware gets into your computer and what it does once it gets there.

    B. Spyware installs itself silently, often "piggybacking" onto other downloaded programs such as file-sharing applications and games.

        1. Links in pop-up ads and the "unsubscribe" button in spam are known sources.

2. Some types track your Web-browsing habits and sell this information to marketers.

3. "Adware" loads ads onto the computer but doesn't monitor browsing habits.

4. The most dangerous type, called keystroke logging, records and transmits keystrokes to steal such personal information as passwords and social security numbers.

TRANSITION: There's a lot of confusion regarding the difference between spyware and computer viruses—and even whether there is any.

C. Spyware is different from a virus in a variety of ways.

1. Viruses are generally written in their own codes by individuals in order to brag about causing damage. (CNET.com video)

2. Spyware is written by teams employed by companies, not all of them shady, to make money.

3. Viruses have been around for more than two decades; everyone agrees on how to define them; and they are illegal.

TRANSITION: Leaving aside the finer distinctions between spyware and other types of computer menaces, what is clear is that spyware represents a serious threat.

II. Users can learn to recognize symptoms of spyware.

A. Signs of infiltration include a constant stream of pop-up ads, strange toolbars on the desktop, and hijacked browser settings. (Vara, *WSJ*, July 18th, 2005)

B. Files may become displaced or disappear, and the computer may crash.

III. Spyware is the leading cause of computer-related problems today.

A. Tanner Nielson of Totally Awesome Computers in Salt Lake City, Utah, reports that the majority of problems brought into his store are spyware related. (Nielson interview)

B. A 2008 *Consumer Reports* national survey finds that spyware is a leading cause of computer malfunction. (*Consumer Reports*, 2008)

1. In 2008, 1 in 14 computer owners experienced severe computer problems, including erased hard drives.

    2. Costs to consumers from spyware during
       2007–2008 totaled $3.6 billion.

TRANSITION: So spyware can do some nasty things to
                   your computer as well as your wallet.

IV. Prevention is the best way to avoid spyware's harmful
    and potentially dangerous effects.

    A. Keep your browser up-to-date to take advantage of
       security updates.

    B. Invest in one of the three top antispyware programs
       recommended by *PC Magazine*: Webroot's
       Antivirus with AntiSpyware, PC Tools' Spyware
       Doctor, and Symantec's Norton Internet Security
       (*PC Magazine*, 2008)

    C. Enable your computer's firewall or purchase one
       from a company such as McAfee or Symantec.

    D. Download free software only from sites you know
       and trust.

    E. Don't click on links in pop-up windows.

    F. Don't reply to or even open spam or any e-mail that
       isn't from someone you know.

    G. Don't hit the "unsubscribe" button because spyware
       is known to lurk here.

    H. Exercise extreme caution when surfing online.
       Spyware tends to be loaded onto disreputable sites
       containing pornography, and even on Web sites
       advertising spyware solutions.

    I. Beware of spyware lurking in ads on social network-
       ing sites such as Facebook and MySpace.

TRANSITION: The makers of spyware are in it for the
                   money, so the problem is likely to be long
                   lasting. (*Signals close of speech*)

CONCLUSION

I. Spyware can do serious damage to your computer and to
   your finances. (*Summarizes main points*)

    A. The steps I've laid out should help you protect your
       computer from becoming infected.

    B. One final piece of advice is to keep abreast of devel-
       opments related to spyware by reading reputable
       computer publications such as *PC Magazine* and
       visiting reputable Web sites such as CNET.com.
       (*Leaves audience with something to think about*)

II. Forewarned is forearmed. Good luck. (*Memorable close*)

Sources

Federal Trade Commission, "Monitoring Spyware on Your PC: Spyware, Adware, and Other Software," Mar. 2005. Retrieved August 8, 2005, from www.ftc.gov/os/2005/03/050307spywarerpt.pdf.

Federal Trade Commission, Web Site for the Consumer. "Consumer Alert on Spyware." Retrieved August 8, 2005, from www.ftc .gov/cp/conline/pubs/alerts/spywarealrt.htm.

"Virus vs. Spyware," CNET.com, CNET Videos section. Retrieved August 9, 2005, from reviews.cnet.com/Virus vs spyware/ 4660-10620_7-6273711.html.

Vauhini Vara, "Lurking in the Shadows," *Wall Street Journal*, July 18, 2005; July 19, 2005. online.wsj.com/article/ 0,,SB112128460774484814,00-search.html.

Tanner Nielson, personal interview, May 12, 2005.

"Protect Yourself Online," *Consumer Reports*, September, 2008. Retrieved Nov. 9, 2008, from www.consumerreports.org/ cro/electronics-computers/computers-internet/ internet-and-other-services/protect-yourself-online/ overview/protect-yourself-online-ov.htm.

Neil J. Rubenking, "Nine Ways to Wipe Out Spyware," *PC Magazine* Feb. 5, 2008. Retrieved Nov. 9, 2008, from www.pcmag.com/article2/0,2817,2255857,00.asp.

Use a Speaking Outline for Delivery

Using the same numbering system as the working outline, condense the full sentences into key words or phrases. Place the speaking outline on large (at least 4×6-inch) notecards or 8.5×11-inch sheets of paper. Print large enough so that you can see the words at a glance.

QUICK TIP

Sometimes Only Exact Wording Will Do

Even though the delivery outline should contain key words or phrases almost exclusively, when exact wording is critical to an accurate representation of your speech material (as in presenting highly technical material or conveying quotations, facts, or statistics verbatim), you may want to write it out in full sentences.

Indicate Delivery Cues

Include any **delivery cues** that will be part of the speech. To draw attention to the cues, capitalize them, place them in parentheses, and/or highlight them.

DELIVERY CUE	EXAMPLE
Transitions	(TRANSITION)
Timing	(PAUSE) (SLOW DOWN)
Speaking Rate/Volume	(SLOWLY) (LOUDER)
Presentation Aids	(SHOW MODEL) (SLIDE 3)
Source	(ATLANTA CONSTITUTION, August 2, 2005)
Statistic	(2010, boys to girls = 94,232; U.S. Health Human Services)
Quotation	Eubie Blake, 100: "If I'd known I was gonna live this long, I'd have taken better care of myself."
Difficult-to-Pronounce or -Remember Names or Words	Eowyn (A-OH-win)

CHECKLIST: Tips on Using Notecards or Sheets of Paper

___ 1. Leave some blank space at the margins. This will help you find your place as you glance at the cards.

___ 2. Number your notecards or sheets so that you can follow them with ease.

___ 3. Instead of turning the cards or sheets, slide them under one another.

___ 4. Do not staple notes or sheets together.

___ 5. If you use a lectern, place the notes or sheets near eye level.

___ 6. Don't use the cards or sheets in hand gestures, as they become distracting pointers or flags.

Practice the Speech

The key to the successful delivery of any speech, particularly when using a key-word outline, is practice. The more you rehearse your speech, the more comfortable you will become when you speak. For more information on practicing the speech, see Chapter 19, "Using the Body."

SAMPLE SPEAKING OUTLINE

Staying ahead of Spyware

JOHN COULTER
Salt Lake Community College

TOPIC:	Problems and solutions associated with spyware
SPECIFIC PURPOSE:	To inform my audience of the dangers of spyware so that they may take appropriate steps to prevent infection
THESIS STATEMENT:	Computer users must understand the nature of spyware and how it works in order to take the necessary steps to protect themselves.

INTRODUCTION

I. Imagine feel? (*Attention getter*)

II. Can happen; spyware installs, harvests

III. To protect, understand how (*Thesis*)

IV. What, harm, who affects, avoid (*Preview*)

TRANSITION:	So, what exactly . . . ?
(TRANSITION:	So, what exactly is spyware?)
[PAUSE]	

BODY

I. Decades old, many guises

    A. Until 2000, monitoring devices on cameras (FTC, March 2004 report)

        1. First link to software content, *Zone Alarm*.

        2. FTC defined: installs, gathers data, sends to remote computer, no consent

            a) Install advertising

            b) Collect personal data

   B. Installs silently, "piggybacks"

      1. Known sources—pop-up ads, "unsubscribe" button in spam

      2. Some track browsing habits, sell info

      3. Adware loads ads; no monitoring

      4. Keyloggers steal info [SHOW SLIDE]

(TRANSITION: There's lots of confusion . . .)

   C. Different from virus

      1. Individuals; to brag, damage (CNET.com video)

      2. Spyware—teams, companies, money

      3. Viruses two decades; all defined; illegal

(TRANSITION: Leaving aside finer distinctions, serious threat . . .)

II.   Recognize symptoms, problems

   A. Stream pop-ups, toolbars, browsers hijacked (Vara, *WSJ*, July 18th, 2005) [SHOW SLIDE]

   B. Files displaced, disappear, crash

III. Leading cause computer problems

   A. Tanner Nielson majority of problems

   B. *Consumer Reports* 2008 survey

      1. 2008. 1 in 14 owners severe; erase

      2. Costs 2007–2008, $3.6 billion

(TRANSITION: Nasty things to computer, wallet)

IV. Prevention key

   A. Update browser; security updates

   B. Antispyware: Webroot's Antivirus with AntiSpyware, PC Tools' Spyware Doctor, and Symantec's Norton Internet Security (*PC Magazine*, 2008) [SHOW BOX]

   C. Enable firewall or purchase

   D. Beware free downloads

   E. Don't click links pop-up

   F. Don't click links spam, strangers

   G. Unsubscribe button

    H. Caution! Disreputable sites, even spyware
       solutions!

    I. Facebook. MySpace ads

[PAUSE]

(TRANSITION: The makers of spyware are in it for the
                money, so the problem is likely to be long
                lasting) (*Signals close of speech*)

CONCLUSION

I. Damage computer, finances, right step

    A. Solutions, browsers, antispyware

    B. Steps laid out

    C. *PC Magazine*, CNET.com

II. Forewarned is forearmed. Good luck!

✓ **CHECKLIST: Steps in Creating a Speaking Outline**

____ 1. Create the outline on sheets of paper or large
      notecards.

____ 2. Write large and legibly using at least 14-point font or
      easy-to-read ink and large letters.

____ 3. For each main and subpoint, choose a key word or a
      phrase that will jog your memory accurately.

____ 4. Include delivery cues.

____ 5. Write out full quotations and other critical
      information.

____ 6. Using the speaking outline, practice at least five
      times.

Part 4
Starting, Finishing, and Styling

15 Developing the Introduction and Conclusion

Many novice speakers think that if the body of their speech is well developed they can "wing" the introduction and conclusion. Leaving these elements to chance, however, is a formula for failure. A good opening previews what's to come in a way that invites listeners to give you their attention and goodwill. Conclusions ensure that the audience remembers the speech and reacts in a way that the speaker intends.

Any kind of supporting material—examples, stories, testimony, facts, or statistics—can be used to open and conclude a speech as long as it accomplishes these objectives.

Preparing the Introduction

The choices you make about the introduction can affect the outcome of the entire speech. In the first several minutes (one speaker pegs it at ninety seconds),[1] audience members will decide whether they are interested in the topic of your speech, whether they will believe what you say, and whether they will stay the course.

CHECKLIST: Guidelines for Preparing the Introduction

✓ Prepare the introduction after you've completed the speech body. This way, when you turn to the introduction, you will know exactly what you need to preview.

✓ Keep the introduction brief—as a rule, no more than 10 to 15 percent of the body of the speech. Nothing will turn off an audience more quickly than waiting interminably for you to get to the point.

✓ Practice delivering your introduction until you feel confident you've got it right.

A good introduction serves to:

• Gain the audience's attention and willingness to listen.

• Preview the topic, purpose, and main ideas of the speech.

• Establish your credibility to speak on the topic.

• Motivate the audience to accept your goals.

The Power of First and Last Impressions
Two psychological principles illustrate why introductions and conclusions are so important. The "primacy effect" suggests that initial impressions tend to stay with us. According to the "recency effect," we recall best what we hear last. Thus, even if audience members don't retain everything you say in the body of your speech, they will probably remember the impression you made in your introduction and the message you left them with in your conclusion. First impressions tend to be lasting ones, and final impressions linger.

Gain Audience Attention

An introduction must first of all gain the audience's attention. Some time-honored techniques include sharing a compelling quotation or story, posing a question, relating unusual information, using humor, and referring to the audience and the occasion.

USE A QUOTATION   A Czech proverb says, "Do not protect yourself by a fence but rather by your friends." A good quotation, one that elegantly and succinctly expresses an idea related to the speech theme, is an effective way to draw the audience's attention. Quotations can be culled from literature, poetry, and film, or directly from people.

TELL A STORY   Noted speechwriter and language expert William Safire once remarked that stories are "surefire attention getters."[2] Stories personalize issues, encouraging identification and making things relevant. Research confirms that speakers who use brief stories based on real life (called *anecdotes*; see Chapter 8) to open a speech motivate the audience to listen and promote greater understanding and retention of the speaker's message.[3]

POSE QUESTIONS   Are you concerned about student loans? Posing a question such as this can be an effective way to draw the audience's attention to what you are about to say. Questions can invite a response (as in polling audience members) or they can be rhetorical. **Rhetorical questions** do not invite actual responses. Instead, they make the audience think.

RELATE UNUSUAL INFORMATION   Did you know that virtually no one is having babies anymore in parts of Western Europe? Surprising audience members with startling or unusual facts and statistics is one of the surest ways to get their attention. Statistics are a powerful means of illustrating consequences and relationships and tend to quickly bring things into focus.

USE HUMOR   Handled well, humor is an excellent way to build rapport, put people at ease, make key points, and introduce the theme of a speech. However, humor is culturally specific, and if audience members do not share your frames of reference, they may not react as you expect. As one scholar notes, "Humor goes beyond language; it takes us into the heart of cultural understanding."[4] Use humor with discretion, taking care that it is truly appropriate for your particular audience, topic, and occasion.

REFER TO THE AUDIENCE   Audiences are won over when speakers express interest in them and show that they share in the audiences' concerns and goals. This creates goodwill and a feeling of common ground, or *identification*. Finding common ground helps overcome the natural human divisions that separate people.[5] Use your knowledge of the audience to touch briefly on areas of shared experience.

REFER TO THE OCCASION   Introductions that include references to the speech occasion and to any relevant facts about the audience make listeners feel recognized as individuals. People appreciate the direct reference to the event, and they are interested in the meaning the speaker assigns to it.

Preview the Topic and Purpose

The introduction should alert the audience to the speech topic and purpose. Surprisingly, many beginning speakers forget to do this, leaving listeners confused. Make sure to declare what your speech is about and what you hope to accomplish.

Topic and purpose are clearly explained in this introduction to a speech by Marvin Runyon, postmaster general of the United States:

> This afternoon, I want to examine the truth of that statement—"Nothing moves people like the mail, and no one moves the mail like the U.S. Postal Service." I want to look at where we are today as a communications industry, and where we intend to be in the days and years ahead.[6]

Preview the Main Points

Once you've revealed the topic and purpose, briefly preview the main points of the speech. A *preview statement* identifies the main points of the speech, thus helping audience members to be alert to key ideas. It also helps you, the speaker, to keep their attention. Preview statements can be straightforward. You simply tell the audience what the main points will be and in what order you will address them. Rather than elaborate on them, save your in-depth discussion of each point for the body of your speech.

Robert L. Darbelnet introduces his topic, purpose, and main points with this preview statement; it not only previews content but motivates listeners:

> My remarks today are intended to give you a sense of AAA's ongoing efforts to improve America's roads. Our hope is that you will join your voices to ours as we call on the federal government to do three things:
>
> Number one: Perhaps the most important, provide adequate funding for highway maintenance and improvements.
>
> Number two: Play a strong, responsible, yet flexible role in transportation programs.
>
> And number three: Invest in highway safety.
>
> Let's see what our strengths are, what the issues are, and what we can do about them.[7]

Motivate the Audience to Accept Your Goals

A final function of the introduction is to motivate the audience to care about your topic and believe what you have to say about it. For this to occur, audience members must believe that (1) the topic is relevant and (2) you are qualified to address it.

MAKE THE TOPIC RELEVANT   Listeners need to know early on why they should care about the speech. One way to demonstrate your topic's relevance is to address its practical implications and what the audience stands to gain by listening to you. Another is to demonstrate that your speech goal is consistent with their motives and values. A student speech about the value of formal interview training shows how this can be accomplished:

> Let me start by telling you why you need interview training. It boils down to competition. As in sports, when you're not training, someone else is out there training to beat you. All things being equal, the person who has the best interviewing skills has got the edge.

ESTABLISH CREDIBILITY AS A SPEAKER   During the introduction, audience members make a decision about whether they

---

QUICK TIP

When Establishing Credibility Is Especially Key
Although it is always important to establish your credibility in the introduction, it is particularly so when the audience does not know you well and you must clearly establish your expertise.[8] In these situations, be sure to stress the reasons why audience members should trust you and believe what you have to say.

---

are interested not just in your topic but also in you. They want to know why they should believe you. To build credibility, make a simple statement of your qualifications for speaking on the topic. Briefly emphasize some experience, knowledge, or perspective you have that is different from or more extensive than that of your audience. If your goal, for example, is to persuade your audience to be more conscientious about protecting city parks, you might state, "I have felt passionate about conservation issues ever since I started volunteering with the city's local chapter of the Nature Conservancy four summers ago."

CHECKLIST: How Effective Is Your Introduction?

Does your introduction . . .

____ 1. Capture the audience's attention?

____ 2. Alert listeners to the speech purpose and topic?

____ 3. Motivate listeners to accept your speech goals?

____ 4. Make the topic relevant to listeners?

____ 5. Establish your credibility?

Preparing the Conclusion

A well-constructed conclusion ensures that you go out with a bang and not a whimper. Conclusions give you the opportunity to drive home your purpose and make the kind of impression that will accomplish the goals of your speech. A good conclusion serves to:

• Signal to the audience that the speech is coming to an end and provide closure.

- Summarize the key points.
- Reiterate the topic and speech purpose.
- Challenge the audience to respond.
- End the speech memorably.

> **CHECKLIST: Guidelines for Preparing the Conclusion**
>
> ✓ As with the introduction, prepare the conclusion after you've completed the speech body.
>
> ✓ Keep the conclusion brief—as a rule, no more than 10 percent of the body of the speech. Conclude soon after you say you are about to end.
>
> ✓ Carefully consider your use of language. More than in other parts of the speech, the conclusion can contain words that inspire and motivate (see Chapter 16 on using language).
>
> ✓ Practice delivering your conclusion until you feel confident you've got it right.

Signal the End of the Speech and Provide Closure

People who listen to speeches take a journey of sorts, and they want and need the speaker to acknowledge the journey's end. The more emotional the journey, as in speeches designed to touch hearts and minds, the greater the need for logical and emotional closure.

One way to alert the audience that a speech is about to end is to use a transition statement or phrase. Phrases such as *Finally, Looking back, In conclusion,* and *Let me close by saying* all signal closure.

You can also signal closure more subtly, by your manner of delivery. For example, you can vary your tone, pitch, rhythm, and rate of speech to indicate that the speech is winding down.

Once you've signaled the end of your speech, do finish in short order (though not abruptly).

Summarize the Key Points

One bit of age-old advice for giving a speech is "Tell them what you are going to tell them (in the introduction), tell them (in the body), and tell them what you told them (in the conclusion)." In other words, emphasizing the main points three times will help the audience remember them.

The summary or review should be more than a rote recounting, however. Consider how Holger Kluge, in a speech titled "Reflections on Diversity," summarized his main points:

> I have covered a lot of ground here today. But as I draw to a close, I'd like to stress three things.
>
> First, diversity is more than equity. . . .
>
> Second, weaving diversity into the very fabric of your organization takes time. . . .
>
> Third, diversity will deliver bottom line results to your businesses and those results will be substantial, if you make the commitment. . . .[9]

A restatement of points like this brings the speech full circle.

Reiterate the Topic and Speech Purpose

The conclusion should reiterate the topic and speech purpose—to imprint it on the audience's memory. In the conclusion to a persuasive speech, about the U.S. immigration debate, Elpidio Villarreal reminds his listeners of his central idea:

> Two paths are open to us. One path would keep us true to our fundamental values as a nation and a people. The other would lead us down a dark trail; one marked by 700-mile-long fences, emergency detention centers and vigilante border patrols. Because I really am an American, heart and soul, and because that means never being without hope, I still believe we will ultimately choose the right path. We have to.[10]

Challenge the Audience to Respond

A strong conclusion challenges audience members to put to use what the speaker has taught them. In *informative speeches*, the speaker challenges audience members to use what they've learned in a way that benefits them. In *persuasive speeches*, the challenge to audience members usually comes in the form of a **call to action**, a challenge to see the problem in a new way, change their beliefs about the problem, or change both their actions and their beliefs about the problem.

Hillary Rodham Clinton makes a strong call to action in her conclusion to an address presented to the United Nations Fourth World Conference on Women:

> We have seen peace prevail in most places for a half century. We have avoided another world war. But we have not solved older, deeply rooted problems that continue to diminish the

potential of half the world's population. *Now it is time to act on behalf of women everywhere.* If we take bold steps to better the lives of women, we will be taking bold steps to better the lives of children and families too. . . . Let this conference be our—and the world's—call to action.[11]

Make the Speech Memorable

A good conclusion increases the odds that the speaker's message will linger after the speech is over, and a speech that makes a lasting impression is one that listeners are most likely to remember and act on. To accomplish this, make use of the same devices for capturing attention described for use in introductions—quotations, stories, questions, startling statements, humor, and references to the audience and the occasion.

QUICK TIP

Bring Your Speech Full Circle
In addition to using a quotation, line of poetry, or anecdote that captures the essence of your message, picking up on a story or idea you mentioned in the introduction can be a memorable way to close a speech and bring the entire presentation full circle.

CHECKLIST: How Effective Is Your Conclusion?

Does your conclusion . . .

____ 1. Alert the audience that the speech is ending?

____ 2. Come to an end soon after you say you will finish?

____ 3. Last no more than about one-sixth of the speech body?

____ 4. Reiterate the main points?

____ 5. Remind listeners of the topic and speech purpose?

____ 6. Challenge the audience to respond?

____ 7. Make a lasting impression?

16 Using Language

In public speaking, choosing the right words is crucial to creating a dynamic connection with your audience and helping listeners understand, believe in, and retain your message.[1] **Style** is the specific word choices and **rhetorical devices** (techniques of language) speakers use to express their ideas. A speaker's style can make a speech colorful and convincing or bland and boring.

Prepare Your Speeches for the Ear

Unlike readers, listeners have only one chance to understand a spoken message. They cannot go back and reread a difficult passage or pause to look up an unfamiliar word. Speeches should therefore be prepared for the ear, using familiar words, easy-to-follow sentences, repetition, and a direct form of address.

Strive for Simplicity

When selecting between two synonyms, choose the simpler term. Translate **jargon**—the specialized, "insider" language of a given profession—into commonly understood terms. As speechwriter Peggy Noonan notes in her book *Simply Speaking*:

> Good hard simple words with good hard clear meanings are good things to use when you speak. They are like pickets in a fence, slim and unimpressive on their own but sturdy and effective when strung together.[2]

Be Concise

As a rule, try to use fewer rather than more words to express your thoughts, and shorter rather than longer sentences. Consider the following examples. Which would you rather hear?

> It is difficult to believe that the United States government is attempting to tax us at every level of our personal and professional lives, whether it be capital gains taxes, value-added taxes, or, of course, your favorite and mine: income taxes.

> It's hard to believe but true. The U.S. government is taxing us to death. It's got its hands in every conceivable pocket. Capital gains taxes. Value-added taxes. And, of course, your favorite and mine: income taxes.

131

Make Frequent Use of Repetition

Good speeches, even very brief ones, often repeat key words and phrases. Repetition adds emphasis to important ideas, helps listeners follow your logic, and imbues language with rhythm and drama.

QUICK TIP

Experiment with Phrases and Sentence Fragments
To make your speech come alive, experiment with using phrases and sentence fragments in place of full sentences. This speaker, a physician, demonstrates one way of doing this: "I'm just a simple bone-and-joint guy. I can set your broken bones. Take away your bunions. Even give you a new hip. But I don't mess around with the stuff between the ears. . . . That's another specialty."[3]

Use Personal Pronouns

The direct form of address, using personal pronouns such as *we, us, I,* and *you* draw the audience into the message. Note how the following speaker uses personal pronouns to encourage involvement in his message:

> My talk today is about you. Each one of you personally. I know you hear many presentations. For the most part, they tend to be directed mostly to others with very little for you. My presentation today is different; the topic and the information will be important to every one of you. . . . I'm going to show and tell each of you how to become a verbal visionary.[4]

Choose Concrete Words and Vivid Imagery

Concrete words and vivid imagery help audience members grasp meaning and encourage their involvement.

Use Concrete Language

Concrete language conveys meaning that is specific, tangible, and definite. In contrast, **abstract language** is general or nonspecific, leaving meaning open to interpretation. Politicians use abstract language to appeal to mass audiences, or to be noncommittal. In most speaking situations, however, listeners will appreciate concrete nouns and verbs:

ABSTRACT		LESS ABSTRACT		CONCRETE
summer	→	hot weather	→	sweltering heat
congestion	→	traffic jam	→	gridlock

Experiment with concrete imagery to clarify key speech points. Rather than merely saying, "The American dream is fading," give listeners a mental picture. Note how Joe Biden accomplished this in his 2008 acceptance speech for the vice-presidential nomination:

> Almost every single night, I take the train home to Wilmington. . . . As I . . . look out that window, I see those flickering lights of the homes that pass by; I can almost hear the conversation they're having at their kitchen tables after they put their kids to bed. . . . Should Mom move in with us now that Dad's gone? Fifty, sixty, seventy dollars just to fill up the gas tank? How in God's name, with winter coming, how are we going to heat the home?[5]

Offer Vivid Imagery

Imagery is concrete language that uses the senses of smell, taste, sight, hearing, and touch to paint mental pictures. Listeners respond more positively to speeches that use ample imagery than those that do not.[6] Create vivid images by modifying nouns and verbs with descriptive adjectives and adverbs. For example, rather than simply identifying the hour that the Japanese bombed Pearl Harbor, President Franklin D. Roosevelt described it as "the dark hour"[7] to drive home the gravity of the attack.

Figures of speech are expressions, such as metaphors, similes, and analogies, in which words are used in a nonliteral fashion to achieve a rhetorical effect.

A **simile** explicitly compares one thing to another, using *like* or *as*: "He works like a dog" and "The old woman's hands were as soft as a baby's." A **metaphor** also compares two things but does so by describing one thing as actually being the other: "Education is an uphill climb" and "The U.S. is a melting pot."

An **analogy** is an extended metaphor or simile that clarifies an unfamiliar concept by comparing it to a more familiar one.[8] For example, note how African American minister Phil Wilson used metaphoric language when he preached to his congregation in Los Angeles about the dangers of AIDS:

> Our house is on fire! The fire truck arrives, but we won't come out, because we're afraid the folks from next door will see that we're in that burning house. AIDS is a fire raging in our community and it's out of control![9]

> **QUICK TIP**
>
> ### Avoid Clichés and Mixed Metaphors
> *Try not to use tired metaphors and similes, known as clichés. A* **cliché** *is an expression used so often that it no longer has the power to move us: "sold like hotcakes" (a clichéd simile), "pearly white teeth" (a clichéd metaphor). Beware too of mixed metaphors, those that juxtapose unlike images or expressions. For example, "burning the midnight oil at both ends" incorrectly joins two (clichéd) expressions "burning the midnight oil" and "burning the candle at both ends."*

Choose Words That Build Credibility

To gain trust and credibility, use language that is appropriate, accurate, assertive, and respectful.

Use Words Appropriately

As a rule, strive to uphold the conventional rules of grammar and usage associated with general American English (GAE), but as prepared for the ear. The more formal the occasion, the closer you will want to remain within conventional bounds. Listeners view speakers who use general American English as more competent—though not necessarily more trustworthy or likable—than those who speak in a distinctive dialect (regional variation of speech).[10]

There are times, however, when it may be appropriate to mix casual language, dialects, or even slang into your speech. Done carefully, the selective use of dialect, sometimes called **code-switching**, can imbue your speech with friendliness, humor, earthiness, honesty, and nostalgia.[11] The key is to ensure that your meaning is clear and your use is appropriate for your audience. Former President Bill Clinton, for example, drew a laugh when he used Arkansas "backwoods-speak" to describe a Republican budget proposal: "It is their dog. And it was a mangy old dog, and that's why I vetoed that dog."[12]

Use Words Accurately

Audiences lose confidence in speakers who misuse words. Check that your words mean what you intend, and beware of **malapropisms**—the inadvertent, incorrect uses of a word or phrase in place of one that sounds like it[13] ("It's a strange receptacle" for "It's a strange spectacle").

QUICK TIP

Avoid the "Shock Jock" Syndrome
"Shock Jock" is an informal term for a radio host who uses suggestive language, bathroom humor, and obscene references. These (ab)uses of language are never appropriate in a public speech event. Even those audience members who otherwise might not object to off-color material will react to it unfavorably.

Use the Active Voice

Speaking in the active rather than passive voice will make your statements clear and assertive instead of indirect and weak. **Voice** is the feature of verbs that indicates the subject's relationship to the action. A verb is in the active voice when the subject performs the action, and in the passive voice when the subject is acted upon or is the receiver of the action:

PASSIVE:	A test was announced by Ms. Carlos for Tuesday.
	A president is elected by the voters every four years.
ACTIVE:	Ms. Carlos announced a test for Tuesday.
	The voters elect a president every four years.

Use Culturally Sensitive and Gender-neutral Language

Demonstrate respect for your listeners' cultural beliefs, norms, and traditions by using culturally sensitive and unbiased language. Review and eliminate from your speech statements that reflect unfounded assumptions, negative descriptions, or stereotypes. Consider whether certain seemingly well-known names and terms may be foreign to some listeners and include brief explanations for them. Sayings specific to a certain region or group of people (termed **colloquial expressions** or idioms), such as "back the wrong horse" and "ballpark figure" can add color and richness to a speech, but only if listeners understand them.

Word your speech with gender-neutral language: Avoid the third-person generic masculine pronouns (*his, he*) in favor of inclusive pronouns such as *his or her, he or she, we, our, you, your,* or other gender-neutral terms:

INSTEAD OF. . .	USE. . .
mankind, early man, man	humankind, early peoples, humans
he, his	he or she, his or her, one, you, our, they
policeman, mailman, anchorman, chairman, middleman	police officer, mail carrier, news anchor, chair, intermediary

Choose Words That Create a Lasting Impression

Oral language that is artfully arranged and infused with rhythm draws listeners in and leaves a lasting impression on audience members. You can create a cadenced arrangement of language through rhetorical devices such as repetition, alliteration, and parallelism.

QUICK TIP

Denotative versus Connotative Meaning
*When drafting your speech, choose words that are both denotatively and connotatively appropriate to the audience. The **denotative meaning** of a word is its literal, or dictionary, definition. The **connotative meaning** of a word is the special (often emotional) association that different people bring to bear on it. For example, you might like to be called "slender" but not "skinny," "thrifty" but not "cheap." Consider how the connotative meanings of your word choices might affect the audience's response to your message.*

Use Repetition to Create Rhythm

Repeating key words, phrases, or even sentences at various intervals throughout a speech creates a distinctive rhythm and thereby implants important ideas in listeners' minds. Repetition works particularly well when delivered with the appropriate voice inflections and pauses.

In one form of repetition called **anaphora**, the speaker repeats a word or phrase at the beginning of successive phrases, clauses, or sentences. For example, in his speech delivered in 1963 in Washington, DC, Dr. Martin Luther King Jr. repeated the phrase "I have a dream" many times, each with an upward inflection followed by a pause. In another example, President Barack Obama, in his November 4, 2008, election night speech repeated the phrase, "It's the answer" (noted in italics below):

> If there is anyone out there who still doubts that America is a place where all things are possible . . . tonight *is your answer*. . . .*It's the answer* told by lines that stretched around schools. . . . *It's the answer* spoken by young and old. . . . *It's the answer*.[14]

Speakers have made use of anaphora since earliest times. For example, Jesus preached:

> Blessed are the poor in spirit. . . .
> Blessed are the meek. . . .
> Blessed are the peacemakers. . . . [15]

Use Alliteration for a Poetic Quality

Alliteration is the repetition of the same sounds, usually initial consonants, in two or more neighboring words or syllables. Alliteration drives home themes and leaves listeners with a lasting impression. Examples of alliteration in speeches include phrases such as Jesse Jackson's "Down with dope, up with hope" and former U.S. Vice-President Spiro Agnew's disdainful reference to the U.S. press as "nattering nabobs of negativism."

Experiment with Parallelism

The arrangement of words, phrases, or sentences in a similar form is known as **parallelism**. Parallel structure can help the speaker emphasize important ideas in the speech. Like repetition, it also creates a sense of steady or building rhythm.[16] You can easily make use of parallelism by doing the following:

- Orally numbering your points ("first," "second," and "third")
- Grouping speech concepts or ideas into three parallel grammatical elements or triads ("Of the people, by the people, and for the people")
- Setting off two strongly contrasting ideas in balanced (parallel) opposition (the device of **antithesis**, e.g., "One small step for man, one giant leap for mankind")
- Repeating a key word or phrase that emphasizes a central or recurring idea of the speech, often in the introduction, body, and conclusion

CHECKLIST: Use Language Effectively

✓ Use familiar words, easy-to-follow sentences, and straightforward syntax.

✓ Root out **biased language.**

✓ Avoid unnecessary jargon.

✓ Use fewer rather than more words to express your thoughts.

✓ Make striking comparisons with *similes, metaphors,* and *analogies.*

✓ Use the active voice.

✓ Repeat key words, phrases, or sentences at various intervals (*anaphora*).

✓ Experiment with *alliteration* — words that repeat the same sounds, usually initial consonants, in two or more neighboring words or syllables.

✓ Experiment with *parallelism* — arranging words, phrases, or sentences in similar form.

Part 5
Delivery

Choosing a Method of Delivery

The delivery of a speech is the moment of truth. For most of us, delivery makes us feel anxious because this is the moment when all eyes are upon us. In fact, effective delivery rests on the same natural foundation as everyday conversation.[1] Focusing on the quality of naturalness can help you reduce the fear of delivery and make your presentations more effective.

Strive for Naturalness and Enthusiasm

Effective **delivery** is the skillful application of vocal and non-verbal conversational behavior in a way that is natural, enthusiastic, confident, and direct. Speakers who deliver well-received speeches or presentations share these characteristics at the podium.

- *Strive for naturalness.* Think of your speech as a particularly important conversation. Rather than behaving theatrically, act naturally.

- *Show enthusiasm.* Inspire your listeners by showing enthusiasm for your topic and for the occasion. Speak about what interests and excites you.

- *Project a sense of confidence.* Focus on the ideas you want to convey rather than on yourself. Inspire the audience's confidence in you by appearing confident to them.

- *Be direct.* Engage your listeners by establishing eye contact, using a friendly tone of voice, and smiling whenever it is appropriate. Consider positioning yourself so that you are physically close to the audience.

> **QUICK TIP**
>
> **Build Rapport by Being Direct**
> *Connect with listeners by being direct: Maintain eye contact; use a friendly tone of voice; animate your facial expressions, smile; and get physically close to the audience. An enthusiastic and confident delivery helps you feel good about your speech, and it focuses your audience's attention on the message.*

Select a Method of Delivery

For virtually any type of speech or presentation, you can choose from four basic methods of delivery: speaking from manuscript; speaking from memory; speaking impromptu; and speaking extemporaneously.

Speaking from Manuscript

When **speaking from manuscript**, you read a speech *verbatim*—that is, from prepared written text that contains the entire speech, word for word. As a rule, speaking from manuscript restricts eye contact and body movement, and may also limit expressiveness in vocal variety and quality. Watching a speaker read a speech can be monotonous and boring for the audience.

There are times, however, when it is advisable or necessary to read a speech—for example, when you must convey a very precise message, when you will be quoted and must avoid misinterpretation, or when you must address an emergency and need to convey exact descriptions and directions (see Chapter 33 on crisis response presentations).

If you must read from a prepared text, do what you can to deliver the speech naturally:

- Vary the rhythm of your words.
- Become familiar enough with the speech so that you can establish some eye contact.
- Use a large font and double- or triple-space the manuscript so that you can read without straining.
- Consider using some compelling presentation aids.

Speaking from Memory

The formal name for **speaking from memory** is **oratory**. In oratorical style, you put the entire speech, word for word, into writing and then commit it to memory. In the United States, speaking from memory rarely occurs anymore, though this form of delivery remains common in many parts of the world.[2]

Memorization is not a natural way to present a message. True eye contact with the audience is unlikely, and memorization invites potential disaster during a speech because there is always the possibility of a mental lapse or block. Some kinds of brief speeches, however, such as toasts and introductions, can be well served by memorization. Sometimes it's helpful to memorize a part of the speech, especially when you use direct quotations as a form of support. If you do find an occasion to use memorization, learn that portion of your speech so completely that in actual delivery you can convey enthusiasm and directness.

Speaking Impromptu

Speaking impromptu, a type of delivery that is unpracticed, spontaneous, or improvised, involves speaking on relatively short notice with little time to prepare. Many occasions require that you make some remarks on the spur of the moment. An instructor may ask you to summarize key points from an assignment, for example, or a fellow employee who was scheduled to speak on a new project may be sick and your boss has invited you to take his place.

Try to anticipate situations that may require you to speak impromptu and prepare some remarks beforehand. Otherwise, maximize the time you do have to prepare on the spot:

- Pause to reflect on how you can best address the audience's interests and needs, and shape your remarks accordingly.

- Take a deep breath, and focus on your expertise on the topic or on what you really want to say.

- Jot down in key words or short phrases the ideas you want to cover.

- If your speech follows someone else's, acknowledge that person's statements.

- State your ideas and then summarize them.

- Use transitions such as "first," "second," and "third," both to organize your points and to help listeners follow them.

- Stay on the topic. Don't wander off track.

As much as possible, try to organize your points into a discernible pattern. If addressing a problem, for example, such as a project failure or glitch, consider the problem-solution pattern or the cause-effect pattern of organizational arrangement (see Chapter 13). If called upon to defend one proposal as superior to another, consider using the comparative advantages pattern, in which you illustrate various advantages of the favored proposal over other options (see Chapter 24 on persuasive speeches).

Speaking Extemporaneously

Speaking extemporaneously falls somewhere between impromptu and written or memorized deliveries. In an extemporaneous speech, you prepare well and practice in advance, giving full attention to all facets of the speech—content, arrangement, and delivery alike. Instead of memorizing or writing the speech word for word, you speak from an outline of key words and phrases, having concentrated throughout your preparation and practice on the ideas that you want to communicate.

More speeches are delivered by extemporaneous delivery than by any other method. Because this technique is most conducive to achieving a natural, conversational quality of delivery, many speakers prefer it to the four types of delivery. Knowing your idea well enough to present it without memorization or manuscript gives you greater flexibility in adapting to the specific speaking situation. You can modify wording, rearrange your points, change examples, or omit information in keeping with the audience and the setting. You can have more eye contact, more direct body orientation, greater freedom of movement, and generally better control of your thoughts and actions than any of the other delivery methods allow.

Speaking extemporaneously does present several possible drawbacks. Because you aren't speaking from written or memorized text, you may become repetitive and wordy. Fresh examples or points may come to mind that you want to share, so the speech may take longer than anticipated. Occasionally, even a glance at your speaking notes may fail to jog your memory on a point you wanted to cover, and you momentarily find yourself searching for what to say next. The remedy for these potential pitfalls is frequent practice using a speaking outline.

QUICK TIP

Learn the Extemporaneous Method of Delivery
In most situations, select the extemporaneous method of delivery. Thoroughly prepare and practice your speech in advance of delivery. Speak from a key-word or phrase outline that has been adapted from a full-sentence outline (see Chapter 14).

METHODS OF DELIVERY AND THEIR PROBABLE USES	
WHEN . . .	**METHOD OF DELIVERY**
✓ Precise wording is called for; for instance, when you want to avoid being misquoted or misconstrued, or you need to communicate exact descriptions and directions . . .	Consider *speaking from manuscript* (reading part or all of your speech from fully prepared text)
✓ You must deliver a short special-occasion speech, such as a toast or introduction, or you plan on using direct quotations . . .	Consider *speaking from memory* (memorizing part or all of your speech)
✓ You are called upon to speak without prior planning or preparation . . .	Consider *speaking impromptu* (organizing your thoughts with little or no lead time)
✓ You have time to prepare and practice developing a speech or presentation that achieves a natural conversational style . . .	Consider *speaking extemporaneously* (developing your speech in working outline and then practicing and delivering it with a phrase or key-word outline)

18   Controlling the Voice

Regardless of the quality and importance of your message, if you have inadequate mastery of your voice you may lose the attention of your audience and fail to deliver a successful speech. Fortunately, as you practice your speech, you can learn to control each of the elements of vocal delivery. These include volume, pitch, speaking rate, pauses, vocal variety, and pronunciation and articulation.

Adjust Your Speaking Volume

Volume, the relative loudness of a speaker's voice while delivering a speech, is usually the most obvious vocal element we notice about a speaker, and with good reason. We need to hear the speaker at a comfortable level. *The proper volume for delivering a speech is somewhat louder than that of normal conversation.* Just how much louder depends on three factors: (1) the size of the room and the number of people in the audience, (2) whether or not you use a microphone, and (3) the level of background noise. The easiest way to judge whether you are speaking too loudly or too softly is to be alert to audience feedback.

CHECKLIST: Tips on Using a Microphone

✓ Always do a sound check with the microphone before delivering your speech.

✓ When you first speak into the microphone, ask your listeners if they can hear you clearly.

✓ Speak directly into the microphone; if you turn your head or body, you won't be heard.

✓ To avoid broadcasting private statements, beware of "open" mikes.

✓ When wearing a **lavaliere microphone** attached to your lapel or collar, speak as if you were addressing a small group. The amplifier will do the rest.

✓ When using a *handheld* or *fixed microphone*, beware of *popping*. Popping occurs when you use sharp consonants such as *p, t,* and *d* and the air hits the mike. To prevent popping, move the microphone slightly below your mouth and about six inches away.[1]

Vary Your Intonation

Pitch is the range of sounds from high to low (or vice versa). Vocal pitch is important in speechmaking because it powerfully affects the meaning associated with spoken words. For example, say "stop." Now, say "Stop!" Hear the difference? As you speak, pitch conveys your mood, reveals your level of enthusiasm, expresses your concern for the audience, and signals your overall commitment to the occasion. When there is no variety in pitch, speaking becomes monotonous. A monotonous voice is the death knell to any speech.

Adjust Your Speaking Rate

Speaking rate is the pace at which you convey speech. The normal rate of speech for adults is between 120 and 150 words per minute. The typical public speech occurs at a rate slightly below 120 words per minute, but there is no standard, ideal, or most effective rate. Being alert to the audience's reactions is the best way to know whether your rate of speech is too fast or too slow. An audience will get fidgety, bored, listless, perhaps even sleepy if you speak too slowly. If you speak too rapidly, listeners will appear irritated and confused, as though they can't catch what you're saying.

QUICK TIP

Control Your Rate of Speaking
One recent study suggests that speaking too fast will cause listeners to perceive you as tentative about your control of the situation.[2] To control your rate, choose 150 words from your speech and time yourself as you read them aloud. Do this until you achieve a comfortable speaking rate.

Use Strategic Pauses

Pauses enhance meaning by providing a type of punctuation, emphasizing a point, drawing attention to a key thought, or just allowing listeners a moment to contemplate what is being said. In short, they make a speech far more effective than it might otherwise be. Both the speaker and the audience *need* pauses.

QUICK TIP

Avoid Meaningless Vocal Fillers
*Many novice speakers are uncomfortable with pauses. It's as if there were a social stigma attached to any silence in a speech. We often react the same way in conversation, covering pauses with unnecessary and undesirable **vocal fillers** such as "uh," "hmm," "you know," "I mean," and "it's like." Like pitch, however, pauses are important strategic elements of a speech. Use them purposefully, taking care to eliminate distracting vocal fillers.*

Strive for Vocal Variety

Rather than operating separately, all the vocal elements described so far—volume, pitch, speaking rate, and pauses—work together to create an effective delivery. Indeed, the real key to effective vocal delivery is to vary all these elements.

Enthusiasm is key to achieving effective **vocal variety**. Vocal variety comes quite naturally when you are excited about what you are saying to an audience, when you feel it is important and want to share it with them.

✔️ **CHECKLIST: Practice Check for Vocal Effectiveness**

____ 1. As you practice, does your voice project authority?

____ 2. Is your voice too loud? Too soft?

____ 3. Do you avoid speaking in a monotone? Do you vary the stress or emphasis you place on words to clearly express your meaning?

____ 4. Is your rate of speech comfortable for listeners?

____ 5. Do you avoid unnecessary vocal fillers, such as "uh," "hmm," "you know," and "I mean"?

____ 6. Do you use pauses for strategic effect?

____ 7. Does your voice reflect a variety of emotional expressions? Do you convey enthusiasm?

Carefully Pronounce and Articulate Words

Few things distract an audience more than improper pronunciation or unclear articulation of words. **Pronunciation** is the correct formation of word sounds. **Articulation** is the clarity or forcefulness with which the sounds are made, regardless of whether they are pronounced correctly. It is important to pay attention to and work on both areas.

Articulation problems are also a matter of habit. A very common pattern of poor articulation is **mumbling**—slurring words together at a low level of volume and pitch so that they are barely audible. Sometimes the problem is **lazy speech**. Common examples are saying "fer" instead of "for" and "wanna" instead of "want to."

Like any habit, poor articulation can be overcome by unlearning the problem behavior:

- If you mumble, practice speaking more loudly and with emphatic pronunciation.

- If you tend toward lazy speech, put more effort into your articulation.

- Consciously try to say each word clearly and correctly.

- Practice clear and precise enunciation of proper word sounds. Say *articulation* several times until it rolls off your tongue naturally.

- Do the same for these words: *want to, going to, Atlanta, chocolate, sophomore, California.*

- As you practice, consider words that might pose articulation and pronunciation problems for you. Say them over and over until doing so feels as natural as saying your own name.

Use Dialect (Language Variation) with Care

A **dialect** is a distinctive way of speaking associated with a particular region or social group. Dialects such as Cajun, Appalachian English, and Ebonics (Black English) differ from standard language patterns such as general American English (GAE) in pronunciation, grammar, or vocabulary.

Although dialects are neither superior nor inferior to standard language patterns, the audience must be able to understand and relate to the speaker's language. As you practice your delivery, ensure that your pronunciation and word usage can be understood by all audience members.

REGULAR LANGUAGE PATTERNS IN SELECTED DIALECTS	
Appalachia	The *uh* sound before words ending in "ing" (She's a-fishing today)
Urban African American	The use of *be* to denote activities (She be fishing all the time)
Rural Southern	The absence of the plural *s* inflection (She ran four *mile*)[3]

19 Using the Body

Pay Attention to Body Language

As audience members listen to you, they are simultaneously evaluating the messages sent by your facial expressions, eye behavior, gestures, and general body movements. Audiences do not so much listen to a speaker's words as "read" the **body language** of the speaker who delivers them.[1]

Animate Your Facial Expressions

From our facial expressions, audiences can gauge whether we are excited about, disenchanted by, or indifferent to our speech—and the audience to whom we are presenting it.

Few behaviors are more effective for building rapport with an audience than *smiling*. A smile is a sign of mutual welcome at the start of a speech, of mutual comfort and interest during the speech, and of mutual goodwill at the close of a speech. In addition, smiling when you feel nervous or otherwise uncomfortable can help you relax and gain heightened composure. Of course, facial expressions need to correspond to the tenor of the speech. Doing what is natural and normal for the occasion should be the rule.

CHECKLIST: Tips for Using Effective Facial Expressions

✓ Use animated expressions that feel natural and express your meaning.

✓ Avoid a deadpan expression.

✓ Never use expressions that are out of character for you or inappropriate to the speech occasion.

✓ In practice sessions, loosen your facial features with exercises such as widening the eyes and moving the mouth.

✓ Establish rapport with the audience by smiling naturally when appropriate.

Maintain Eye Contact

If smiling is an effective way to build rapport, maintaining eye contact is mandatory in establishing a positive relationship with your listeners. Having eye contact with the audience is one of the most, if not *the* most, important physical actions in public speaking. Eye contact does the following:

• Maintains the quality of directness in speech delivery

• Lets people know they are recognized

• Indicates acknowledgment and respect

• Signals to audience members that you see them as unique human beings.

With an audience of one hundred to more than a thousand, it's impossible to look at every listener. But in most speaking situations you are likely to experience, you should be able to make the audience feel recognized by using a technique called **scanning**. When you scan an audience, you move your gaze from one listener to another and from one section to another, pausing to gaze at one person long enough to complete one sentence. Be certain to give each section of the room equal attention.

QUICK TIP

Use Eye Contact to Connect with the Audience

One way to make audience members feel connected to you is to maintain sustained eye contact with one person in the audience at a time. Fully complete one thought or sentence before removing your gaze and shifting it to another listener. Although the individuals sitting near the person sustaining your eye contact aren't receiving your gaze directly, they will feel your energy and recognition.[2] Move from one side, to the middle section, to the other side, and do the same thing. Make sure not to neglect the people in the back.

Use Gestures That Feel Natural

Words alone seldom suffice to convey what we want to express. Physical gestures fill in the gaps, as in illustrating the size or shape of an object (e.g., by showing the size of it by extending two hands, palms facing each other), or expressing the depth of an emotion (e.g., by pounding a fist on a podium). Gestures should arise from genuine emotions and should conform to your personality.[3]

- Use natural, spontaneous gestures.
- Avoid exaggerated gestures, but use gestures that are broad enough to be seen by each audience member.
- Eliminate distracting gestures, such as fidgeting with pens or pencils, brushing back hair from your eyes, or jingling coins in your pockets.
- Analyze your gestures for effectiveness in practice sessions.
- Practice movements that feel natural to you.

Be Aware of General Body Movement

General body movement is also important in maintaining audience attention and processing of your message. Audience members soon tire of listening to a "**talking head**" that remains steadily positioned in one place behind a microphone or a podium. As space and time allow, try to get out from behind the podium and stand with the audience. As you do, move around at a comfortable, natural pace.

QUICK TIP

Stand Straight

A speaker's posture sends a definite message to the audience. Listeners perceive speakers who slouch as being sloppy, unfocused, or even weak. Strive to stand erect, but not ramrod straight. The goal should be to appear authoritative but not rigid.

Dress Appropriately

Superficial as it may sound, the first thing an audience is likely to notice about you as you approach the speaker's position is your clothing. The critical criteria in determining appropriate dress for a speech are audience expectations and the nature of the speech occasion. If you are speaking as a representative of your business, for example, you will want to complement your company's image.[4]

An extension of dress is the possession of various objects on or around your person while giving a speech — pencil and pen, a briefcase, a glass of water, or papers with notes on them. Always ask yourself if these objects are really necessary. A sure way to distract an audience from what you're saying is to drag a briefcase or a backpack to the speaker's stand and open it while speaking, or to fumble with a pen or other object.

 CHECKLIST: Broad Dress Code Guidelines

✓ For a "power" look, wear a dark-colored suit.

✓ Medium or dark blue paired with white can enhance your credibility.

✓ Yellow and orange color tones convey friendliness.

✓ The color red focuses attention on you.

✓ Flashy jewelry distracts listeners.

Practice the Delivery

Practice is essential to effective delivery. The more you practice, the greater your comfort level will be when you actually deliver the speech. More than anything, it is uncertainty that breeds anxiety. By practicing your speech using a fully developed speaking outline, you will know what to expect when you actually stand in front of an audience.

Focus on the Message

The primary purpose of any speech is to get a message across, not to display extraordinary delivery skills. Keep this goal foremost in your mind. Psychologically, too, focusing on your message is likely to make your delivery more natural and confident.

QUICK TIP

Create a Feeling of Immediacy

*As a rule in most Western cultures, listeners learn more and respond most positively to speakers who create a perception of physical and psychological closeness, called **nonverbal immediacy**, between themselves and audience members.[5] An enthusiastic vocal delivery, frequent eye contact, animated facial expressions, and natural body movements are the keys to establishing immediacy.*

Plan Ahead and Practice Often

If possible, begin practicing your speech at least several days before you are scheduled to deliver it.

- Practice with your speaking notes.
- Revise those parts of your speech that aren't satisfactory, altering your speaking notes as you go.
- Focus on your speech ideas rather than on yourself.
- Time each part of your speech—introduction, body, and conclusion.
- Practice with any presentation aids you plan to use.
- Practice your speech several times, and then record it with a tape recorder.
- If possible, videotape yourself twice—once after several practice sessions, and again after you've worked to incorporate any changes into your speech.

- Visualize the setting in which you will speak and practice the speech under realistic conditions, paying particular attention to projecting your voice to fill the room.

- Practice in front of at least one volunteer, and seek constructive criticism.

- Schedule your practice sessions early in the process so that you have time to prepare.

QUICK TIP

Practice Five Times

Many expert speakers recommend practicing your speech about five times in its final form. Given that few speeches are longer than twenty minutes, and most are shorter, this represents a maximum of two hours of practice time—time certainly well spent.

Part 6
Presentation Aids

20 Types of Presentation Aids

Presentation aids can help listeners to understand and remember key points, to see relationships among concepts, and to evaluate complex ideas and data more quickly.[1] Designed well and used wisely—a not so simple task—presentation aids enhance speaker credibility.

Offering information visually as well as verbally appeals to the two basic ways we process information.[2] Indeed, studies show that we remember only about 30 percent of what we hear, but more than 60 percent of what we hear *and see*.[3]

QUICK TIP

Use Presentation Aids to Supplement Your Main Ideas

The strength of a presentation aid lies in the context in which it is used. No matter how powerful a photograph or chart or video may be, the audience will be less interested in merely gazing at it than in discovering how you will relate it to a specific point. Even superior-quality aids that are poorly related to the speech will turn off listeners. Use your presentation aids to supplement rather than to serve as the main source of your speech ideas.

Select an Appropriate Aid

Presentation aids include props and models, graphs, charts, video, audio, and multimedia. Select the aid, or combination of aids, that will illustrate your speech points most effectively.

Consider a Prop or Model

A **prop** can be any inanimate or live object—a stone or a snake, for instance—that captures the audience's attention and illustrates or emphasizes key points. A **model** is a three-dimensional, scale-size representation of an object. Presentations in engineering, architecture, medicine, and many other disciplines often make use of models.

When using a prop or model,

- Keep the prop or model hidden until you are ready to use it, in most cases.
- Make sure it is big enough for everyone to see (and read, if applicable).
- Practice your speech using the prop or model.

155

Create a Graph

A **graph** represents the relationship between variables. Four types of graphs that speakers use include line graphs, bar graphs, pie graphs, and pictograms.

A *line graph* displays one measurement, usually plotted on the horizontal axis, and units of measurement or values, plotted on the vertical axis. Each value or point is connected with a line. Line graphs are especially useful in representing information that changes over time, such as trends.

A *bar graph* uses bars of varying lengths to compare quantities or magnitudes; the bars may be arranged either vertically or horizontally. *Multidimensional bar graphs*, bar graphs distinguished by different colors or markings, compare two or more different kinds of information or quantities in one chart.

When creating line and bar graphs,

- Label both axes appropriately.
- Start the numerical axis at zero.
- Compare only like variables.
- Put no more than two lines of data on one line graph.
- Assign a clear title to the graph.

A *pie graph* depicts the division of a whole into slices. Each slice constitutes a percentage of the whole. When creating pie graphs,

- Restrict the number of pie slices to a maximum of seven.
- Identify and accurately represent the values or percentages of each pie slice.
- Consider using color or background markings to distinguish the different slices of the pie.

A *pictogram* uses picture symbols (icons) to illustrate relationships and trends; for example, using a generic-looking human figure repeated in a row to demonstrate increasing enrollment in college over time.

When creating pictograms,

- Clearly label what the pictogram symbolizes.
- To avoid confusing the eye, make all pictograms the same size.
- Clearly label the axes of the pictogram.

BEST USE OF DIFFERENT TYPES OF GRAPHS AND CHARTS

TYPE OF GRAPH OR CHART		BEST USE
Line graph	U.S. Fruit Production, 2001–2005	To represent trends or information that changes over time
Bar graph	Percent of Recycled Solid Waste	To compare individual points of information, magnitudes
Pie graph		To show proportions, such as sales by region, shares
Pictogram	New College Students	To show comparisons in picture form
Flowchart	Should You Change Your Oil?	To show processes
Diagram		To show how something works or is constructed
Table	COMMUTER BUS SCHEDULE TOWARD HAIGHT DISTRICT AND GOLDEN GATE PARK	To show large amounts of information in an easily viewable form

Produce a Chart

Like a graph, a **chart** visually represents data and their relationship to other data in a meaningful form. Several different
types of charts help listeners grasp key points.

A **flowchart** diagrams the progression of a process, helping viewers visualize sequence or directional flow.

A **diagram** (also called a "schematic drawing") visually
plots how something works or is made or operated.

A tabular chart, or **table**, systematically groups data in
column form, allowing viewers to examine and make
comparisons about information quickly.

Incorporate Audio and Video

Introducing an *audio clip*—a short recording of sounds,
music, or speech—into a speech can add interest, illustrate
ideas, and even bring humor to the mix. *Video*—including
movie, television, and other recording instruments—can
also be a powerful presentation aid that combines sight,
sound, and movement. With various presentation software
programs, you can easily incorporate audio and video into
an electronic presentation. **Multimedia** combines several
(stills, sound, video, text, and data) into a single production. When incorporating audio and video into your
presentation:

- Cue the audio or videotape to the appropriate segment
  before the presentation.

- Alert audience members to what they will be viewing
  before you show the tape.

- Reiterate the main points of the audio or video clip once
  it is over.

- Check to see whether the audio or video material you are
  using is copyrighted, and that you are using it in a manner
  that is consistent with copyright laws. (See Chapter 22
  for further guidance on using video in presentations.)

Choose a Method of Display

Options for showing the aids to the audience include, on the
more traditional side, overhead transparencies, slide transparencies, flip charts, chalkboards, and handouts. Many presenters display computer-generated graphics with digital
projectors.

Project Overhead Transparencies

An **overhead transparency** is an image printed on a transparent sheet of acetate that can be viewed by projection. If you write on the transparency during the presentation, it can be used much like a chalkboard.

When using overhead transparencies:

- Check that the projector is in good order before the speech.
- Stand to the *side* of the projector and face the *audience,* not the projected image.
- Use a pointer to indicate specific sections of a transparency— point to the transparency, not to the screen.
- If creating transparencies by writing or drawing during the presentation, use a water-soluble transparency pen and be sure to write clearly.
- Cover the transparencies when you are finished using them. Use heavy paper or cardboard so they will not be moved by the projector's fan.[4]
- Practice using your transparencies before your presentation.

Use LCD Panels or Digital Projectors

Many speakers today project aids using **LCD** (liquid crystal display) **panels** and projectors or the newer **DLP** (digital light processing) **projectors**. Aids displayed digitally are created with presentation software such as PowerPoint and transferred directly to the projector. Stand-alone slides or acetates aren't necessary, and you can use the software to generate speaker's notes and handouts (see Chapter 22).

Prepare a Flip Chart

A **flip chart** is simply a large (27–34 inch) pad of paper on which a speaker can draw visual aids. They are often

---

QUICK TIP

Hold the Handouts

*A **handout** conveys information that either is impractical to give to the audience in another manner or is intended to be kept by audience members after the presentation. To avoid distracting listeners, unless you specifically want them to read the information as you speak,* wait until you are finished before you distribute the handout. *If you do want the audience to view a handout during the speech, pass it out only when you are ready to talk about it.*

prepared in advance; then, as you progress through the speech, you simply flip through the pad to the next exhibit. You can also write and draw on the paper as you speak.

Use Posters

A **poster** is (generally) a large (36 × 56 inch) stiff paper board on which the speaker places, alone or in combination, text, data, and pictures. Speakers use posters to introduce topics or concepts to survey a topic. Many disciplines make use of posters in a form of presentation called the *poster session* (see Chapter 26). You can create posters by hand or generate them using presentation software (see Chapter 22).

Rehearse, Rehearse, Rehearse

Coordinating aids with a speech requires planning. Because timing is critical, you must rehearse the entire speech at least twice—once days before the event and again shortly before delivery. In your speaker's notes, cue each aid to where you want to introduce it (see table of common delivery cues in Chapter 14) and practice reading through the speech with the aids. If you're comfortable doing so, record the speech so that you can view it as the audience will see it.

CHECKLIST: Incorporating Presentation Aids into Your Speech

✓ Talk to your audience rather than to the screen—insofar as possible, don't turn your back to the audience.

✓ Maintain eye contact with the audience.

✓ Avoid putting the aid directly behind you. Place it to one side so that the entire audience can see it.

✓ Display the aid only when you are ready to discuss it and put it away when you are finished.

✓ Practice your speech with the aids until you are confident you can handle them without causing undue distractions.

✓ If you decide to use a pointer, don't brandish it about. Once you've indicated your point, put it down.

✓ In case problems arise, make sure you are prepared to give your presentation without the aids.

21 Designing Presentation Aids

Whether you create your presentation aids with pen and paper or generate them on a computer, apply the principles of simplicity and continuity to each aid you create. Remember that the purpose of a presentation aid is to reinforce, support, or summarize what you say, not to repeat verbatim what you've already stated in your speech.

Strive for Simplicity

Visuals that try to communicate too many messages will quickly overwhelm the audience. On average, audience members have thirty seconds or less to view an aid, so present one major idea per aid. To convey your points effectively on a slide:

- Follow the **eight by eight rule**; don't use more than eight words in a line or more than eight lines on one slide.

- State your points in short phrases.

- Construct your text in active verb form and parallel grammatical structure.

- Create concise titles that tell viewers what to look for and that reinforce your message.

- Avoid cluttering with unnecessary graphics and text (see Quick Tip on chartjunk below).

QUICK TIP

Beware of "Chartjunk"
Certain kinds of information — especially statistical data and sequences of action — are best understood through visual reasoning. However, speakers should avoid what design expert Edward Tufte coined "chartjunk" — slides jammed with too many graphs, charts, and other meaningless design elements that obscure rather than illuminate information. Tufte counsels using as few slides as possible and only those design elements that truly enhance meaning.[1]

Use Design Elements Consistently

Apply the same design decisions you make for one presentation aid to all of the aids you display in a speech. Doing so will ensure that viewers don't become distracted by a jumble of unrelated visual elements. Carry your choice of any key design elements—colors for objects or backgrounds, fonts, upper- and lowercase letters, styling (boldface, underlining, italics), page layout, repeating elements such as titles and logos—through to each aid.

QUICK TIP

Save the Text for Handouts

Audience members quickly become bored reading text on slides, especially text that repeats exactly what the speaker is saying. For this reason, design experts suggest limiting the number of words in slides, instead offering visuals such as charts, diagrams, illustrations, photos, and video. If you do have a lengthy message you want to display in text, save it for a handout.

Select Appropriate Typeface Styles and Fonts

A **typeface** is a specific style of lettering, such as Arial, Times Roman, and Courier. Typefaces come in a variety of **fonts**, or sets of sizes (called the point size), and upper and lower cases. Designers divide the thousands of available typefaces into two major categories: serif and sans serif. (Additional categories, such as script [calligraphy] typefaces, aren't recommended for presentation aids because they are difficult to read from a distance.) **Serif typefaces** include small flourishes, or strokes, at the tops and bottoms of each letter. **Sans serif typefaces** are more blocklike and linear; they are designed without these tiny strokes.

When selecting a typeface, consider the audience's distance from the aid; make sure it is simple and easy to read. Check its legibility by going some distance from it and squinting as you try to read it.[2] In addition:

• Check that your lettering stands apart from your background; for example, don't put black type on a dark blue background.

• Use upper- and lowercase type; this combination is easier to read than all capital letters.

QUICK TIP

Using Serif and Sans Serif Type
For reading a block of text, serif typefaces are easier on the eye. Small amounts of text, however, such as headings, are best viewed in sans serif type. Thus, consider a sans serif typeface for the heading and a serif typeface for the body of the text. If you include only a few lines of text, consider using sans serif type throughout.

- Don't overuse **boldface**, <u>underlining</u>, or *italics*. Use them sparingly to emphasize the most important points.
- Experiment with 32- to 44-point type for major headings and 24- to 32-point type for text.[3]
- Use a sans serif typeface for major headings. Experiment with a serif typeface for the body of the text.
- Avoid ornate fonts—they are difficult to read.
- Use no more than two different typefaces in a single visual aid.

Use Color Carefully

Color can draw attention to key points and help listeners see comparisons, contrasts, and emphases. However, poor color combinations will set the wrong mood, render an image unattractive, or make it unreadable.

- Use colors consistently across all aids.
- For the background, use neutral colors such as tan, blue, green, or white.
- For type and graphics, use colors that contrast rather than clash with or blend into the background.
- Emphasize important points with bold, bright colors. Yellow, orange, and red rank highest in visibility, so use these to highlight text or objects. But be careful: These colors can be difficult to see from a distance.
- Use no more than four colors; using two or three is better.

Consider Subjective Interpretations of Color

Colors can evoke distinct associations for people, so take care not to summon an unintended meaning or mood. For example, for financial managers, blue signifies cooperation and reliability; for health-care professionals, however, it signifies death. Control engineers see red and think danger, whereas a financial manager will think unprofitability and a health-care professional, health.[4]

CHECKLIST: Apply the Principles of Simplicity and Continuity

✓ Concentrate on presenting one major idea per visual aid.

✓ Apply design decisions consistently to each aid.

✓ Use type that is large enough for audience members to read comfortably.

✓ Use color to highlight key ideas and enhance readability.

✓ Check that colors contrast rather than clash.

22 | A Brief Guide to Microsoft PowerPoint

Various presentation software packages—and even some free Web-based applications, such as Google Docs (docs.google.com)—offer public speakers powerful tools for creating and displaying professionally polished visual aids. The best known and most available of these programs is Microsoft's PowerPoint. Preloaded templates provide expert guidelines for font, color, and background combinations, but you can also design your own. Multimedia displays may be produced by importing video and audio into your slides.

Give a Speech, Not a Slide Show

Many speakers mistake the PowerPoint display itself for the presentation, or they believe the slide show will somehow save an otherwise poorly planned speech. Some speakers become so enamored of creating glitzy multimedia presentations that they forget their primary mission: to communicate through the spoken word and their physical presence. PowerPoint slides, like all presentation aids, can sometimes help listeners process information, but only as long as they truly work to engage your audience and achieve your speech goal.

Develop Effective Slides

The fundamental principle for using PowerPoint slides for a speech is the same as for any visual aid: Make sure that the slides add value to your speech rather than distract from or become your speech.

The best place to begin planning your slides is with your speaking outline. Think through which points in your speech might be better explained to your audience with some kind of visual; decide what the content of your slides should be, how many slides you'll need, and how to arrange them. Ask yourself, "Are some of the points more suited to visual display than others? What features should be used for each slide?" There is no fixed formula for answering these questions, so you must rely on your own creativity and critical thinking.

CHECKLIST Using PowerPoint Presentations Effectively

✓ Don't let the technology get in the way of relating to your audience.

✓ Talk to your audience rather than to the screen. Maintain eye contact as much as possible.

✓ Have a backup plan in case of technical errors and prepare to give the speech without slides.

✓ If you use a pointer (laser or otherwise), turn it off and put it down as soon as you have made your point.

✓ Incorporate the aids into your practice sessions until you are confident that they strengthen, rather than detract from, your core message.

Avoid Technical Glitches

For all its promise, the use of PowerPoint slides can be fraught with peril. To minimize problems, do the following:

- Check for compatibility of the equipment, operating system, and software. Incompatibilities between versions can distort your graphics, audio, and video; in some cases one version may not recognize another.

- Properly save all the files associated with your presentation (e.g., images, sound files, videos) into the same folder and onto the disk you will use in your presentation.
- Familiarize yourself with the layout and functioning of the equipment.
- Prepare a hard copy of your presentation as backup. Use the Handout Master and handout printing option to print out your slides for distribution.

Using Microsoft PowerPoint

PowerPoint allows you to generate slides containing text, artwork, photos, charts, graphs, tables, clip art, video, and audio. You can upload PowerPoint presentations onto the Web for viewing elsewhere, and with additional software you can broadcast your PowerPoint presentation online in real time. This section offers a brief overview of PowerPoint's primary features.

Presentation Options

Begin by familiarizing yourself with the toolbars and icons at the top and bottom of the main screen (see Figure 22.1). PowerPoint provides three options for composing a set of presentation slides: *AutoContent Wizard, Design Template,* and *Blank Presentation Mode.*

AUTOCONTENT WIZARD   The *AutoContent Wizard* (or *Slide Layout* in PowerPoint 2007) lets you choose the type of presentation you want from about two dozen alternatives, such as Marketing Plan, Introducing a Speaker, Product/Services Overview, and Presenting a Technical Report. AutoContent Wizard then applies an outline for your presentation (see Figure 22.2). You select the presentation medium (on-screen, Web, overheads) in which to enter the information to be presented. The AutoContent Wizard sets

FIGURE 22.1 PowerPoint Toolbars

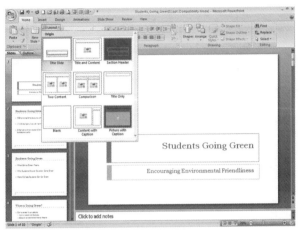

FIGURE 22.2 PowerPoint's AutoContent Wizard or Slide Layout

up from six to twelve slides with preloaded slide titles, points, subpoints, colors, and designs.

DESIGN TEMPLATE The *Design Template* option includes approximately forty-eight predesigned templates (see Figure 22.3). You decide how to organize your points and subpoints; the template you select then applies a consistent layout and color scheme to each slide in the presentation. Each template is designed to convey a consistent look or feel.

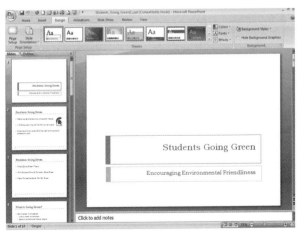

FIGURE 22.3 Design Template

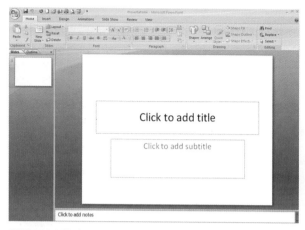

FIGURE 22.4 Blank Presentation Mode

BLANK PRESENTATION MODE   With *Blank Presentation mode*, you customize every aspect of the presentation: layout, color, font, type and size, organization of content, and graphics (see Figure 22.4). This option allows the greatest degree of flexibility. Once you have designed a slide with the feature you want, you can opt to have each subsequent slide share the same features, or you can design each slide independently.

View Options

Current versions of PowerPoint offer three different ways to view slides as you create them: *normal view*, *slide-sorter view*, and *slide-show view*.

- *Normal view* allows you to view and edit one entire slide on the screen. To the left of the screen is a text outline of the entire presentation or, alternatively, a thumbnail view of each slide as it is created. Below the slide is a space to add notes.

- *Slide-sorter view* provides a matrix-type view of all the slides in the order they are created. Here you can delete slides or click and drag slides to reorganize the presentation sequence.

- *Slide-show view* is the actual view to use for projecting the presentation to an audience. Each slide fills the entire screen.

Masters

For each presentation you create using a Design Template, PowerPoint creates a *Slide Master* and a *Handout Master*. The Slide Master contains the elements (text or images) that you want to appear on every slide, such as a logo, image, or line of text. The Handout Master shows a page-size view depicting a number of slides per page (six by default) and lets you alter the orientation of slides on the page. When printed, this view serves as a handout of the slides. To display a master, go to the View menu and scroll down to Master.

Transitions and Animation Effects

When moving from one slide to the next in your presentation, or from one point to another within a single slide, you may wish to add special effects in the form of transitions and text animations. *Transitions* add motion and sound effects as you click from one slide to another. For example, you can play a "swoosh" sound when the slide appears, or you can make the slides dissolve into black or red as you shift from one to another.

Animation effects—sometimes referred to as *builds*—allow you to reveal text or graphics within a slide during a presentation. For example, you can reveal one letter, word, or paragraph at a time as you discuss each item. Or you can make text or objects look dimmer or change color when you add another element.

As a rule of thumb, your PowerPoint presentation will be just as effective without transitions and animation effects, but if you decide to use them, use sparingly. Unnecessary use of effects can harm the presentation.

QUICK TIP

Using Animation Effects

Used sparingly, animations and transitions can add to a presentation, but beware of using them so much that they distract from your message. Keep all text animations consistent from one slide to the next. For example, if you use the "fly in from left" effect for one slide, use it on all slides. The same guidelines apply to transitions. Keep them consistent throughout the entire slide show or within different sections.

Entering and Editing Text

Whenever you choose a slide layout other than a blank layout, you replace the sample text in a placeholder or textbox with your own text. PowerPoint text can be edited much like text in a word processor—you can apply bold, italics, and other text modifications. When you finish entering text, deselect the placeholder by clicking a blank area of the slide. After entering text, making changes is as easy as clicking and retyping.

Inserting Objects

PowerPoint allows you to create or import photos, pictures, clip art, and other objects into the slides to supplement or illustrate speech points.

CLIP ART   The PowerPoint ClipArt Gallery contains more than one thousand drawings that cover a wide range of topics. Other programs or Web sites such as Microsoft's online Clip Gallery (office.microsoft.com/clipart) offer thousands of graphic images and sounds, including photographs and Web animations.

You can insert clip art into a slide in several ways. If you are using AutoLayout, you simply double-click on the clipart placeholder. You can also choose the Insert ClipArt command or select from the category list (Clip Art, Pictures, Sounds, Videos).

TABLES AND WORKSHEETS   To insert a table or a worksheet into your PowerPoint presentation, follow these steps:

1. Choose Insert Microsoft Word Table or Insert Microsoft Excel Worksheet in the standard toolbar. A drop-down grid of cells appears.

2. Click and drag the mouse pointer across the cells in the grid to indicate how many rows or columns you want in your table or worksheet. Upon releasing the mouse button, PowerPoint inserts a special object into your slide, replacing the PowerPoint toolbars for either Word or Excel toolbars. In effect, the special object allows you to use either Word or Excel inside a PowerPoint window.

3. To create the content of the table or worksheet, use the mouse, the tab key, or the arrow keys to move from cell to cell and type in the text. When you are finished, select Exit to insert the object into the slide.

Inserting Videos and Sounds

The growing availability of amateur video on Web sites such as YouTube (www.youtube.com) and Google Video (video.google.com) and the increasing ease of transferring video to computers from portable devices such as iPods, pocket-size hard drives, and cell phones makes the embedding of video even simpler. However, unlike objects that can truly be embedded into the PowerPoint presentation, video clips are *merely linked*. This means that if you move your PowerPoint presentation from one computer to another (by saving it to a CD or to a USB flash drive or by e-mailing it), you will break the link to your video file unless you saved the file in the same folder as your PowerPoint presentation. To add video to a slide, follow these steps:

1. In Normal view, click the slide to which you want to add a movie or animated file.

2. On the Insert tab, in the Media Clips group (or Movie tab), click the arrow under Movie.

3. Do one of the following:

    • Click Movie from File, locate the folder that contains the file, and then double-click the file that you want to add.

    • Click Movie from Clip Organizer, scroll to find the clip that you want in the Clip Art task pane, and then click it to add it to the slide.

You can also go to Microsoft's PowerPoint Web site (office .microsoft.com/en-us/powerpoint/default.aspx) and follow the instructions for adding and playing a movie in a presentation. Note that you cannot insert portions of a digital movie from a DVD to a PowerPoint slide, but you can use some third-party software to synchronize a DVD video during a PowerPoint presentation.

PowerPoint also allows you to insert a playable music track from a compact disc or a file from your computer. To do so, select Sound from the Insert menu and then select whether you want to play from a file or from a CD audio track.

Avoiding Copyright Infringement

Much like plagiarism, it is easy to unwittingly commit copyright infringement when downloading and using visual and audio materials from the Internet. Be certain to abide by copyright restrictions (often individual objects, e.g., clip art, carry a copyright indicator) and read the site's terms of use for the materials. Recognize when material is available under Fair-use provisions (see Chapter 4, p. 29). Even if fair use applies, you must still appropriately cite the source of the material in your presentation.

Be sure to consult your school's information technology (IT) office for statements of policy pertaining to copyrighted and fair-use materials. It is important for you to be familiar with these policies before using any textual, visual, or audio resources acquired electronically, especially from undocumented sources such as peer-to-peer (P2P) sharing. You might have to pay for or seek the originator's permission to use these materials. Your improper acquisition or use of a copyrighted object could lead to loss of privileges on your campus computer network or, worse, to legal consequences including stiff fines and jail time.

CHECKLIST: Ensuring Legal Use of Media Acquired Electronically

✓ Be sure to cite the source of all copyrighted material in your presentation. For example, include a bibliographic footnote on the slide containing the material.

✓ Be wary of sites purporting to offer "royalty free" media objects; there might actually be other costs associated with the materials. For instance, some sites require that you present their logo along with any of their materials you use. Not doing so is an infringement of copyright.

✓ Some librarians are experts on the use of copyrighted and fair-use materials. Check with your library about who to consult if you have questions or concerns.

✓ When time, resources, and ability allow, create and use your own pictures, video, or audio for your presentation slides.

Running the Presentation

During your actual presentation, you can control your slides using the commands listed in the table on the next page:

COMMANDS TO RUN A POWERPOINT SLIDE SHOW	
FUNCTION	**METHOD**
Show the next slide	Click the left mouse button or press the space bar, N, right arrow, down arrow, or Page Down
Show the preceding slide	Click the right mouse button or press Backspace, P, left arrow, up arrow, or Page Up
Show a specific slide	Type the number and press Enter
Access Meeting Minder or pointers	Click the right mouse button and select the appropriate option
Toggle the mouse pointer on or off (show or hide)	Type A or the equal sign
Toggle between a black screen and a current screen	Type B or a period
Toggle between a white screen and a current screen	Type W or a comma
End the show	Press ESC, hyphen, or CTRL-Break
Pause and resume an automatic slide show	Type S or the plus sign

23 | Informative Speaking

To *inform* is to communicate knowledge. An **informative speech** provides new information, new insights, or new ways of thinking about a topic. Your speech might be an explanation of a concept or practice; a description of a person, place, or event; or a physical demonstration of how something works. As long as the audience learns something, the options are nearly limitless.

QUICK TIP

Enlighten Rather than Advocate
Whereas a persuasive speech would seek to modify attitudes or ask an audience to adopt a specific position, an informative speech stops short of this. Yet there are always elements of persuasion in an informative speech, and vice versa. Nevertheless, if you keep your focus on building understanding, you will be able to deliver an informative speech whose primary function is to enlighten rather than to advocate.

Gain and Sustain Involvement

Audience members are not simply empty vessels into which you can pour facts and figures and then expect them to automatically process them. Before they retain information, they must be able to recognize, understand, and relate to it.

Demonstrate the Topic's Relevance Early On

Early on in your speech (in your preview statement, for example) tell listeners why the topic is relevant to them and point to what they will gain from learning about it. Give them reasons to care about what's to follow.

Use Audience Analysis

Use audience analysis to discover what listeners might want and need to know about your topic, as well as their familiarity with it (see Chapter 6). Then adapt your speech accordingly. If speaking about collecting violins to a general audience, for example, you might describe its parts, the sounds it produces, and name the Italian families who made the most prized instruments. Only a specialized audience of musicians will want or need to hear about staccato bowings, sforzandos, or other technical information.[1]

Present New and Interesting Information

Try to uncover information that is fresh and compelling. Seek out unusual—but credible—sources, novel—but sound—interpretations, startling facts, cogent examples, and moving stories. As professional speaker Vickie K. Sullivan notes:

> The first point that transforms an ordinary speaker into an industry beacon is a new perspective on a major problem.... If the speech does not convey provocative information, audience members feel their time has been wasted (and rightfully will feel offended). They expect their thinking to be challenged.[2]

Help Listeners Follow Along

Audience members cannot reread, "rewind," or put a speaker on "pause," so help them to stay on track:

- *Preview main points.* In the introduction, preview your main points and summarize what you want listeners to gain from the speech; for example, "I'll begin by.... Next I will.... By the end of this presentation I hope that you will understand...." See also the section on preview statements in Chapter 15.

- *Use clear transitions.* Transition words, phrases, and sentences that tie speech ideas together will help audience members follow your points (see Chapter 12).

- *Use repetition.* Repeat key ideas and concepts to help listeners grasp and retain information (see Chapter 16).

- Use internal previews to forecast key points and internal summaries to revisit them (see p. 102).

Subject Matter of Informative Speeches

Broadly speaking, informative speeches may be about *objects* or *phenomena, people, events, processes, concepts,* or *issues.* These are not hard and fast divisions—a speech can be about both the process of dance and the people who perform it, for example—but they show the range of informative subjects and can point to a logical organizational pattern (see Chapter 13).

SUBJECT MATTER OF INFORMATIVE SPEECH	SAMPLE TOPICS
Objects or phenomena • Define and describe object or phenomenon. • Offer explanations and/or demonstration.	• digital cameras • Texas English • MP3 players • campaign for city council • El Niño winds in the western U.S.
People • Describe the person or group. • Explain their significance.	• athletes • authors • inventors • political leaders • war refugees
Current or historical events • Use description to paint a vivid picture. • Analyze the event's meaning.	• Lady Gaga concerts • 1937 Paris World's Fair • The National College Cheerleading Finals • The Battle of Britain
Processes • If physically showing a physical process, rely on demonstration. • If explaining a process, vary strategies as needed.	• isolation of DNA in cells • podcasting • lightning formation • Power Yoga movements
Concepts • Offer multiple definitions. • Use analogies. • Discuss underlying processes/causes.	• artificial intelligence • nanotechnology • free speech • slow time movement • nuclear fission
Issues • Focus on description and explanation. • Avoid advocating one position versus another.	• racial profiling • outsourcing • plastic in the world's oceans • climate change

Decide How to Communicate Your Information

Typically, speakers communicate information by defining, describing, demonstrating, and/or explaining. Some speeches rely almost exclusively on a single approach (e.g., to demonstrate how something works or to describe what something is). Many speeches, however, employ a combination of approaches. As you prepare your speech, ask yourself, "By which of these means can I best convey my ideas?"

DEFINITION   Informative speaking often involves defining information—identifying the essential qualities and meaning of something. When your speech focuses on addressing the meaning of a complex concept or one that is new to the audience—such as "What is cholesterol?" or "What does 'equilibrium price' mean?"—pay particular attention to using definition.

You can approach definition in a number of ways, including the following:

- Defining the topic by explaining what it does (**operational definition**); for example, *A computer is something that processes information.*

- Defining the topic by describing what it is not (**definition by negation**); for example, *Courage is not the absence of fear.*

- Defining the topic by providing several concrete examples (**definition by example**); for example, *Health professionals include doctors, nurses, EMTs, and ambulance drivers.*

- Defining the topic by comparing it to something with which it is synonymous (**definition by synonym**); for example, *A friend is a comrade or a buddy.*

- Defining the topic by illustrating the root meaning of the term in question (**definition by word origin** [etymology]); for example, *Our word* rival *derives from the Latin word* rivalis, *"one living near or using the same stream."*[3]

DESCRIPTION   Vivid and concise language helps turn abstract concepts into concrete examples. When you describe something, you provide an array of descriptive details that paint a mental picture of the person, place, event, or process. Concrete and colorful words, metaphors, and other figures of speech will help listeners visualize your ideas (see Chapter 16).

QUICK TIP

Use Visual Reinforcement

People process and retain information best when they receive it in more than one format. Well-conceived drawings, models, videos, and other graphic illustrations allow listeners to see the "big picture."[4] Messages that are reinforced with presentation aids—such as slides, objects, props, and video—are often more memorable and believable than those that are simply verbalized.

DEMONSTRATION Sometimes the purpose of an informative speech is to explain how something works or to actually demonstrate it, using an object, a representation, or some other visual aid. Topics such as "how to use social bookmarks" and "treating a burn" may not include an actual physical demonstration, but the speaker will nevertheless verbally demonstrate the steps involved.

EXPLANATION Explanation provides reasons or causes, demonstrates relationships, and offers interpretation and analysis. The classroom lecture is a classic example of explanation. But many kinds of speeches rely on explanation, from those that address difficult or confusing theories and processes (*What is the relationship between the glycemic index and glycemic load?*) to those that present ideas that challenge conventional thinking (*Why do researchers say that sometimes emotion makes us more rather than less logical?*) See the checklist on p. 181 for strategies for explaining complex processes.

Take Steps to Reduce Confusion

New information can be hard to grasp, especially when it addresses a difficult concept or term (such as *equilibrium* in engineering), a difficult-to-envision process (such as *cash-flow management* in business), or a counterintuitive idea[5] (such as *drinking a glass of red wine a day can be healthy*).

Useful in nearly all informative speeches, the following strategies for communicating information are especially helpful when attempting to clarify complex information.

Use Analogies to Build on Prior Knowledge

Audience members will understand a new concept more easily if the speaker uses an analogy to relate it to something that they already know[6] (see also Chapter 16). For example, to explain the unpredictable paths that satellites often take when they fall to earth, you can liken the effect to dropping a penny into water: "Sometimes it goes straight down, and sometimes it turns end over end and changes direction. The same thing happens when an object hits the atmosphere."[7]

Demonstrate Underlying Causes

Listeners may fail to understand a process because they believe that something "obviously" works a certain way when in fact it does not. To counter faulty assumptions, first acknowledge common misperceptions and then offer an accurate explanation of underlying causes.[8]

Appeal to Different Learning Styles

People have different **learning styles**, or preferred ways of processing information. One learning theory model suggests four preferences: visual, aural, read/write, and kinesthetic[9] (see table on different learner types). Some of us are *multimodal learners*, in that we combine two or more preferences.

Audience analysis can sometimes give you a sense of individuals' learning styles. For example, mechanics of all types have strong spatial visualization abilities and thus would be classified as visual learners; they may also be kinesthetic learners who want to "test" things for themselves. Often, however, you may not have enough information to determine your listeners' learning style, *so plan on conveying and reinforcing information in a variety of modes.*

COMMUNICATING INFORMATION TO DIFFERENT TYPES OF LEARNERS	
TYPE	ADVICE FOR COMMUNICATING INFORMATION
Visual	Will most easily grasp ideas communicated through pictures, diagrams, charts, graphs, flow charts, maps.
Aural	Will most easily grasp ideas communicated through the spoken word, either in live lectures, tapes, group discussions, Webcasts.
Read/Write	Will most easily grasp ideas communicated through text-based delivery, handouts, PowerPoint with text-based slides.
Kinesthetic	Will most easily grasp ideas communicated through real-life demonstrations, simulations, and movies, and through hands-on applications.

Check for Understanding

Audience feedback becomes especially important when explaining new information. Be alert to nonverbal signals, such as blank stares, that indicate a lack of focus, and invite questions accordingly.

Arrange Points in a Pattern

Our understanding of a speech is directly linked to how well it is organized.[10] Informative speeches can be organized using any of the patterns described in Chapter 13, including the topical,

CHECKLIST: Strategies for Explaining Complex Information

To explain a concept or term:

✓ Build on prior knowledge.

✓ Use analogies that link concepts to something familiar.

✓ Define terms in several ways.

✓ Simplify terminology wherever possible.

✓ Check for understanding.

To explain a process or structure, do all of the above *and:*

✓ Make ample use of visual aids, including models and drawings.

To explain a counterintuitive idea, do all of the above *and:*

✓ Address the commonly held assumption first.

✓ Acknowledge its plausibility.

✓ Demonstrate its limitations using familiar examples.

chronological, spatial, problem-solution, cause-effect, narrative, comparative advantage, and circular patterns. A speech defining the French Impressionist movement in painting, for example, could be organized *chronologically*, in which main points are arranged in sequence from the movement's early period to its later falling out of favor. The speech could be organized *causally*, by demonstrating that French Impressionism came about as a reaction to the art movement that preceded it. It could also be organized *topically*, by focusing on the major figures associated with the movement, famous paintings linked to it, or notable contemporary artists who paint in the style.

In a student speech on "How to Buy a Guitar," Richard Garza organizes his main points chronologically:

GENERAL PURPOSE: Buying and caring for a guitar involve knowing what to look for when purchasing it and understanding how to maintain it once you own it.

MAIN POINTS: I. Decide what kind of guitar you need.

II. Inspect the guitar for potential flaws.

III. Maintain the guitar.

In a speech on the nonmonetary uses of gold, Krista Kim organizes her main points topically, dividing her points by category:

THESIS STATEMENT: Although generally unknown to the general population, gold has many nonmonetary applications in medicine and science.

MAIN POINTS: I.   Gold has many unique and useful qualities.

II. Gold has many applications in medicine.

III. Gold has several applications in the NASA space program.

CHECKLIST: Possible Matches of Organizational Patterns with Speech Types

✓ Objects — spatial, topical

✓ People — chronological, topical, narrative

✓ Events — chronological, cause-effect, narrative

✓ Processes — chronological, narrative

✓ Concepts — topical, circle, cause-effect

✓ Issues — chronological, cause-effect, topical, circle

SAMPLE INFORMATIVE SPEECH

The following speech by student David Kruckenberg describes a promising new way to treat cancer. David clarifies information with definitions and analogies and uses transitions and repetition to help listeners follow along. He also cites sources wherever he offers information gathered and reported by others.

David's topic could suggest a chronological pattern of arrangement. For example, he could have arranged his main points to trace the invention from inception to ongoing trials. Instead, he uses the *topical pattern of arrangement* (see Chapter 13) to move back and forth between describing the history of the new cancer treatment and explaining key concepts related to it.

John Kanzius and the Quest to Cure Cancer

DAVID KRUCKENBERG
Santiago Canyon College

One night in 2003, Marianne Kanzius awoke to a tremendous clamor coming from downstairs. She found her husband John sitting on the kitchen floor, cutting up her good aluminum pie pans with a pair of shears.

This is David's "attention getter."

As Peter Panepento describes the scene in an article titled "Sparks of Genius," published in the May 2006 edition of *Reader's Digest,* when Marianne asked him why he was wiring the pans to his ham radio, John told her to go back to bed. So off she went, knowing that her single-minded husband wasn't the kind of person to quit until he was satisfied.

Marianne soon learned that John's late-night experiment with pie pans was an attempt to use radio waves to kill cancer cells—and to rid himself of the rare form of leukemia threatening his life. In the next five years, John Kanzius would radically modify an existing cancer treatment technique called *radiofrequency ablation,* making it potentially far more effective than existing treatments. Soon, the work of this retired TV and radio engineer might give additional hope to the 1.4 million Americans diagnosed with cancer every year, according to the 2008 American Cancer Society "Facts and Figures" section of its Web site.

David draws listeners in with an unusual story.

Thesis statement.

To understand John's discovery, we'll explore how the medical profession currently makes use of radio waves to treat cancer, learn about John's truly promising new approach, and consider the implications for the future.

David previews the main points then moves into a transition.

But first, to understand radiofrequency energy, we need a crash course in wave physics.

Energy moves in a wave and is measured in *frequency,* how quickly it moves up and down. *High frequency waves,* like Superman's x-ray vision—and real x-rays—move quickly and penetrate most matter, but can alter the chemical and genetic material in cells. *Low frequency waves,* such as radio waves, move slowly and don't disturb the atomic balance of matter they pass through. Radio

David increases understanding using an analogy to x-ray vision, definitions of high and low frequency waves, and recognizable examples of each.

waves are harmless to healthy cells, making them a promising tool for ablation.

Let me explain the term. Ablation, according to the National Cancer Institute's *Dictionary of Cancer Terms,* available on its Web site, is the medical term for "the removal or destruction of a body part or tissue or its function," using hormone therapy, conventional surgery, or radiofrequency. *Radiofrequency ablation,* or RFA, uses radiofrequency energy to "cook" and kill cancer cells, according to the Society of Interventional Radiology. The least invasive RFA technique practiced today is through the skin; it's also done laparoscopically.

> David defines terms that the audience may not know.

Here's how the Radiological Society of North America explains radiofrequency ablation on its Web site, last updated December 17, 2008.

> This transition helps listeners focus on the ensuing explanation.

First, a doctor makes a small incision in the skin and inserts a needle electrode or a straight hollow needle containing retractable electrodes.

The doctor guides the needle to the site of the tumor using an imaging technique such as ultrasound.

The needle in turn is connected to an electric generator, and once in place, electrodes extend out of it and into the tumor.

Next, contact pads, also wired to the generator, are placed on the patient's skin; this completes an electric circuit so that when the generator is turned on, electric energy in the form of radio waves pass through the body, going back and forth between the needles and the contact pads.

> Such signal words as *first* and *next* help listeners follow the procedure's chronologically organized steps.

Here's the critical part:

Every time that the radio waves meet the resistance of the electrodes at the treatment site, they create heat. It's kind of like an atomic mosh pit, with a crowd of atoms suddenly agitated by radio waves; the electrons begin to bounce around and collide, creating friction and thus heat. This heat gets up to 212 degrees Fahrenheit, the temperature at which water boils. The heat destroys the cancerous cells in the tumor, essentially cooking them, but leaving noncancerous cells alone.

> David's mosh-pit analogy helps listeners understand a complex concept.

In many ways, it's a great treatment option right now. However, while it is called "minimally invasive" surgery, the needles required by this method can damage tissue and even organs near the tumor site, limiting its usefulness.

Enter John Kanzius.

This transition adds drama.

John was diagnosed with leukemia in 2002, and his ordeal with chemotherapy motivated him to find a better way to attack cancer cells.

Now John had no medical training, but he had worked 18 in the radio industry for forty years, and he knew all about radio waves. He recalled that a colleague wearing wire-rimmed glasses got burned as he stood too close to a radio transmitter. As Peter Panepento describes it in *Reader's Digest*, this led Kanzius to theorize that if you could infuse cancer cells with a conductive substance, you could use a transmitter to heat them with radio waves, while avoiding invasive needles. The cells marked with the substance would act like "tiny antennas," as Panepento put it.

David is careful to credit direct quotations.

It was this chain of thought which spurred John's late- 19 night kitchen experiment with the pie pans and his ham radio.

Two things were amazing about John's initial experi- 20 ment.

First, John was able to replicate RFA in his kitchen. 21 Second, John made a huge improvement upon the technique, alone and at home. Instead of inserting needles into a tumor, he injected tiny metal minerals into a stand-in hotdog. He then placed the hotdog between the radio transmitter and receiver so that the radio waves would pass through the meat. When he cut the hotdog open, the area around the minerals was cooked, but the rest remained raw. Kanzius later repeated the experiment with liver, then steak, obtaining the same results.

Could there really be a way to use radiofrequency without side effects, and to treat more types of cancer with it?

Here he uses a transition in the form of a rhetorical question.

As told by Charles Schmidt in the *Journal of the National Cancer Institute* on July 16, 2008, John shared his results with several leading oncologists, who immediately recognized the potential. He then filed for a patent for his RF machine.

Researchers at two prominent cancer centers decided 24 to test John's theory, starting in August 2005 with the University of Pittsburgh's Liver Cancer Center. As detailed in the University of Pittsburgh Medical Center newsletter of March 22, 2006, instead of using a hotdog, the researchers placed a thin test tube between the radio transmitter and the receiver. Inside this tube was a solution of carbon nanoparticles—actually pieces of metal about 1/75,000 times smaller than the width of a human hair. A speck of dandruff is like a mountain to a nanoparticle. When they turned on the electricity, the carbon nanoparticles successfully heated to 130 degrees Fahrenheit—the perfect temperature at which to kill cancer cells, according to Peter Panepento's *Reader's Digest* piece.

Because the size of a nanometer is hard to visualize, David compares it to something with which listeners are familiar—a strand of hair and dandruff.

Now that I've explained John's major improvement over current RFA procedures, let's consider the implications of his discovery. 25

John's non-invasive radiofrequency cancer treatment holds tremendous promise as an alternative to existing cancer therapies. First, because RFA uses electromagnetic energy in the form of radio waves, it's much safer than chemotherapy and traditional radiation treatment. As noted, radio waves are harmless to healthy cells, as compared to x-rays. 26

Second, as explained in the January 2008 issue of the *Journal of Nanobiotechnology* by Gannon et al., the current RFA procedure can only be used in cancers that are not difficult to reach, such as liver, breast, lung, and bone; John's new method potentially can target tumors anywhere in the body.

Using full oral citations supports David's credibility and allows the audience to seek further information on the topic.

Third, the current RFA procedure must be performed several times to target multiple tumors, but John's method could make it possible to target multiple tumors in just a single treatment. 28

Intensive research is now underway at the renowned M. D. Anderson Cancer Center in Houston. The goal is to find ways to make the nanoparticles target cancer cells exclusively. Success occurred in late 2007, when in a preclinical trial researchers at the M.D. Anderson Cancer Center used the technique to completely destroy liver cancer tumors in rabbits, as described in the December 2007 issue of the journal *Cancer*. 29

Another area they are trying to resolve, according to Schmidt, is the potential toxicity of nanoparticles in the bloodstream. Human trials may begin in two to three years, according to Dr. Steven Curley, lead investigator on the Kanzius project at M.D. Anderson, as reported this summer by David Bruce in the *Erie Times News*. 30

Today we learned how a man with vision discovered   31
how to cook a hotdog with a ham radio. We explored first
the current procedure, then John's new
approach, and, finally, the implications of
this new hope for treating cancer.

David gives a clear signal of the speech's conclusion with a summary of the main points.

John's cancer is in remission, and he's
established the John Kanzius Cancer
Research Foundation, which you can read about online.
He is continuing to refine his technique and is working on
clinical trials.

Marianne Kanzius was upset when she saw her hus-   33
band destroying her good pie pans, but
now it's clear that the loss of a few pie pans
and a hotdog may soon save millions of
lives.

A return to David's opening story brings the speech full circle.

Works Cited

Bruce, David. "Community Unites Behind Kanzius, Human Trials"
   Erie Times-News, July 27, 2008, doc ID: 1222E79CB5E00DA0.

"Cancer Facts and Figures, 2008," American Cancer Society,
   www.cancer.org/docroot/STT/content/STT_1x_
   Cancer_Facts_and_Figures_2008.asp

Dictionary of Cancer Terms, National Cancer Institute.
   www.cancer.gov/templates/db_alpha.aspx?expand=A
   (accessed December 15, 2008).

Gannon, Christopher J. Chitta Ranjan Patra, Resham Bhattacharya,
   Priyabrata Mukherjee, and Steven A. Curley, "Intracellular
   Gold Nanoparticles Enhance Non-invasive Radiofrequency
   Thermal Destruction of Human Gastrointestinal Cancer Cells,"
   Journal of Nanobiotechnology 2008, 6:2doi:10.1186/1477-
   3155-6-2.

Gannon, Christopher J., et al. "Carbon nanotube-enhanced thermal
   destruction of cancer cells in a noninvasive radiofrequency
   field." *Cancer*. Published Online: Oct 24 2007 12:19PM_DOI:
   10.1002/cncr.23155.

Panepento, Peter. "Sparks of Genius: Efforts Done by John Kanzius,
   a Cancer Patient, to Find a Better Cure for Cancer," *Reader's
   Digest* (May 2006): 132–36.

"Radiofrequency Ablation of Liver Tumors," Radiological Society of
   North America, www.radiologyinfo.org/en/info.cfm?PG=rfa
   (accessed December 17, 2008).

"Radiofrequency Catheter Ablation." Society of Interventional
  Radiology. http://www.sirweb.org (accessed June 23, 2009).
Schmidt, Charles. "A New Cancer Treatment from an Unexpected
  Source," *Journal of the National Cancer Institute* 2008
  100(14):985–86; doi:10.1093/jnci/djn246, July 16, 2008.
University of Pittsburgh Medical Center Web Site, *Match*
  (a publication of the Thomas E. Starzl Transplantation
  Institute), March 22, 2006.

24 Persuasive Speaking

To persuade is to advocate, to ask others to accept your views.
The goal of a **persuasive speech** is to influence the attitudes,
beliefs, values and acts of others (see Chapter 6). Some persuasive speeches attempt to modify audience attitudes and
values so that they move in the direction of the speaker's
stance. Others aim for an explicit response, as when a speaker
urges listeners to donate money for a cause or to vote for a
candidate. Sometimes a speech will attempt to modify both
attitudes and actions.

Focus on Motivation

Success in persuasive speaking requires attention to human
psychology—to what motivates listeners. Audience analysis
is therefore extremely important in persuasive appeals.

Research confirms that you can increase the odds of
achieving your persuasive speech goal if you:

- Make your message personally relevant to the audience.[1]
- Demonstrate how any change you propose will benefit
  the audience.[2]
- Set modest goals. Expect minor rather than major
  changes in your listeners' attitudes and behaviors.
- Target issues that audience members feel strongly about.
  If they don't care much about an issue, it's unlikely they
  will pay much attention to the speech.[3]

- Demonstrate how an attitude or a behavior might keep listeners from feeling satisfied and competent, thereby encouraging receptivity to change.

- Expect to be more successful when addressing an audience whose position differs only moderately from your own.

- Establish your credibility with the audience.

QUICK TIP

Expect Modest Results
Regardless of how thoroughly you have conducted audience analysis, or how skillfully you present your point of view, don't expect your audience to respond immediately or completely to a persuasive appeal. Persuasion does not occur with a single dose. Changes tend to be small, even imperceptible, especially at first.

Balance Reason and Emotion

Persuasion is a complex psychological process of reasoning and emotion, and effective persuasive speeches target not one but both processes in audience members. Emotion gets the audience's attention and stimulates a desire to act; reason provides the justification for the action.

Persuasive speeches are built upon **arguments**—stated positions, with support, for or against an idea or issue. Appealing to reason and logic—or to what Aristotle termed **logos**—is important in gaining agreement for your position; it is especially critical when asking listeners to reach a conclusion regarding a complicated issue or to take a specific action. To truly persuade listeners to care about your argument, however, you must also appeal to their emotions—to what Aristotle termed **pathos**. Feelings such as pride, love, anger, shame, and fear underlie many of our actions and motivate us to think and feel as we do.

You can evoke pathos in a speech by using vivid imagery and emotionally charged words (see Chapter 16). Consider the following example from a speech by Elpidio Villarreal about the value of immigrants to the United States. In this excerpt, Villarreal movingly describes the death of his uncle, an immigrant from Mexico, during combat in World War II.

Villarreal's strong imagery effectively conveys the loyalty and sacrifice of Mexican Americans:

> On June 6, 1944, [my Uncle Lupe] landed at a place called Omaha Beach in Normandy, France. He was killed while leading an attack on an enemy Bunker. . . . I was privileged to walk the battlefields of Normandy, including Omaha Beach, and I visited the great American Cemetery there where lie 17,000 Americans who gave the "last full measure of devotion," as Lincoln so beautifully put it. Simple white marble crosses, interspersed with occasional Stars of David, stretch out for 70 acres. . . .
>
> I thought about all the brave Americans buried there and of the meaning of their deaths, but I thought especially about my Uncle Lupe, the one who went to war knowing he would die for no other reason than that his country, the one that treated him as a second-class citizen, asked him to.[4]

QUICK TIP

Base Your Emotional Appeals on Sound Reasoning
Although emotion is a powerful means of moving an audience, relying solely on naked emotion will fail most of the time.[5] What actually persuades an audience is the interplay between emotion and logic. When using emotions to appeal to an audience, always do so on the basis of sound reasoning.

Stress Your Credibility

Audiences want more than arguments from a speaker; they want what's relevant to them from someone who cares. Aristotle termed this effect of the speaker on the audience **ethos**, or moral character. Modern-day scholars call it speaker credibility.

Audience members' feelings about your credibility strongly influence how receptive they will be to your proposals, and studies confirm that attitude change is related directly to the extent to which listeners perceive speakers to be truthful and competent (well prepared).[6]

The following steps will help you establish credibility:

- Demonstrate your trustworthiness by presenting the topic honestly and in a way that shows concern for your listeners.

- Establish a feeling of identification, or commonality, and goodwill (see Chapter 6).

- If relevant, acknowledge personal knowledge or expertise vis-à-vis the topic.
- Be vibrant and charismatic in your presentation, using eyes, voice, and body effectively (see Chapter 19).

Target Listeners' Needs

Audience members are motivated to act on the basis of their needs; thus, one way to persuade listeners is to point to some need they want fulfilled and then give them a way to fulfill it. According to psychologist Abraham Maslow's classic **hierarchy of needs** (see Figure 24.1), each of us has a set of basic needs ranging from essential, life-sustaining ones to less critical, self-improvement ones. Our needs at the lower, essential levels (physiological and safety needs) must be fulfilled before the higher levels (social, self-esteem, and self-actualization needs) become important and motivating. Using Maslow's hierarchy to persuade your listeners to wear seat belts, for example, you would appeal to their need for safety. Critics of this approach suggest that we may be driven as much by *wants* as by needs; nevertheless, the theory points to the fact that successful appeals depend on understanding what motivates the audience.[7] Below are Maslow's five basic needs, along with suggested actions a speaker can take to appeal to them.

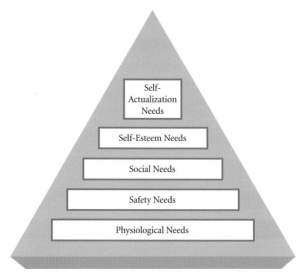

FIGURE 24.1 Maslow's Hierarchy of Needs

NEED	SPEECH ACTION
Physiological needs (basic sustenance, including food, water, and air)	• Plan for and accommodate the audience's physiological needs—are they likely to be hot, cold, hungry, or thirsty?
Safety needs (to feel protected and secure)	• Appeal to safety benefits—how wearing seat belts or voting for a bill to stop pollution will remove a threat or protect the audience members from harm.
Social needs (to find acceptance; to have lasting, meaningful relationships)	• Appeal to social benefits—if you want teenagers to quit smoking, stress that if they quit they will appear more physically fit and attractive to their peers.
Self-esteem needs (to feel good about ourselves; self-worth)	• Appeal to emotional benefits—stress that the proposed change will make listeners feel better about themselves.
Self-actualization needs (to achieve goals; to reach our highest potential)	• Appeal to your listeners' need to fulfill their potential—stress how adopting your position will help them "be all that they can be."

QUICK TIP

Show Them the Money

In order for change to endure listeners must be convinced they will be rewarded in some way. For example, to persuade people to lose weight and keep it off, you must make them believe that they will be healthier and happier if they do so. Skillful persuaders motivate their listeners to help themselves.

Encourage Mental Engagement

Audience members will mentally process your persuasive message by one of two routes, depending on their degree of involvement in the message.[8] When they are motivated and able to think critically about a message, they engage in **central processing**. That is, these listeners seriously consider what your message means to them and are the ones who are most likely to act on it. When listeners lack the motivation (or the ability) to judge the argument based on its merits, they engage in **peripheral processing** of information—they pay little attention and respond to the message as being irrelevant, too complex to follow, or just plain unimportant. Even though such listeners may sometimes buy into your message, they will do so not on the strength of the arguments but on the basis of such superficial factors as reputation, entertainment value, or personal style. Some viewers of the television show *Oprah*, for example, buy books she recommends simply because they like her, rather than because they've critically considered the book's contents.[9] Listeners who use peripheral processing are unlikely to experience meaningful changes in attitudes or behavior.

To encourage listeners to engage in central rather than peripheral processing (and thus increase the odds that your persuasive appeal will produce lasting, rather than fleeting, changes in their attitudes and behavior), make certain to do the following:

• Link your argument to practical concerns of listeners and emphasize direct consequences to them.	"Hybrid cars may not be the best-looking or fastest cars on the market, but as gas prices continue to soar, you will save a great deal of money."
• Present your message at an appropriate level of understanding.	For a *general audience*: "The technology behind hybrid cars is relatively simple . . ." For an *expert audience*: "To save even more gas, you can turn an EV into a PHEV with a generator and additional batteries . . ."
• Demonstrate common bonds (i.e., foster identification; see p. 40).	"It took me a while to convince myself to buy a hybrid . . ."
• Stress your credibility to offer the claims.	"Once I selected the car, I found I saved nearly $1,000 this year."

Construct Sound Arguments

In an *argument*, you offer a conclusion about some state of affairs, support it with evidence, and then link the evidence to the claim with reasons (also called *warrants*). The **claim**

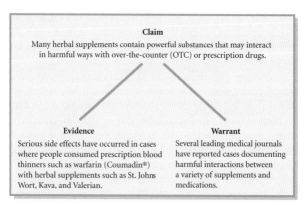

FIGURE 24.2 Core Components of Argument

(also called a *proposition*) states the speaker's conclusion, based on evidence. The **evidence** substantiates the claim. Reasoning links claims to evidence. A line of reasoning is called a **warrant**. A warrant explains (reasons) why the evidence proves the claim (see Figure 24.2, "Core Components of Argument").

Identify the Nature of Your Claims

Depending on the nature of the issue being addressed, an argument may address three different kinds of claims: of *fact*, of *value*, and of *policy*. Each type of claim requires evidence to support it. A persuasive speech may address only one type of claim or consist of several arguments addressing different kinds of claims.

- **Claims of fact** focus on whether something is or is not true or whether something will or will not happen. They usually address issues for which two or more competing answers exist, or those for which an answer does not yet exist. An example of the first is, "Does affirmative action discriminate against nonminority job applicants?" An example of the second (*speculative claim*) is, "Will a woman win in the next U.S. presidential election?"

- **Claims of value** address issues of judgment by attempting to show that something is right or wrong, good or bad, worthy or unworthy. Examples include "Is assisted suicide ethical?" and "Should late-term abortions be permitted when a woman's health is at stake?" The evidence in support of a value claim tends to be more subjective than for a fact claim.

- **Claims of policy** recommend that a specific course of action be taken or approved. Such claims often use the word "should" and often involve claims of fact and value as well. Examples include "Full-time students who commute to campus should be granted reduced parking fees" and "Property taxes should be increased to fund classroom expansions in city elementary schools." Notice that in each claim the word "should" appears. A claim of policy speaks to an "ought" condition, proposing that certain better outcomes would be realized if the proposed condition were met.

CHECKLIST: Structure the Claims in Your Persuasive Speech

✓ When addressing whether something is or is not true, or whether something will or will not happen, frame your argument as a *claim of fact*.

✓ When addressing issues that rely upon individual judgment of right and wrong for their resolution, frame your argument as a *claim of value*.

✓ When proposing a specific outcome or solution to an issue, frame your argument as a *claim of policy*.

Use Convincing Evidence

Every key claim must be supported with convincing *evidence*, supporting material that provides grounds for belief. Chapter 8 describes several forms of evidence: *examples*, *narratives*, *testimony*, *facts*, and *statistics*. These most common forms of evidence—called "external evidence" because the knowledge does not generate from the speaker's own experience—are most powerful when they impart new information that the audience has not previously used in forming an opinion.[10]

You can also use the *audience's preexisting knowledge and opinions*—what listeners already think and believe—as evidence for your claims. Nothing is more persuasive to listeners than a reaffirmation of their own attitudes, beliefs, and values, especially for claims of value and policy. To use this form of evidence, however, you must first identify what the audience knows and believes about the topic, and then present information that confirms these beliefs.

Finally, when the audience will find your opinions credible and convincing, consider using your own *speaker expertise* as evidence. Be aware, however, that few persuasive speeches can be convincingly built solely on speaker experience and knowledge. Offer your expertise in conjunction with other forms of evidence.

QUICK TIP

Address the Other Side of the Argument

All attempts at persuasion are subject to counterpersuasion. Listeners may be persuaded to accept your claims, but once they are exposed to counterclaims they may change their minds. If listeners are aware of counterclaims and you ignore them, you risk a loss of credibility.[11] Yet you need not painstakingly acknowledge and refute all opposing claims. Instead, raise and refute the most important counterclaims and evidence that the audience would know about. Ethically, you can ignore counterclaims that don't significantly weaken your argument.[12]

Use Effective Reasoning

Reasoning is the process of drawing conclusions from evidence. Arguments can be reasoned inductively, deductively, or causally. Arguments using *deductive reasoning* begin with a general principle or case, followed by a specific example of the case, which then leads to the speaker's conclusion.

In a deductive line of argument, if you accept the general principle and the speaker's specific example of it, you must accept the conclusion:

GENERAL CASE: All men are mortal.

SPECIFIC CASE: Socrates is a man.

CONCLUSION: Therefore Socrates is mortal.

Reversing direction, an argument using *inductive reasoning* moves from specific cases to a general conclusion supported by those cases. The speaker offers evidence that points to a conclusion that *appears to be*, but *is not necessarily*, true:

SPECIFIC CASE 1: In one five-year period, the average daily temperature (ADT) on Continent X rose three degrees.

SPECIFIC CASE 2: In that same period, ADT on Continent Y rose three degrees.

SPECIFIC CASE 3: In that same period, ADT on Continent Z rose three degrees.

CONCLUSION: Globally, average daily temperatures appear to be rising by three degrees.

Arguments based on inductive reasoning can be *strong* or *weak*; that is, listeners may decide the claim is probably true, largely untrue, or somewhere in between.

Arguments can also follow lines of **causal reasoning**, in which the speaker argues that one event, circumstance, or idea (the cause) is the reason (effect) for another. For example, "Smoking causes lung cancer." Sometimes a speaker can argue that multiple causes lead to a single effect, or that a single cause leads to multiple effects. (For more details on the cause-effect pattern, see Chapter 13.)

Avoid Fallacies in Reasoning

A **logical fallacy** is either a false or erroneous statement or an invalid or deceptive line of reasoning.[13] In either case, you need to be aware of fallacies in order to avoid making them in your own speeches and to be able to identify them in the speeches of others. Many fallacies of reasoning exist; the following are merely a few.

LOGICAL FALLACY	EXAMPLES
Begging the question An argument that is stated in such a way that it cannot help but be true, even though no evidence has been presented	• "War kills." • "Intelligent Design is the correct explanation for biological change over time because we can see godly evidence in our complex natural world."

LOGICAL FALLACY	EXAMPLES
Bandwagoning An argument that uses (unsubstantiated) general opinion as its (false) basis	• "Nikes are superior to other brands of shoes because everyone wears Nikes." • "Everybody on campus is voting for her so you should, too."
Either-or fallacy An argument stated in terms of two alternatives only, even though there may be many additional alternatives	• "If you don't send little Susie to private school this year, she will not gain admission to college." • "Either you're with us or against us."
Ad hominem argument An argument that targets a person instead of the issue at hand in an attempt to incite an audience's dislike for that person	• "I'm a better candidate than X because, unlike X, I work for a living." • "How can you accept my opponent's position on education when he has been divorced?"
Red herring An argument that relies on irrelevant premises for its conclusion	• "The previous speaker suggests that Medicare is in shambles. I disagree and recommend that we study why the young don't respect their elders." • "I fail to see why hunting should be considered cruel when it gives pleasure to many people and employment to even more."[14]
Hasty generalization An argument in which an isolated instance is used to make an unwarranted general conclusion	• "As shown by the example of a Labrador retriever biting my sister, this type of dog is dangerous and its breeding should be outlawed." • "My neighbor who works for K-Mart is untrustworthy; therefore, K-Mart is not a trustworthy company."

LOGICAL FALLACY	EXAMPLES
Non sequitur ("does not follow") An argument in which the conclusion is not connected to the reasoning	• "Because she lives in the richest country in the world, she must be extremely wealthy." • "If we can send a man to the moon, we should be able to cure cancer in five years."
Slippery slope A faulty assumption that one case will lead to a series of events or actions	• "Helping refugees in the Sudan today will force us to help refugees across Africa and around the world." • "If we outsource jobs from the United States, then other companies will outsource jobs, and then the U.S. economy will collapse."
Appeal to tradition An argument suggesting that audience members should agree with a claim because that is the way it has always been done	• "A marriage should be between a man and a woman because that is how it has always been done." • "The president of the United States must be a man because a woman has never been president."

Address Culture

Persuasion depends on appeals to values; culture shapes these values. Thus the audience's cultural orientation will significantly affect their responses to persuasion.[15]

CORE VALUES   Audience members of the same culture share core values; for example, individualist cultures such as that of the United States, promote *self-reliance* and *individual achievement.* Collectivist cultures such as those of China and India promote *interdependence* and *group harmony.* Usually, appeals that clash with core values are unsuccessful, although globalization may be leading to some cross-pollination of values.[16]

CULTURAL NORMS *Cultural norms* are a group's rules for behavior. Attempts to persuade listeners to think or do things contrary to important norms usually will fail.[17] The argument that intermarriage leads to happier couples, for example, will find greater acceptance among Reform rather than Orthodox Jews, since the latter group has strong prohibitions against the practice.

CULTURAL PREMISES Listeners sharing a common culture usually hold culturally specific values about identity and relationships, called *cultural premises.* Prevalent among the Danes and Israelis, for example, is the premise of egalitarianism, the belief that everyone should be equal. A different premise exists in Korea, Japan, and other Asian societies, where status most often is aligned strictly with one's place in the social hierarchy. Bear in mind that it is difficult to challenge deeply held cultural premises.[18]

EMOTIONS Culture also influences our responses to emotional appeals. Appeals that touch on *ego-focused* emotions such as pride, anger, happiness, and frustration, for example, tend to find more acceptance among members of individualist cultures;[19] those that use *other-focused* emotions such as empathy, indebtedness, and shame are more apt to encourage identification in collectivist cultures.[20] Usually, it is best to appeal to emotions that lie within the audience's "comfort zone."[21] Eliciting a range of emotions may help you appeal to diverse audience members.

CHECKLIST: Be a Culturally Sensitive Persuader

✓ Do you appeal to any *core values* (deeply held ideas of what's important in life) that might clash with those held by audience members?

✓ Do you attempt to persuade listeners to think or do things contrary to their *norms* (rules for behavior)?

✓ Do you challenge any *cultural premises* (deeply held values about identity and relationships)?

✓ Do you appeal to emotions that lie outside of the audience's "comfort zone"?

Strengthen Your Case with Organization

Once you've developed your speech claims, the next step is to structure your speech points using one (or more) of the organizational patterns described in Chapter 13 and in this chapter.

First, however, consider where your target audience stands in relation to your position. Are they likely to be receptive to your claims? Hostile to them? Persuasion scholar Herbert Simon describes four types of potential audiences and suggests various reasoning strategies and different organizational patterns for each:[22]

PERSUASIVE STRATEGIES AND AUDIENCE TYPE	
AUDIENCE	STRATEGIES
Hostile audience or those that strongly disagree	• Stress areas of agreement. • Address opposing views. • Don't expect major change in attitudes. • Wait until the end before asking the audience to act, if at all. • Save your major claim or conclusion until last (e.g., "We should raise tuition."), and lead instead with your evidence (e.g., "We've run out of space for students"; "We need to hire more instructors."). • Consider the *refutation* pattern (see p. 206).
Critical and conflicted	• Present strong arguments and audience evidence. • Address opposing views, perhaps by using the *refutation* pattern.
Sympathetic audience	• Use motivational stories and emotional appeals to reinforce positive attitudes. • Stress your commonality with listeners. • Clearly tell the audience what you want them to think or do. • Consider the *narrative* (storytelling) pattern.
Uninformed, less-educated, or apathetic audience	• Focus on capturing their attention. • Stress personal credibility and "likeability." • Stress the topic's relevance to listeners.

Problem-Solution Pattern

One commonly used design for persuasive speeches, especially those based on *claims of policy*, is the problem-solution
pattern. Here you organize speech points to demonstrate the
nature and significance of a problem and then to provide justification for a proposed solution:

I. Problem (define what it is)

II. Solution (offer a way to overcome the problem)

Most problem-solution speeches require more than two
points to adequately explain the problem and to substantiate
the recommended solution. Thus a three-point **problem-
cause-solution pattern** may be in order:

I.   The nature of the problem (explain why it's a problem,
     for whom, etc.)

II. Reasons for the problem (identify its causes, incidence)

III. Proposed solution (explain why it's expected to work,
     noting any unsatisfactory solutions)

When arguing a claim of policy, it may be important to
demonstrate the proposal's feasibility. To do this, use a four-
point *problem-cause-solution-feasibility pattern,* with the last
point providing evidence that the solution can be implemented.

This organization can be seen in the following claim of
policy about changing the NBA draft:

THESIS: The NBA draft should be changed so that
              athletes like you aren't tempted to throw
              away their opportunity for an education.

I.   The NBA draft should be revamped
     so that college-age athletes are not
     tempted to drop out of school
     (*need/problem*).

II. Its present policies lure young ath-
     letes to pursue unrealistic goals of
     superstardom while weakening the
     quality of the game with immature
     players (*reasons for the problem*).

III. The NBA draft needs to adopt a
     minimum age of twenty (*solution to
     the problem*).

IV. National leagues in countries X and
     Y have done this successfully (*evi-
     dence of the solution's feasibility*).

Monroe's Motivated Sequence

The **motivated sequence**, developed in the mid-1930s by Alan Monroe,[23] is a five-step process that begins with arousing listeners' attention and ends with calling for action. This time-tested variant of the problem-solution pattern is particularly effective when you want the audience to do something—buy a product, donate to a cause, and so forth. Yet it is equally useful when you want listeners to reconsider their present way of thinking about something or to continue to believe as they do but with greater commitment.

STEP 1: ATTENTION The *attention step* addresses listeners' core concerns, making the speech highly relevant to them. Here is an excerpt from a student speech by Ed Partlow on becoming an organ donor:

> Today I'm going to talk about a subject that can be both personal and emotional. I am going to talk about becoming an organ donor. Donating an organ is a simple step you can take that will literally give life to others—to your husband or wife, mother or father, son or daughter—or to a beautiful child whom you've never met.
>
> There is one thing I want to acknowledge from the start. Many of you may be uncomfortable with the idea of becoming an organ donor. I want to establish right off that it's OK if you don't want to become a donor.
>
> Many of us are willing to donate our organs, but because we haven't taken the action to properly become a donor, our organs go unused. As a result, an average of 17 people die every day because of lack of available organs.

STEP 2: NEED The *need step* isolates and describes the issue to be addressed. If you can show the members of an audience that they have an important need that must be satisfied or a problem that must be solved, they will have a reason to listen to your propositions. Continuing with the organ donor speech, here the speaker establishes the need for donors:

> According to statistics compiled by the U.S. Department of Health and Human Services' Organ Procurement and Transplantation Network, found on the OPTN Web site, there are approximately 91,000 people on the waiting list for an organ transplant. Over 67,000 are waiting for a kidney transplant alone, and the stakes are high: the majority of patients who receive a kidney from a living donor can live at least 10 years, and oftentimes much longer, after the transplant. One of the

people on the waiting list is Aidan Malony, who graduated two years ago from this college. Without a transplant, he will die. It is agonizing for his family and friends to see him in this condition. And it is deeply frustrating to them that more people don't sign and carry organ donor cards. I have always carried my organ donor card with me, but didn't realize the extreme importance of doing so before talking to Aidan. Every 12 minutes, according to the United Network for Organ Sharing, another name joins that of Aidan Malony and is added to the National Transplant Waiting List.

STEP 3: SATISFACTION   The *satisfaction step* identifies the solution. This step begins the crux of the speech, offering the audience a proposal to reinforce or change their attitudes, beliefs, and values regarding the need at hand. Here is an example from the speech on organ donation:

It takes only two steps to become an organ donor. First, fill out an organ donor card and carry it with you. You may also choose to have a note added to your driver's license next time you renew it.

Second and most important, tell your family that you want to become an organ donor and ask them to honor your wishes when the time arrives. Otherwise, they may discourage the use of your organs should something happen to you.

Check with your local hospital to find out about signing a family pledge—a contract where family members share their wishes about organ and tissue donation. This is an absolutely essential step in making sure the necessary individuals will honor your wish to become an organ donor.

STEP 4: VISUALIZATION   The *visualization step* provides the audience with a vision of anticipated outcomes associated with the solution. The purpose of this step is to carry audience members beyond accepting the feasibility of your proposal to seeing how it will actually benefit them:

There are so many organs and such a variety of tissue that may be transplanted. One organ donor can help up to 50 people. Who can forget the story of 7-year-old American Nicholas Green, the innocent victim of a highway robbery in Italy that cost him his life? Stricken with unfathomable grief, Nicholas's parents, Reg and Maggie Green, nevertheless immediately decided to donate Nicholas's organs. As a direct result of the donation, seven Italians thrive today, grateful recipients of Nicholas's heart, corneas, liver, pancreas cells, and kidneys. The young woman who received Nicholas's liver has recently given birth to a boy she's named Nicholas. Today, organ donations in Italy have nearly tripled since 1994, the year of Nicholas's death. The Italians called this phenomenon "The Nicholas Effect."

STEP 5: ACTION Finally, in the *action step* the speaker asks audience members to act according to their acceptance of the message. This may involve reconsidering their present way of thinking about something, continuing to believe as they do but with greater commitment, or implementing a new set of behaviors. Here, the speaker makes an explicit call to action:

> It takes courage to become an organ donor.
> You have the courage to become an organ donor!
> All you need to do is say yes to organ and tissue donation on your donor card and/or driver's license and discuss your decision with your family. You can obtain a donor card at www.organdonor.gov.
>   Be part of "The Nicholas Effect."

Comparative Advantage Pattern

When your audience is already aware of an issue or problem that needs a solution, consider the **comparative advantage pattern**. In this arrangement, speech points are organized to show how your viewpoint or proposal is superior to one or more alternatives. To maintain credibility, make sure to identify alternatives that your audience is familiar with and ones supported by opposing interests. With the comparative advantage pattern, the main points in a speech addressing the best way to control the deer population might look like these:

THESIS:	Rather than hunting, fencing, or contraception alone, the best way to reduce the deer population is by a dual strategy of hunting *and* contraception.
	I. A combination strategy is superior to hunting alone because many areas are too densely populated by humans to permit hunting; in such cases, contraceptive darts and vaccines can address the problem (*advantage over alternative #1, hunting*).
	II. A combination strategy is superior to relying solely on fencing because fencing is far too expensive for widespread use (*advantage over alternative #2, fencing*).

III. A combination strategy is superior to relying solely on contraception because only a limited number of deer are candidates for contraceptive darts and vaccines (*advantage over alternative #3, contraception*).

 CHECKLIST: Steps in the Motivated Sequence

✓ *Step 1: Attention* Address listeners' core concerns, making the speech highly relevant to them.

✓ *Step 2: Need* Show listeners that they have an important need that must be satisfied or a problem that must be solved.

✓ *Step 3: Satisfaction* Introduce your proposed solution.

✓ *Step 4: Visualization* Provide listeners with a vision of anticipated outcomes associated with the solution.

✓ *Step 5: Action* Make a direct request of listeners that involves changing or strengthening their present way of thinking or acting.

Refutation Pattern

When you feel confident that the opposing argument is vulnerable, consider the **refutation organizational pattern**, in which each main point addresses and then refutes (disproves) an opposing claim to your position. Note that it is important to refute strong rather than weak objections to the claim, since refuting weak objections won't sway the audience.[24] If done well, refutation may influence audience members who either disagree with you or are conflicted about where they stand.

Main points arranged in a refutation pattern follow a format similar to this:

Main Point I: State the opposing position.

Main Point II: Describe the implications or ramifications of the opposing claim.

Main Point III: Offer arguments and evidence for your position.

Main Point IV: Contrast your position with the opposing claim to drive home the superiority of your position.

Consider the speaker who argues for increased energy conservation versus a policy of drilling for oil in protected land in Alaska.

THESIS: Rather than drilling for oil in Alaska's Arctic National Wildlife Refuge (ANWR), we should focus on energy conservation measures as a way of lessening our dependence on foreign oil.

I. Proponents claim that drilling in the Arctic Refuge is necessary to decrease dependence on foreign oil sources, hold down fuel costs while adding jobs; and that with modern drilling techniques and certain environmental restrictions, it will have little negative impact on the environment (*describes opposing claims*).

II. By calling for drilling in the Refuge, these proponents sidestep the need for stricter energy conservation policies and the need to protect one of the last great pristine lands. They also ignore the fact that Alaskan oil would make a negligible dent in oil imports—from 68 percent to 65 percent by 2025 (*describes implications and ramifications of opposing claims*).

III. The massive construction needed to access the tundra will disturb the habitat of caribou, polar bear, and thousands of species of birds and shift the focus from energy conservation to increased energy consumption, when the focus should be the reverse (*offers arguments and evidence for the speaker's position, as developed in subpoints*).

IV. The proponents' plan would encourage consumption and endanger the environment; my plan would encourage energy conservation and protect one of the world's few remaining wildernesses (*contrasts the speaker's position with opposing claims, to drive home the superiority of this position*).

SAMPLE PERSUASIVE SPEECH (PROBLEM-CAUSE-SOLUTION)

The following speech by college student Lisa Roth investigates the crisis in emergency room care and advocates a claim of policy—that our emergency room system should be overhauled. Note that the speech is organized in a problem-cause-solution pattern. Lisa offers a variety of types of claims, evidence, and reasoning to build her argument.

Emergency in the Emergency Room

LISA ROTH
Illinois Central College

Last year, 49-year-old Beatrice Vance began experiencing some alarming symptoms—nausea, shortness of breath, and chest pain. She called her daughter, Monique, who raced her to the emergency room at Vista Medical Center in Lake County, Illinois. At sign-in, a nurse briefly met with Beatrice and told her to wait until she could be seen by a doctor. She advised the women that patients were treated in order of severity. 1

This dramatic incident serves as an effective attention getter.

Two hours later, when her name was finally called, Beatrice didn't respond. Hospital officials found her slumped over in her chair, ten feet or so from the admitting station, unconscious and without a pulse. According to an ABC *Nightly News* report on September 17th, 2007, Beatrice had already died from a massive heart attack while waiting to be seen by a doctor.

Lisa's vivid description appeals to listeners' emotion (pathos) and indicates that a problem exists.

Sadly, Beatrice is not the only one who has suffered from the hands of overwhelmed, sometimes inconsistent, and sometimes incompetent emergency room staff members. Similar scenes occur in hospitals across the country. According to experts on the frontline, such as Dr. Brent Eastman, Chief Medical Advisor at Scripps Health Hospital in San Diego, America's emergency rooms are in a crisis that could jeopardize everyone in this room and all their loved ones. 3

Lisa states her thesis and backs it up with an expert's opinion; to ensure her source's credibility, she names his title and affiliation.

Today, we'll uncover the catastrophic conditions existing in America's emergency rooms, discover what is causing these conditions, and look at how to restore our faith

Lisa's preview statement indicates a problem-cause-solution pattern.

in a system that has—to quote from an editorial in the June 21st, 2006 edition of the *New York Times*—"reached a breaking point."

To begin, emergency rooms are desperately overcrowded. According to a landmark series of three reports on the breakdown of our emergency-room system conducted by the Institute of Medicine, the need for emergency rooms has increased by 26 percent since 1993; during the same period, 425 emergency departments closed their doors. The average emergency room wait is now almost four hours, according to a report broadcast on *Good Morning America* on September, 18th, 2006, but patients could be asked to wait up to 48 hours before they are allowed into an inpatient bed.

> Lisa introduces the first problem plaguing the ER system.

> Citing recent statistics from a credible source about the ER system emphasizes the gravity of the situation.

The United States emergency care system is also seriously understaffed, especially with regard to specialists. As reported in the *New York Times* editorial, emergency rooms find it very difficult to get specialists to take emergency room and trauma center calls. Specialists such as neurosurgeons shy away from emergency room procedures because of the lack of compensation associated with treating so many uninsured patients, as well as the risk of seeing their malpractice premiums rise.

> Lisa introduces the second problem—understaffing.

Not only are emergency rooms understaffed; existing staff often are unprepared for disasters. An investigation in the July 6th, 2006 edition of the *Columbus Dispatch* found that EMTs received only one hour of training for major disaster preparation. What's even scarier, says Maria Perotin in the June 15th, 2006 edition of the *Fort Worth Star Telegram*, with one major disaster—if a terrorist's bomb exploded or an epidemic broke out—our emergency care service could fall apart completely.

7

The third problem with our current system is not surprising. There is simply not enough money to adequately fund our emergency rooms.

> Lisa introduces the third problem plaguing the ER system.

The *New York Times* reports that emergency rooms are notorious money losers. Most emergency rooms operate in the red even while being asked to operate securely and safely. Additionally, as reported in the June 15th, 2006, edition of the *Pittsburgh Tribune Review*, because of the lack of money, there are now 200,000 less hospital beds in

9

the United States than there were in 1993, even as the need for them has increased tremendously.

She briefly summarizes the nature of the problem before transitioning to the causes.

So, our emergency rooms are broke, overcrowded, and understaffed. Don't you feel secure?

We can pinpoint three specific causes for the emergency room crisis. These include the highly fragmented emergency medical care system, the uninsured patients, and the lack of money.

Lisa now turns to the causes of the crisis.

Fragmentation occurs on all levels because there are no standardized procedures and no clear chain of command. On the regional level, emergency vehicles fail to communicate effectively with ER and trauma care centers, causing poorly managed patient flow. On the national level, there are no standardized procedures for the training and certification of emergency room personnel.   12

To complicate matters even more, there is no lead agency to control emergency room and trauma care centers.   13

So, as you can see, this lack of organization, from poorly managed patient flow to the absences of standardized training and certifying personnel, causes chaos and confusion in what should be a streamlined and secure service industry.

An internal summary of the first cause of the problem.

Consider the second cause of the crisis.

Transitioning into the second cause.

Uninsured patients cause about as much chaos in the emergency room as does fragmentation. According to the July 6th, 2006 *Columbus Dispatch*, through no fault of their own, there are now 46 million uninsured in the United States. This of course leads to more unpaid ER bills, which leads to more financial problems for the emergency rooms.

But please understand, I am not blaming the patients who simply cannot afford or are not offered health insurance. They are merely the effect of a larger cause: a society that doesn't place a premium on affordable health care. A lack of affordable health care only perpetuates the cycle in which no affordable health care means no insurance, which in turn leads to unpaid ER bills.   17

The vast numbers of uninsured leads us to the third and final cause of the emergency room breakdown. Emergency rooms are

Lisa transitions from the second to the third cause of the crisis.

plagued by insufficient reimbursements from insurers and insufficient funding by the government.

Lack of money is a major cause of the shortage of capacity and staffing stability in the emergency rooms. Maria Perotin of the *Fort Worth Star Telegram* reports that emergency rooms received only 4 percent of the $3.38 billion that was allotted to them by the Homeland Security Department in 2002 and 2003 for emergency medical preparation. As government budgets continue to be slashed, the quality of our health care will continue to deteriorate.

So, how can we renovate a cycle that seems beyond control? Well, we can look to solutions on a national level and then on a personal level.

> Lisa turns to solutions to the problem.

The first step to defeating the chaos in the emergency rooms is to create a coordinated, regionalized system with national standards and a lead agency. Everyone—from 911, to ambulances, to emergency care services—needs to coordinate their operations effectively and efficiently in order to ensure each patient a safe and secure emergency room visit. Additionally, the Institute of Medicine suggests that a lead agency be started in the Department of Health and Human Services in order to control emergency room and trauma care centers.

On a personal level, the National Association of Emergency Physicians asks us to be responsible before going to the emergency room. Before going to the emergency room, ask yourself, do I really need to go to the emergency room, or can my primary care physician take care of my needs? Urge your community leaders to lessen the impact of the uninsured on emergency rooms by following the lead of the people of Columbus, Ohio, who, according to the July 6th, 2006 edition of the *Columbus Dispatch*, are building affordable primary care clinics in some of the poor neighborhoods.

> She offers listeners a concrete solution; this also serves as a call to action.

Today we have uncovered some of the catastrophic conditions existing in America's emergency rooms. Armed with a greater understanding of what is causing these issues—overcrowding, lack of specialization and training, and funding—we can now look to the future and focus our energy on solving this national crisis.

> Lisa's summary of the main points signals a close to the speech.

19

21

22

Unfortunately, while it is too late for Beatrice Vance, 24
authorities did rule that her death was a homicide because
she was not given an EKG within 10 minutes
of admission to the emergency room. This
paves the way for criminal prosecution of the
Vista Medical Center and puts emergency
rooms across the country on notice that they too could be
found liable should they be found similarly negligent.

Lisa brings the speech full circle by returning to her opening story.

Perhaps this terrible tragedy will turn out to be the 25
wake-up call that the United States has needed in order to
restore safety and stability to our emergency care system.

Works Cited

Amen, Rob. "Emergency Rooms Turn Away More Patients,"
      Pittsburgh Tribune Review, June 16, 2006.

Campo-Flores, Arian. "How to Stop the Bleeding," *Newsweek,*
      May 8, 2007. Retrieved September 26, 2007, from
      www.newsweek.com/id/34803.

"Code Blue," *Columbus Dispatch,* July 6, 2006, 18A, editorial.
      Retrieved September 29, 2007, from www.dispatch.com.

Committee on the Future of Emergency Care in the United States
      Health System, *Emergency Medical Services: At the Crossroads*
      (Bethesda, MD: National Academies Press, 2007).

"Emergency in the Emergency Rooms," *New York Times,* June 21,
      2006, Opinion. Retrieved September 29, 2007, from
      www.nytimes.com/2006/06/21/opinion/21Wed4.html?ex=
      1189137600&en=fdd466fef8f1534c&ei=5070.

"Illinois Woman's ER Wait Death Ruled a Homicide," *Good Morning
      America.* September 17, 2006. Retrieved September 26, 2007,
      from abcnews.go.com/GMA/Health/story?id=2454685&page=1.

"Inexcusable Death," *ABC Nightly News,* September 18, 2006.
      Retrieved September 26, 2007, from
      abcnews.go.com/Video/playerIndex?id=2457808

National Association of EMS Physicians, summary of "Future of
      Emergency Care: Hospital-Based Emergency Care at the
      Breaking Point" Recommendations. Retrieved September 26,
      2007, from www.naemsp.org.

Perotin, Maria M. "Serious Condition," *Fort Worth Star Telegram,*
      June 15, 2006, C1.

SAMPLE PERSUASIVE SPEECH (MONROE'S MOTIVATED SEQUENCE)

In this speech, Stephanie Poplin argues that by volunteering we can enrich our lives (a claim of value). Stephanie organizes the speech using Monroe's five-step motivated sequence pattern. She begins with the *attention step,* making the speech relevant to listeners. She next points to audience members' innate thirst for fulfillment in life (the *need step*) and suggests that volunteering can satisfy or solve this need (the *satisfaction step*). Next, Stephanie offers vivid examples of how listeners will feel when they volunteer (the *visualization step*). She concludes by directly asking the audience to get involved (the *action step*).

The Importance of Community Engagement and Volunteerism

STEPHANIE POPLIN
University of Oklahoma

"Great social forces are the mere accumulation of individual actions." Think about that—"*Great social forces are the mere accumulation of individual actions.*" This was said by noted economist and antipoverty activist Jeffrey Sachs in a March, 2005 *Time* magazine essay about helping the world's poor. And it's true, right? Every great volunteer organization and every great social movement, from the Red Cross to the Peace Corps to the Civil Rights Movement achieved what it did through individual actions, yet all those actions were history changing. 1

> Stephanie establishes the *attention step* by stating that listeners have the power to make profound changes in the world.

I'm Stephanie Poplin, and I would like to speak to you today about why it is imperative that you give yourself the opportunity to live a more successful and meaningful life. One way of achieving this is by contributing—by putting yourself into the community that surrounds you. I'm referring to community service and civic engagement. Today, I will talk to you about what you can personally gain from your involvement and participation in your community. 2

Volunteering may seem like it requires too much time and energy. In truth, it's a requirement for happiness. Marian Wright Edelman, founder of the Children's

> Stephanie introduces the *need step* by claiming that volunteering is a "requirement for happiness."

Defense Fund, made this observation: "We make a living by what we get, we make a life by what we give." Echoing this, Helen Keller, who was both blind and deaf, yet devoted her life to others, said, "The unselfish effort to bring cheer to others will be the beginning of a happier life for ourselves."

Stephanie quotes two credible sources to illustrate her point.

Now, traditionally, when you hear the words *community service* and *volunteer*, what do you think of? Some of us become confused by "community service," since it can refer to both an alternative to jail time and to an altruistic act of giving to the community. Here I am speaking about the latter. And what about the term *volunteer*? Here, we think of someone who wants to do good—someone who wants to improve the lives of those who are less fortunate. And while this remains true, attitudes towards volunteering are changing. Volunteers are realizing that in addition to satisfying altruistic goals, community services offers some major personal benefits.

Clarifying potentially unclear terms is important, regardless of speech type.

In today's job market, for example, it's becoming evident that college graduates need more than just paper qualifications. We'll need to be able to stand out from the crowd, to be resourceful, to be initiators, to be team players, and to possess a get-up-and-go attitude. These are now the desired skills of employers, and volunteering can provide all of this.

She establishes the need step by appealing to her listeners' core concerns and self-actualization needs.

Research bears this out. Student Volunteering UK conducted large-scale research into the benefits of volunteering. Results show that volunteering can enhance employability and develop and strengthen new and different job skills. In our own country, the Corporation for National and Community Service has found that volunteering makes us better problem solvers, a key trait employers look for. I think we'd all agree this is a necessity for us, especially given the stages our lives are in right now.

Demonstrating how volunteering can solve our innate need for fulfillment, Stephanie transitions into the satisfaction step.

Stephanie uses sources that her college audience is likely to find credible.

Virtually every paid job can be mirrored by a volunteering opportunity, according to both the Corporation for National and Community Service and Student Volunteering UK. Taking part in community service is a new and pioneering form of work experience. Not only is it seen as work experience, but employers view job applicants who have volunteered as having greater initiative and commitment than applicants without volunteer experience.

Research from Student Volunteering UK and the Corporation for National and Community Service also lists outcomes, other than résumé building, that students felt they had gained through their participation in volunteering. Here's some of what they found:

Stephanie demonstrates the visualization step, which reinforces outcomes associated with the solution (volunteering).

- Volunteering built confidence.
- It helped them decide on a career path.
- Making a difference gave them a feeling of exhilaration.
- Their service opened up unexpected opportunities and challenges.

Volunteering also benefits physical and emotional 9 health. The Corporation for National and Community Service did a review of recent research on the health benefits of volunteering. It found that volunteering builds social support networks and enhances a sense of achievement and meaning, which in turn leads to lowered rates of depression and even lowered mortality rates.

Just as volunteering can help individuals become happier and healthier, it helps strengthen communities. *Community building* is an incredibly important social outcome of volunteering. According to the Corporation for National and Community Service, volunteers are absolutely crucial to creating and sustaining healthy communities.

Fortunately, since the tragedy of 9/11 now nearly a 11 decade ago, as well as the election of President Barack Obama and his call to national service, there has been a surge in student volunteers. Volunteering has increased so much since 2001 that today's student volunteers are sometimes called the "9/11 generation" by leaders of charitable organizations. The Corporation reports, for example, that each year since 2001, 3.3 million college students— over 30 percent of the college population—gave their time, up from 27 percent before 9/11. Tutoring and mentoring are the most popular volunteer activities, with 44 percent of students spending at least 12 hours a week on these activities. Students who take service learning courses and who work part time volunteer more often than those who don't have jobs.

Knowing that people tend to adopt a behavior if they know that people like themselves have done so, Stephanie mentions examples of student volunteers.

I have experienced the benefits of community service first-hand through my involvement in Habitat for Humanity. Habitat for Humanity is an international organization fueled by hundreds of thousands of volunteers who join with future homeowners to build simple and affordable houses.

Still in the visualization step, Stephanie offers personal testimony to demonstrate how volunteering can make a real impact.

It wasn't until my first experience building a home, here in Norman, that I realized the impact this organization has on its volunteers and the families involved. I've always had a bedroom of my own to escape to, and I've always had a kitchen to make breakfast in the morning, but there are two little boys who now have this for the first time, thanks to the University of Oklahoma's chapter of Habitat for Humanity. I have always taken my home for granted, but now I can be a part of giving these little boys a home of their own.

13

Sometimes big changes follow from small events, such as my sheet-rocking an empty space that will eventually become a living room that these little boys and their mom and dad can enjoy together.

These words link back to the speech's central idea to promote thematic unity.

Someone once told me, "You don't find yourself; you create yourself." As college students, we have every opportunity in the world to create a life that is successful and meaningful. Use your good fortune, and choose to create a life that is service-oriented. Walk over to OU's Volunteer Programs office on West California, or go to their Web page. You'll find great ways to combine volunteering with earning your degree. You can also go to *Step Up*'s community volunteer network—just Google "Step Up!"—to find volunteer opportunities in your area. Visit the *Habitat for Humanity* Web site and click on "Local Affiliates" to find the branch nearest you. These are just a few ways to find volunteer opportunities. Many others exist, from countless nonprofits, to houses of worship, to local, state, and Federal government programs.

Here Stephanie transitions to the fifth and final step, the *action step*.

To encourage action, Stephanie offers contact information for volunteer organizations.

We have seen how you can personally benefit from contributing to your community. Whether you want to make new friends, improve your job prospects, test a potential career, or build confidence, help build communities, beat depression, and

Stephanie signals the conclusion.

Stephanie briefly reiterates the main points.

even live longer, volunteering can be the answer. People who have spent time volunteering report they get back in personal fulfillment and satisfaction more than they ever expend in inconvenience and effort.

We all have the power to make an impact one way or another. After all, "Great social forces are the mere accumulation of individual actions."

Stephanie concludes by repeating the quote from the introduction, bringing the speech full circle.

Works Cited

Corporation for National and Community Service, *College Students Helping America,* October 2006. Retrieved January 8, 2008, from www.nationalservice.gov/pdf/06_1016_RPD_college_full.pdf.

Motivational Quotes Web site, quotes on volunteering page, www.motivationalquotes.com/pages/volunteer-quotes.html.

Sachs, Jeffrey D. "The End of Poverty," *Time,* March 6, 2005.

Student Volunteering UK, The Art of Crazy Paving: Volunteering for Enhanced Employability, n.d. Retrieved January 8, 2008, from www.studentvolunteering.org.uk/

25   Speaking on Special Occasions

A **special occasion speech** is one that is prepared for a specific occasion and for a purpose dictated by that occasion. Special occasion speeches can be either informative or persuasive or, often, a mix of both. However, neither of these functions is the main goal; the underlying function of a special occasion speech is to entertain, celebrate, commemorate, inspire, or set a social agenda:

- In speeches that *entertain*, listeners expect a lighthearted, amusing speech; they may also expect the speaker to offer a certain degree of insight into the topic at hand.

- In speeches that *celebrate* (a person, place, or event), listeners look to the speaker to praise the subject of the celebration; they also anticipate a degree of ceremony in accordance with the norms of the occasion.

- In speeches that *commemorate* an event or person (at dedications of memorials or at gatherings held in someone's honor), listeners expect the speaker to offer remembrance and tribute.

- In speeches that *inspire* (including inaugural addresses, keynote speeches, and commencement speeches), listeners expect to be motivated by examples of achievement and heroism.

- In speeches that *set social agendas* (such as occur at gatherings of cause-oriented organizations, fund-raisers, campaign banquets, conferences, and conventions), listeners expect the articulation and reinforcement of the goals and values of the group.

Special occasion speeches include speeches of introduction, speeches of acceptance, speeches of presentation, roasts and toasts, eulogies and other speeches of tribute, after-dinner speeches, and speeches of inspiration.

Speeches of Introduction

The object of a **speech of introduction** is to prepare or "warm up" the audience for the main speaker—to heighten audience interest and build the speaker's credibility. A good speech of introduction balances four elements: the speaker's background, the subject of the speaker's message, the occasion, and the audience.

- *Describe the speaker's background and qualifications.* Describe the speaker's achievements, offices held, and other facts to demonstrate why the speaker is relevant to the occasion. Mention the speaker's achievements, but not so many that the audience glazes over.

- *Briefly preview the speaker's topic.* Give the audience a sense of why the subject is of interest, bearing in mind that it is not the introducer's job to evaluate the speech or otherwise comment on it at length. The rule is: Get in and out quickly with a few well-chosen remarks.

- *Ask the audience to welcome the speaker.* This can be done simply by saying something like "Please welcome Anthony Svetlana."

- *Be brief.* Speak just long enough to accomplish the goals of preparation and motivation. One well-known speaker recommends a two-minute maximum.[1]

CHECKLIST: Preparing a Speech of Introduction

✓ Identify the speaker correctly. Assign him or her the proper title, such as "vice president for public relations" or "professor emeritus."

✓ Practice a difficult-to-pronounce name several times before introducing the speaker.

✓ Contact the speaker ahead of time to verify any facts about him or her that you plan to cite.

✓ Consider devices that will capture the audience's attention, such as quotes, short anecdotes, or startling statements.

Speeches of Acceptance

A **speech of acceptance** is made in response to receiving an award. Its purpose is to express gratitude for the honor bestowed on the speaker. The speech should reflect that gratitude.

- *Prepare in advance.* If you know or even suspect that you are to receive an award, decide before the event what you will say.

- *Express what the award means to you.* Convey to the audience the value you place on the award. Express yourself genuinely and with humility.

- *Express gratitude.* Thank by name each of the relevant persons or organizations involved in giving you the award. Acknowledge any team players or others who helped you attain the achievement for which you are being honored.

Upon winning an Oscar in 2001, film director Steven Soderbergh gave a brief and unusual acceptance speech. Rather than thanking individuals, he used the occasion to praise all who labor to create:

> There are a lot of people to thank, but rather than thank some of them publicly, I'm going to thank all of them privately. I do want to thank anyone who spends part of their day creating, I don't care if it's a book, a film, a painting, a dance, a piece of theater, a piece of music. Anybody who spends part of their day sharing their experience with us. I think the world would be unlivable without art.[2]

Speeches of Presentation

The goal of the **speech of presentation** is twofold: to communicate the meaning of the award and to explain why the recipient is receiving it.

- *Convey the meaning of the award.* Describe what the award is for and what it represents. Mention the sponsors and describe the link between the sponsors' goals and values and the award.

- *Explain why the recipient is receiving the award.* Explain the recipient's achievements and special attributes that qualify him or her as deserving of the award.

- *Plan the physical presentation.* To avoid any awkwardness, consider logistics before the ceremony. For example, if you hand the award to the recipient, do so with your left hand so that you can shake hands with your right.

Roasts and Toasts

A **roast** is a humorous tribute to a person, one in which a series of speakers jokingly poke fun at him or her. A **toast** is a brief tribute to a person or an event being celebrated. Both roasts and toasts call for short speeches whose goal is to celebrate an individual and his or her achievements.

- *Prepare.* Impromptu though they might appear, the best roasts and toasts reflect time spent drafting and rehearsing. As you practice, time the speech.

- *Highlight remarkable traits of the person being honored.* Restrict your remarks to one or two of the person's most unusual or recognizable attributes. Convey the qualities that have made him or her worthy of celebrating.

- *Be positive.* Even if the speech is poking fun at someone, as in a roast, keep the tone positive. Remember, your overall purpose is to pay tribute to the honoree.

- *Be brief.* Usually several speakers are involved in roasts and toasts. Be considerate of the other speakers by refraining from taking up too much time.

Just days before the 2008 election, then presidential candidates John McCain and Barack Obama appeared together at a charity roast. Using self-deprecating humor, Obama poked fun at himself: "Contrary to the rumors you have heard, I was not born in a manger. I was actually born on Krypton and sent here by my father Jorel to save the Planet Earth."[3]

Eulogies and Other Tributes

The word **eulogy** derives from the Greek word meaning "to praise." Those delivering eulogies, usually close friends or family members of the deceased, are charged with celebrating and commemorating the life of someone while consoling those who have been left behind.

- *Balance delivery and emotions.* The audience looks to the speaker for guidance in dealing with the loss and for a sense of closure, so stay in control. If you do feel that you are about to break down, pause, take a breath, and focus on your next thought.

- *Refer to the family of the deceased.* Families suffer the greatest loss, and a funeral is primarily for their benefit. Show respect for the family, and mention each family member by name.

- *Be positive but realistic.* Emphasize the deceased's positive qualities while avoiding excessive praise.

QUICK TIP

Commemorate Life—Not Death

A eulogy should pay tribute to the deceased person as an individual and remind the audience that he or she is still alive, in a sense, in our memories. Rather than focus on the circumstances of death, focus on the life of the person. Talk about the person's contributions and achievements, and demonstrate the person's character. Consider telling an anecdote that illustrates the type of person you are eulogizing. Even humorous anecdotes may be appropriate if they effectively humanize the deceased.

After-Dinner Speeches

Its name notwithstanding, the contemporary **after-dinner speech** is just as likely to occur before, during, or after a lunch seminar or other type of business, professional, or civic meeting as it is to follow a formal dinner. In general, an after-dinner speech is expected to be lighthearted and entertaining. At the same time, listeners expect to gain insight into the topic at hand.

- *Recognize the occasion.* Connect the speech with the occasion. Delivering a speech that is unrelated to the event may leave the impression that the speech is

canned—one that the speaker uses again and again in different settings.

- *Keep remarks sufficiently low-key to accompany the digestion of a meal.* Even when charged with addressing a serious topic, keep the tone somewhat low-key.

Speeches of Inspiration

A **speech of inspiration** seeks to motivate listeners to positively consider, reflect on, and sometimes act on the speaker's words. Effective speeches of inspiration touch on deep feelings in the audience. Through emotional force, they urge us toward purer motives and harder effort and remind us of a common good.

- *Appeal to audience members' emotions.* Two means of invoking emotion are *vivid description* and *emotionally charged words.* These and other techniques of language, such as repetition, alliteration, and parallelism, can help transport the audience from the mundane to a loftier level (see Chapter 16).

- *Use real-life stories.* Few things move us as much as real-life examples and stories, such as that of an ordinary person whose struggles result in triumph over adversity and the realization of a dream.

- *Be dynamic.* If it fits your personality, use a dynamic speaking style to inspire through delivery. Combining an energetic style with a powerful message can be one of the most successful strategies for inspirational speaking.

- *Make your goal clear.* Inspirational speeches run the risk of being vague, leaving the audience unsure what the message was. Whatever you are trying to motivate your listeners to do, let them know.

- *Consider a distinctive organizing device.* Many successful inspirational speakers use devices such as *acronyms* or steps to help the audience to remember the message. For example, a football coach speaking at a practice session might organize an inspirational speech around the word *WIN*. His main points might be "Work," "Intensity," and "No excuses," forming the acronym *WIN*.

- *Close with a dramatic ending.* Use a dramatic ending to inspire your audience to feel or act. Recall from Chapter 15 the various methods of concluding a speech, including quotations, stories, rhetorical questions, and a call to action.

QUICK TIP

Tailor Your Message to the Audience and Occasion
Always plan your special occasion speech with audience expectations firmly in mind. People listening to a eulogy, for example, will be very sensitive to what they perceive to be inappropriate humor or lack of respect. Those attending a dedication ceremony for a war memorial will expect the speaker to offer words of inspiration. When a speaker violates audience expectations in situations like these, audience reaction will usually be pronounced.

SAMPLE SPECIAL OCCASION SPEECH (TOAST)

Following is a wedding toast by Ben Platt, a recent college graduate now working as a writer for an animated children's television program. Ben's speech follows the dictates of a toast, offering tribute to the person being honored while remaining brief. Though short, Ben's toast nonetheless required preparation, as he describes:

> I discarded several different takes on this speech before settling on this version, including one made entirely out of Simpsons' quotes and one that featured a poem. I also debated between several different anecdotes about my brother Matthew before settling on Quack and Barf for its mix of relatable little kid humor and the particular qualities of my brother that it brought to light.

Best Man Wedding Toast

BEN PLATT
Delivered at The Grand Hotel, Long Beach, CA, February 7, 2009

A couple years back, long before Matthew asked me to be his best man, I wrote a series of articles for a fledgling Website called GroomGroove.com, whose most recent claim is that it is "the Web's best roadmap for a groom's trip down the aisle."

It can be helpful to consult guides to writing toasts, whether in print or online.

Now, GroomGroove.com also offers advice for the Best Man, so, when the time came to write my speech, I immediately checked to see what sort of pointers they had to offer. Well, they recommended telling an amusing anecdote about the groom. Great! No problem! I've got tons of those! But, they also had a few warnings.

2

"No inside jokes," they said. "If only 20 percent of the   3
guests will understand, skip it." I took this to mean that I
should probably avoid making a speech entirely out of
Simpsons' quotes, so there went plan A. The site's writers
also advise avoiding jokes about "sexual prowess (or lack
thereof), ex-girlfriends, lewdness, police
intervention, and the like."

One of the most effective means of conveying a person's qualities to an audience is through a brief story, or *anecdote*.

No inside jokes? No sexual prowess,
ex-girlfriends, lewdness, or police intervention? That basically left me with . . . well, I
still needed an anecdote.

Finally, it came to me: When we were young, our family used to rent a place up in New Hampshire for a few
weeks each summer, right by Lake Winnipesauke. I have
lots of fond memories of those summers, but the one that
really stands out is when my brother and I were doing
nothing at all.

Matt and I shared what was essentially an unfurnished   6
attic, just bare white walls and a couple of air mattresses.
Not a lot to amuse a seven-year-old and an
eleven-year-old trying to make the most of
their summer vacation. What it did have,
though, was one tiny window that let in the
perfect amount of moonlight each night
for making shadow puppets. So that's what
we did.

The shared history between the speaker and groom adds credibility to his story about the groom's character.

Matt started it. (That's a phrase that served me well   7
throughout childhood, incidentally.) Matt made a duck,
which, being the considerate big brother that he is, he asked
me to name. Feeling creative, I named it "Quack." Then I
made a duck, which we named "Barf." We'd put on shows
for, and with, each other, acting out Quack and Barf's
adventures, which followed a pretty typical pattern—
Quack would quack for a while, then Barf would get
annoyed and eat him, before promptly living up to his own
namesake. (Cue hysterical fits of laughter.) Understand, to
two young boys on vacation who are trying to be quiet
because they're supposed to be asleep, this was "A" material.

Every night while we were on vacation, I couldn't wait   8
for bedtime, because that's when Matt would bust out
Quack and Barf, and that's when the real
fun would begin. Just four white walls and
a couple of air mattresses, and he made it
into something that still makes me laugh
almost twenty years later.

Concrete language helps bring the anecdote to life.

Of course, young boys are easily amused, and I was   9
certainly no exception. But the origins of Quack and Barf

speak to something that's truly wonderful about my brother. It's easy to have a good time when something exciting is happening. But not just *anybody* can make the most mundane situation into something

> Here Ben highlights one of the groom's admirable traits— bringing joy to everyday situations.

special. Whether it's a long car ride, or waiting for the bus, or just laying around doing nothing, if you're with Matt, you're going to be laughing.

Matt, you can make the ordinary into something 10 incredible, and what makes me really happy is that you've found someone who can do the same for you. Megan, you've put a smile on my brother's face since the day the two of you met, and that means more to me than I can possibly tell you. This is the beginning of a lifetime filled with great memories and lots of laughs, and I know that as long as you have each other, even the most ordinary things will never be dull. Congratulations! To Matt and Megan!

> Ben compliments the bride and concludes with warm wishes for the couple's future.

SAMPLE SPECIAL OCCASION SPEECH (COMMENCEMENT ADDRESS)

In this commencement address, delivered to the graduating class of the University of Pennsylvania on May 17, 2004, Bono, activist and lead singer of the rock group U2, skillfully incorporates several qualities of an effective special occasion speech. He combines a serious message about the abolition of poverty and AIDS in Africa with a more relaxed, laid-back attitude typically associated with rock stars. This juxtaposition makes it more likely that Bono's student audience will be receptive to his call to action.

2004 University of Pennsylvania Commencement Address

BONO
Delivered at the University of Pennsylvania, May 17, 2004

My name is Bono and I am a rock star. . . . Doctor of Laws, wow! I know it's an honor, and it really is an honor, but are you sure? . . . I never went to college, I've slept in some strange places, but the library wasn't one of them. I studied rock and roll and I grew up in Dublin in the '70s; music was an alarm bell for me, it woke me up to the world.

> Of course he is. Though the audience knows who Bono is, this opening remark is a guaranteed crowd pleaser.

I was the kid in the crowd who took it at face value. Later I learned that a lot of the rebels were in it for the t-shirt. They'd wear the boots but they wouldn't march. They'd smash bottles on their heads but they wouldn't go to something more painful, like a town hall meeting. By the way, I felt like that myself until recently. I didn't expect change to come so slow. So agonizingly slow. I didn't realize that the biggest obstacle to political and social progress wasn't the . . . Establishment, or the boot heel of whatever you consider the man to be, it was something much more subtle.

> Bono uses personal history to argue that rock music can be revolutionary. He will revisit the theme when he addresses poverty in Africa.

. . . So for better or worse that was my education. I came away with a clear sense of the difference music could make in my own life, in other people's lives if I did my job right, which if you're a singer in a rock band means avoiding the obvious pitfalls, like say a mullet hairdo. If anyone here doesn't know what a mullet is, your education's certainly not complete. I'd ask for your money back. For a lead singer like me, a mullet is, I would suggest, arguably more dangerous than a drug problem. Yes, I had a mullet in the '80s.

> Self-effacing humor establishes rapport with the audience, and shows Bono to be more personable than they might expect of a celebrity.

Now this is the point where the faculty start smiling uncomfortably and . . . asking what on earth I'm doing here, I think it's a fair question: What am I doing here? More to the point: What are you doing here? Because if you don't mind me saying so, this is a strange ending to an Ivy League education. Four years in these historic halls thinking great thoughts and now you're sitting in a stadium better suited for football, listening to an Irish rock star give a speech that is so far mostly about himself. What are you doing here?

> Establishing why the speech will be relevant to the audience.

. . . For four years you've been buying, trading, and selling, everything you've got in this marketplace of ideas. The intellectual hustle. Your pockets are full, even if your parents' are empty, and now you've got to figure out what to spend it on. Well, the going rate for change is not cheap. Big ideas are expensive. The University has had its share of big ideas. Benjamin Franklin had a few, so did Justice Brennan and in my opinion so does Judith Rodin. What a gorgeous girl. They all knew that if you're gonna be good at your word, if you're gonna live up to your ideals and

> References to UPenn history build credibility. Franklin was the founder of the college, Brennan a famous alumnus, and Rodin the president.

your education, it's gonna cost you. So my question, I suppose, is: What's the big idea? What's your big idea? What are you willing to spend your moral capital, your intellectual capital, your cash, your sweat equity in pursuing outside of the walls of the University of Pennsylvania?

Bono introduces the thesis—that the graduates need to use their education to develop a plan of action to help the world.

There's a truly great Irish poet; his name is Brendan 7 Kennelly, and he has this epic poem called the Book of Judas, and there's a line in that poem that never leaves my mind: "If you want to serve the age, betray it." What does that mean to betray the age? Well, to me betraying the age means exposing its conceits, its foibles, its phony moral

Bono quotes a poem to illustrate his message.

certitudes. It means telling the secrets of the age and facing harsher truths. Every age has its massive moral blind spots. We might not see them, but our children will. Slavery was one of them, and the people who best served that age were the ones who called it as it was, which was ungodly and inhuman. Ben Franklin called it when he became president of the Pennsylvania Abolition Society. Segregation. There was another one. America sees this now, but it took a civil rights movement to betray their age. And 50 years ago the U.S. Supreme Court betrayed the age. May 17, 1954, Brown vs. Board of Education came down and put the lie to the idea that separate can ever really be equal. Amen to that.

Fast forward 50 years, May 17, 2004. What are the ideas 8 right now worth betraying? What are the lies we tell ourselves now? What are the blind spots of our age? What's worth spending your post-Penn lives trying to do or undo? It might be something simple. It might be something as simple

The transitional phrase "fast forward" helps listeners follow along.

as our deep down refusal to believe that every human life has equal worth. Could that be it? Could that be it?

Each of you will probably have your own answer, but for me that is it. And for me the proving ground has been Africa. Africa makes a mockery of what we say, at

Bono builds credibility by pointing to his own case.

least what I say, about equality. It questions our pieties and our commitments because there's no way to look at what's happening over there and its effect on all of us and conclude that we actually consider Africans as our equal before God. There is no chance.

An amazing event happened here in Philadelphia in 10 1985, Live Aid, that whole "We Are the World" phenomenon, the concert that happened here. Well, after that concert I went to Ethiopia with my wife, Ali; we were there for a month, and an extraordinary thing happened to me. We used to wake up in the morning and the mist would be lifting; we'd see thousands and thousands of people who'd been walking all night to our food station where we were working. One man—I was standing outside talking to the translator—had this beautiful boy and he was saying to me in Amharic, I think it was, I said I can't understand what he's saying; and this nurse who spoke English and Amharic said to me, he's saying will you take his son. He's saying please take his son; he would be a great son for you. I was looking puzzled and he said, "You must take my son because if you don't take my son, my son will surely die. If you take him he will go back to where he is and get an education." (Probably like the ones we're talking about today.) I had to say no; that was the rules there and I walked away from that man.

> A story humanizes Bono's cause and puts a face on suffering in Africa.

I've never really walked away from it. But I think about 11
that boy and that man and that's when I started this journey that's brought me here into this stadium. Because at that moment I became the worst scourge on God's green earth, a rock star with a cause. Except it isn't the cause. Seven thousand Africans dying every day of preventable, treatable disease like AIDS? That's not a cause. That's an emergency. And when the disease gets out of control because most of the population lives on less than one dollar a day? That's not a cause. That's an emergency.

> Bono drives his point home with repetition.

. . . The fact is that this generation—yours, my 12
generation—we're the first generation that can look at poverty and disease, look across the ocean to Africa and say with a straight face, we can be the first to end this stupid extreme poverty, where, in a world of plenty, a child can die for lack of food in its belly. . . . We can be that generation that says no to stupid poverty. It's a fact, the economists confirm it. It's an expensive fact but cheaper than say the Marshall Plan that saved Europe from communism and fascism. And cheaper I would argue than fighting wave after wave of terrorism's new recruits. . . . So why aren't we pumping our fists in the air and cheering about it? Probably because when we admit we can do something about it, we've got to do something about it. For the first time in history we have the know-how, we have the cash, we have the lifesaving drugs, but do we have the will?

> Multiple examples support Bono's claim that his humanitarian goals are reachable.

Yesterday, here in Philadelphia, at the Liberty Bell, I 13 met a lot of Americans who do have the will. From arch religious conservatives to young secular radicals, I just felt an incredible overpowering sense that this was possible. We're calling it the ONE campaign, to put an end to AIDS and extreme poverty in Africa. They believe we can do it; so do I. I really, really do believe it.

. . . But I don't want to make you cop to idealism, not in 14 front of your parents, or your younger siblings. But what about Americanism? Will you cop to that at least? It's not everywhere in fashion these days. . . . But it all depends on your definition of Americanism. Me, I'm in love with this country called America. I'm a huge fan of America, I'm one of those annoying fans, you know the ones that read the CD notes and follow you into bathrooms and ask you all kinds of annoying questions about why you didn't live up to that. I'm that kind of fan.

> Good use of humor and a nice ironic touch—Bono is used to being on the other side of that kind of fandom.

. . . So what's the problem that we want to apply all this 15 energy and intellect to? Every era has its defining struggle and the fate of Africa is one of ours. It's not the only one, but in the history books it's easily going to make the top five, what we did or what we did not do. It's a proving ground, as I said earlier, for the idea of equality. But whether it's this or something else, I hope you'll pick a fight and get in it. Get your boots dirty; get rough; steel your courage with a final drink there at Smoky Joe's, one last primal scream and go. Sing the melody line you hear in your own head; remember, you don't owe anybody any explanations; you don't owe your parents any explanations; you don't owe your professors any explanations.

> Bono makes his call to action, challenging his audience to pick their fight.

> Mentioning a local bar builds goodwill.

. . . The world is more malleable than you think and it's 16 waiting for you to hammer it into shape. Now if I were a folksinger I'd immediately launch into "If I Had a Hammer" right now, get you all singing and swaying. But as I say I come from punk rock, so I'd rather have the bloody hammer right here in my fist. That's what this degree of yours is, a blunt instrument. So go forth and build something with it. Remember what John Adams said about Ben Franklin, "He does not hesitate at our boldest Measures but rather seems to think us too irresolute." Well this is the time for bold measures, and this is the country, and you are the generation.

> Bono ends his call to action with a memorable music-laden metaphor and a quotation about Philadelphia's storied hometown hero.

Thank you. 17

Part 8
The Classroom and Beyond

Often, you will be called upon to prepare oral presentations in your major classes and in other general-education courses. No matter which major you select or what profession you practice, oral presentations will be part of the mix. Rather than being a formal public speech, **presentational speaking**—reports delivered by individuals or teams addressing classmates or persons in the workplace—has much in common with formal public speaking, yet important differences exist:[1]

- *Degree of formality.* Presentational speaking is *less formal* than public speaking; on a continuum, it would lie midway between public speaking at one end and conversational speaking at the other.

- *Audience factors.* Public-speaking audiences tend to be self-selected or voluntary participants, and they regard the speech as a onetime event. Attendees of oral presentations are more likely to be part of a "captive" audience, as in a classroom or workplace and may be required to attend frequent presentations. Due to the ongoing relationship among the participants, the attendees also share more information with one another than those who attend a public speech and thus can be considered more homogeneous.

- *Speaker expertise.* Listeners generally assume that a public speaker has more expertise or firsthand knowledge than they do on a topic. Presentational speakers, by contrast, are more properly thought of as "first among equals."

Apart from these differences, the rules of public speaking described in this *Pocket Guide* apply equally to both oral presentations and public speeches.

Chapters 27–33 describe various course-specific presentations, from the scientific talk to the design review. Here we consider the following kinds of oral reports commonly assigned across the curriculum including reviews of academic articles, team presentations, debates, and poster sessions (community service learning projects are also frequently assigned; see p. 251).

Review of Academic Articles

A commonly assigned speaking task in many courses is the **review of academic articles**. A biology instructor might ask you to review a study on cell regulation published in *Cell Biology*, for example, or a psychology teacher might require that you talk about a study on fetal alcohol syndrome published in the journal *Neuro-Toxicology*. Typically, when you are assigned to review an academic article, your instructor will expect you to do the following:

- Identify the author's thesis or hypothesis.
- Explain the methods by which the author arrived at his or her conclusions.
- Explain the author's findings.
- Identify the author's theoretical perspective, if applicable.
- Evaluate the study's validity, if applicable.
- Describe the author's sources, and evaluate their credibility.
- Show how the findings of the study might be applied to other circumstances, and make suggestions about ways in which the study might lead to further research.[2]

Team Presentations

Team presentations are oral presentations prepared and delivered by a group of three or more individuals. Regularly used in the classroom and in the business and professional environment, successful team presentations require cooperation and planning. (See Chapter 34 for detailed guidelines on how to prepare and deliver team presentations.)

Debates

Debates are another popular presentation format in many college courses. Debates call upon skills in persuasion (especially the reasoned use of evidence), in delivery, and in the ability to think quickly and critically. Much like a political debate, in an academic debate two individuals or groups consider or argue an issue from opposing viewpoints. Generally there will be a winner and a loser, lending this form of speaking a competitive edge.

Take a Side

Opposing sides in a debate are taken by speakers in one of two formats. In the **individual debate format**, one person takes a side against another person. In the **team debate format**, multiple people (usually two) take sides against another team, with each person on the team assuming a speaking role.

The *pro* side (also called "affirmative") in the debate supports the topic with a *resolution*—a statement asking for change or consideration of a controversial issue. "Resolved, that the United States government should severely punish flag burners" is a resolution that the affirmative side must support and defend. The pro side tries to convince the audience (or judges) to address, support, or agree with the topic under consideration. The *con* side (also called "negative") in the debate attempts to defeat the resolution by dissuading the audience from accepting the pro side's arguments.

Advance Strong Arguments

Whether you take the affirmative or negative side, your primary responsibility is to advance strong arguments in support of your position. Arguments usually consist of the following three parts (see also Chapter 24):

- *Claim*—A claim makes an assertion or declaration about an issue. "Females are discriminated against in the workplace." Depending on your debate topic, your claim may be one of fact, value, or policy.

- *Evidence*—Evidence is the support offered for the claim. "According to a recent report by the U.S. Department of Labor, women make 28 percent less than men in comparable jobs and are promoted 34 percent less frequently."

- *Reasoning*—Reasoning (warrants) is a logical explanation of why the evidence supports the claim. "Females make less money and get promoted less frequently than males."

QUICK TIP

Flowing the Debate

In formal debates (in which judges take notes and keep track of arguments), debaters must attack and defend each argument. "Dropping" or ignoring an argument can seriously compromise the credibility of the debater and her or his side. To ensure that you respond to each of your opponent's arguments, try using a simple technique adopted by formal debaters called "flowing the debate" (see Figure 26.1). Write down each of your opponent's arguments, and then draw a line or arrow to indicate that you (or another team member) have refuted it.

Affirmative	Negative	Affirmative	Negative	Affirmative	Negative
Nonviolent prisoners should be paroled more often.	Nonviolent prisoners can become violent when they are paroled.	Studies show nonviolent prisoners commit fewer crimes upon their release.	Those studies are outdated and involve only a few states.	My studies are recent and include big states like New York and California.	The studies from New York and California were flawed due to poor statistics.

FIGURE 26.1 Flowchart of the Arguments for the Resolution "Resolved, That Nonviolent Prisoners Should Be Paroled More Often"

Debates are characterized by *refutation*, in which each side attacks the arguments of the other. Refutation can be made against an opponent's claim, evidence, reasoning, or some combination of these elements. In the previous argument, an opponent might refute the evidence by arguing, "The report used by my opponent is three years old, and a new study indicates that we are making substantial progress in equalizing the pay among males and females; thus we are reducing discrimination in the workplace."

Refutation also involves rebuilding arguments that have been refuted or attacked by the opponent. This is done by adding new evidence or attacking the opponent's reasoning or evidence.

CHECKLIST: Tips for Winning a Debate

✓ Present the most credible and convincing evidence you can find.

✓ Before you begin, describe your position and tell the audience what they must decide.

✓ If you feel that your side is not popular among the audience, ask them to suspend their own personal opinion and judge the debate on the merits of the argument.

✓ Don't be timid. Ask the audience to specifically decide in your favor, and be explicit about your desire for their approval.

✓ Point out the strong points from your arguments. Remind the audience that the opponent's arguments were weak or irrelevant.

✓ Be prepared to think on your feet (see Chapter 17 on impromptu speaking).

✓ Don't hide your passion for your position. Debate audiences appreciate enthusiasm and zeal.

Poster Sessions

A **poster session** presents information about a study, issue, or concept concisely and visually on a large (usually 3' 8" by 5' 8") poster. Presenters display their key findings on posters, which are hung on freestanding boards; on hand are copies of the written report, with full details of the study. A good poster presenter considers his or her audience, understanding that with so much competing information, the poster must be concise, visually appealing, and restricted to the most important points of the study. Different disciplines (e.g., geology vs. sociology) require unique poster format, so be sure that you follow the guidelines specific to the discipline.

When preparing the poster:

- Select a concise and informative title.
- Include an abstract (a brief summary of the study) describing the essence of the report and how it relates to other research in the field. Offer compelling and "must know" points to hook viewers and summarize information for those who will only read the abstract.
- Ensure a logical and easy-to-follow flow from one part of the poster to another.
- Ruthlessly edit text to a minimum, using clear graphics wherever possible.
- Select a muted color for the poster itself, such as gray, beige, light blue, or white and use a contrasting, clear font color (usually black).
- Make sure your font size is large enough to be read comfortably from at least three feet away.
- Design figures and diagrams to be viewed from a distance, and label each one.
- Include a concise summary of each figure in a legend below each one.
- Be prepared to provide brief descriptions of your poster and to answer questions; keep your explanations short.

Preparing for Different Audiences

Occasionally, instructors may ask that you tailor your oral presentations to a mock (practice) on-the-job audience, with your classmates serving as stand-ins. The types of audiences you will likely address on-the-job include the **expert or insider audience**, **colleagues within the field**, the **lay audience**, and the **mixed audience**. See the next page for a description of each type.

TYPES OF AUDIENCES IN THE WORKING WORLD	
TYPE OF AUDIENCE	CHARACTERISTICS
Expert or insider audience	People who have intimate knowledge of the topic, issue, product, or idea being discussed (e.g., an investment analyst presents a financial plan to a group of portfolio managers).
Colleagues within the field	People who share the speaker's knowledge of the general field under question (e.g., psychology or computer science), but who may not be familiar with the specific topic under discussion (e.g., short-term memory or voice recognition systems, respectively).
Lay audience	People who have no specialized knowledge of the field related to the speaker's topic or of the topic itself (e.g., a physical education teacher discusses the proper diet and exercise regimen with a group of teenagers).
Mixed audience	An audience composed of a combination of people—some with expert knowledge of the field and topic and others with no specialized knowledge. This is perhaps the most difficult audience to satisfy (e.g., an attending surgeon describes experimental cancer treatment to a hospital board comprising medical professionals, financial supporters, and administrative personnel).

27 Science and Mathematics Courses

The primary purpose of most science and math presentations is to inform listeners of the results of original or replicated research. In the classroom, instructors want to know the processes by which you arrived at your experimental results. For example, your biology instructor may assign an oral report on the extent to which you were able to replicate an experiment on cell mitosis. A mathematics instructor may ask you to apply a concept to an experiment or issue facing the field. In a geology course, you might describe how glacial striations in bedrock can help determine the direction of a glacier's movement.

> ### QUICK TIP
>
> #### What Do Science-Related Courses Include?
> *Science-related disciplines include the physical sciences (e.g., chemistry and physics), the natural sciences (e.g., biology and medicine), and the earth sciences (e.g., geology, meteorology, and oceanography). Fields related to mathematics include accounting, statistics, and applied math.*

Research Presentation

In the **research presentation** (also called **oral scientific presentation** or "scientific talk"), you describe original research you have done, either alone or as part of a team. The research presentation usually follows the standard model used in scientific investigation and includes the following elements:

1. *An introduction* describing the research question and the scope and objective of the study.

2. *A description of methods* used to investigate the research question, including where it took place and the conditions under which it was carried out.

3. *The results of the study* summarizing key results and highlighting insights to the questions/hypotheses investigated; this is the "body" of the presentation.

4. *A conclusion* (also called "Discussion"), in which the speaker interprets the data or results and discusses their significance. As in any speech, the conclusion should link back to the introduction, reiterating the research question and highlighting the key findings.

CHECKLIST: Evaluating Your Research Presentation

✓ Have you stated the research question accurately and in a way that will motivate listeners to pay attention?

✓ Have you clearly stated the hypothesis to the research question?

✓ Have you adequately described the study's research design?

✓ Have you described the methods used to obtain the results and why you used them?

✓ Have you explained and evaluated the results of the study, i.e., the data?

✓ Have you addressed the significance of the study?

Methods/Procedure Presentation

The **methods/procedure presentation** describes how an experimental or mathematical process works and under what conditions it can be used. This is generally a ten- to fifteen-minute individual presentation. In a theoretical math class, for example, your assignment might be to describe an approach to solving a problem, such as the use of the Baum Welch algorithm, including examples of how this approach has been used, either inappropriately or appropriately. This type of presentation generally does the following:

1. Identifies the conditions under which the process should be used
2. Offers a detailed description of the process (at times including a demonstration)
3. Discusses the benefits and shortcomings of the process

Research Overview

The *research overview presentation* provides background for a research question that will form the basis of an impending experiment or investigation. Instructors often ask students to organize research overviews with the following sections:

1. Overview of research that is relevant to the question at hand
2. Discussion of key studies that are central to the question
3. Analysis of the strengths and weaknesses of research in light of the current hypothesis or question

The format for the research overview may be an individual presentation or a **panel discussion**, in which a group of people (usually between three and nine) explore specific lines of research that contribute to a general hypothesis or question (see p. 260 for more on panel discussions).

Field Study Presentation

A **field study presentation** describes research conducted in naturalistic surroundings. A geology student may report on a dig or an environmental studies major might describe animal behavior in an oil spill. Field study presentations can be delivered individually, in teams, or in poster-session format. Whatever the nature of the observations, field study presentations address the following:

1. Overview and scope of the field research
2. Description of the site

3. Methods used in the research (e.g., participant observation, type of sample collection, measurement techniques)

4. Interpretation/analysis of the data

5. Future directions for the research

QUICK TIP

Make the Introduction Motivating

As in any kind of oral presentation, if you lose the audience in the introduction phase of a scientific presentation, chances are slim that you'll regain their attention. Instead of simply stating the hypothesis, tell the audience why you believe the research is important and why solving the problem is relevant. Revealing enthusiasm for the research will spark the audience's interest in the research.

Preparing Effective Scientific and Mathematical Presentations

Science and mathematics instructors, and employers and colleagues on the job, will expect your presentations to be grounded in the scientific method. Credible presentations must clearly illustrate the nature of the research question, ideally in a way that audience members will find compelling and relevant, describe the methods used in gathering and analyzing data, and explain the results.

QUICK TIP

Use Presentation Aids to Illustrate Processes

Clearly executed graphics often are critical to effective scientific and mathematical presentations, and instructors generally require them. Aids can range from data tables and graphs to equations drawn on a chalkboard. Condense data in tables to essential information and clearly label axis and variable in graphs. Remember that the more simply you can render complex information visually (without distorting findings), the more likely it is that audience members will grasp your points.

Typically, instructors will expect you to do the following:

- *Use observation, proofs, and experiments as support for your points.*

- *Be selective in your focus on details,* highlighting critical information but not overwhelming listeners with details they can learn about by referring to the written paper and the cited sources.

*   *Use analogies* to associate the unknown with familiar knowledge (see Chapter 23 on strategies).

*   *Use clear graphics* (ranging from slides to equations drawn on a chalkboard) to visually illustrate important processes and concepts.

Scientific and mathematical presentations need not be dry and merely factual. Experimentation is a process of discovery, and the fits and starts that often accompany their completion can make for compelling anecdotes during your talk.

CHECKLIST: Tips for Preparing Successful Scientific Presentations

✓ Create an informative title.

✓ Place your presentation in the context of a major scientific principle.

✓ Focus on a single issue, and adjust it to the interests of your audience.

✓ Identify the underlying question you will address, divide it into subquestions, and answer each question.

✓ Follow a logical line of thought.

✓ Explain scientific concepts unambiguously, with a minimum of jargon.

✓ Use analogies to increase understanding.

✓ End with a clearly formulated conclusion related to your chosen scientific principle.[1]

28   Technical Courses

Oral presentations in technical courses often focus on a project, whether it is a set of plans for a building, a prototype robot, or an innovative computer circuit design. Rather than addressing research, as is often the case in scientific and social scientific reports, the focus of technical presentations usually rests on the product or design itself.

Of the various types of presentations assigned in technical courses, the *design review* is perhaps the most common. Other types of presentations include *requests for funding* and *progress reports* (see Chapter 33, pp. 256–57, for progress reports).

QUICK TIP

What Are the Technical Disciplines?
Technical disciplines include the range of engineering fields (mechanical, electrical, chemical, civil, aerospace, industrial, nuclear), computer science–oriented fields (computer science, computer engineering, software engineering), and design-oriented fields (industrial design, architecture, graphic design).

Engineering Design Review

The **engineering design review** provides information on the results of a design project. Many capstone-engineering courses require that students prepare design reviews, which are generally informative in nature, although their purpose may include convincing the audience that the design decisions are sound. Design reviews often incorporate a **prototype** (model) demonstration. Design reviews often are delivered as team presentations or in poster-sessions and typically include the following:

1. Overview of the design concept
2. Description of design specifications
3. Discussion of any experimental testing that has been completed on the design
4. Discussion of future plans and unresolved problems
5. Discussion of schedule, budget, and marketing issues

Architecture Design Review

The **architecture design review** combines two functions: It enables the audience to visualize the design, and it sells it. A narrative approach, in which you tell the "story" of the design, combined with a *spatial organizational pattern*, in which you arrange main points in order of physical proximity of the design (see Chapter 13), can help you do this. At a minimum, architecture design reviews typically cover:

1. Background on the site
2. Discussion of the design concept
3. Description and interpretation of the design

Request for Funding

In the **request for funding presentation**, a team member or the entire team provides evidence that a project, a proposal, or a design idea is worth funding. Requests for funding, which are persuasive in nature, cover the following ground:

1. Overview of customer specifications and needs
2. Analysis of the market and its needs
3. Overview of the design idea or project and how it meets those needs
4. Projected costs for the project
5. Specific reasons why the project should be funded

QUICK TIP

In Technical Presentations, Lead with Results
Technical disciplines such as engineering are about results — the end product. When organizing a technical presentation, consider telling the audience the most important result first. Then fill in the details.[1]

Preparing Effective Technical Presentations

Technical presentations sell ideas, provide hard data, use concrete imagery, rely on visual aids, and are results oriented:[2]

*   *Sell your ideas.* The technical presenter must persuade clients, managers, or classmates that a design, idea, or product is a good one. As one instructor notes, "You can never assume that your product or design will just sell — *you* have to do that."[3]
*   *Provide hard data.* Good technical presentations are detailed and specific and use numbers as evidence. Instead of general, sweeping statements, provide hard data and clearly stated experimental results.

- *Use ample presentation aids.* Use diagrams, prototypes, and drawings, including design specifications, computer simulations, physical models, and spreadsheets. Construct aids early in the process, and practice the presentation with them.

- *Use concrete imagery* to help listeners visualize how your design will appear in use or its intended site.

- *Gear the information to the appropriate level.* Typically, people who attend technical presentations possess a range of technical knowledge, from little or none to an expert understanding of the topic at hand.

CHECKLIST: Presenting a Technical Report to a Mixed Audience

✓ Find out as much information as you can about the audience.

✓ Prepare both detailed and general content.

✓ Alert the audience to the order of your coverage — each audience segment will know what to expect and when.

✓ Consider devoting one-half to two-thirds of your time to an overview of your subject and saving highly technical material for the remaining time.[4]

✓ Be clear about the level at which you are speaking: "I am going to present the primary results of this project with minimal detailed information, but I'll be happy to review the statistics or experimental results in more detail following the presentation."

✓ If you notice that listeners are experiencing discomfort, consider stopping and asking for feedback about what they want. You might then change course and opt for a different approach.[5]

29 Social Science Courses

Students in the social sciences (including psychology, sociology, political science, and communication) learn to evaluate and conduct **qualitative research** (in which the emphasis is on observing, describing, and interpreting behavior) as well as

quantitative research (in which the emphasis is on statistical measurement).[1] Research methods and areas of investigation can be far-ranging, from experiments on biological bases of behavior to participant observation studies of homelessness.

For students in the social sciences, the focus is often on explaining or predicting human behavior or social forces, answering questions such as "What?," "How?," and "Why?"[2] Instructors may ask you to evaluate a theory or body of research, debate an issue, review the relevant literature, or make policy recommendations. Additionally, as in science and mathematics courses, you might prepare a research, field study, or methods/procedure presentation (see Chapter 27).

Debate Controversial Topics

Students taking social science courses often prepare for *debates* on controversial issues (see Chapter 26 for more on debates). Sometimes an assignment involves advocating a position that you do not support. For example, a sociology instructor might require students who oppose euthanasia to defend the policy. Whatever side of an issue you address, you will need to prepare a well-composed argument with strong supporting evidence.

Provide a Review of the Literature

Frequently, instructors ask students to review the body of research related to a given topic or issue and offer conclusions about the topic based on this research. A communications student, for example, might review the literature on gender bias in the hiring of journalists. In addition to describing the available research, the student would offer conclusions uncovered by the research and suggest directions for future research. A **review of the literature presentation** typically includes the following:

1. Statement of the topic under review
2. Description of the available research, including specific points of agreement and disagreement among sources
3. Evaluation of the usefulness of the research
4. Conclusions that can be drawn from the research
5. Suggested directions for future study

Explain Social Phenomena

Social scientists attempt to analyze and explain social or psychological phenomena such as, "Why do some college students abuse alcohol?" or "What leads to infant neglect?"

This type of **theoretical research presentation** typically addresses the following:

1. Description of the phenomenon under discussion (e.g., *What* is taking place?)

2. Theories of how and why it occurs, as described by the research

3. Evaluation of the research and suggestions for future research

---

QUICK TIP

Narrow Your Topic

Since most of your social scientific research and literature review presentations will be relatively brief, make sure to sufficiently narrow your topic research question and scale your findings to fit the time allotted (see Chapter 7). To ensure that you report the research accurately, maintain a working bibliography of your sources. For guidelines on creating source notes, see "From Source to Speech" guides in Chapters 9 and 10, and Appendix A.

Evaluate Policies and Programs

In addition to explaining social phenomena, social scientists often measure the effectiveness of programs developed to address these issues. Instructors may ask you to evaluate a program or policy, perhaps one you observed in a service learning assignment. Typically, **policy/program evaluation reports** include the following:

1. Explanation of the program's mission

2. Description of the program's accomplishments

3. Discussion of how the accomplishments were measured, including any problems in evaluation

4. Conclusions regarding how well or poorly the program has met its stated objectives

Recommend Policies

As well as evaluating programs and policies, you may be asked to recommend a course of action on an issue or problem. A *policy recommendation report* typically includes the following:

1. Definition and brief discussion of the problem

2. Recommendations to solve the problem or address the issue

3. Application of forecasting methods to show likely results of the recommended policy

4. Plan for implementation of the recommendations

5. Discussion of future needs or parameters to monitor and evaluate the recommendations

Preparing Effective Presentations in the Social Sciences

Good social scientific presentations clearly explain the research question, refer to current research, and use timely data.

- *Illustrate the research question.* Pay special attention to clearly illustrating the nature of the research question and the means by which the results were achieved.

- *Refer to current research.* Credible social scientific presentations refer to recent findings in the field. Instructors are more likely to accept experimental evidence if it is replicable over time and is supported by current research.

- *Use timely data.* Instructors expect student presentations to include timely data and examples. A report on poverty rates for a sociology course must provide up-to-date data, because poverty rates change yearly. A review of treatments for the mentally ill should accurately reflect current treatments.

30 Arts and Humanities Courses

Speaking assignments in arts and humanities courses (including English, philosophy, foreign languages, art history, theater, music, religion, and history) often require that you interpret the meaning of a particular idea, event, person, story, or artifact. Your art history professor, for example, may ask you to identify the various artistic and historical influences on a sculpture or a painting. An instructor of literature may ask you to explain the theme of a novel or a poem. A theater instructor may ask you to offer your interpretation of a new play.

Rather than focusing on quantitative research, presentations in the arts and humanities often rely on your analysis and interpretation of the topic at hand. These interpretations are nonetheless grounded in the conventions of the field and build on research within it.

Oral presentation assignments in arts and humanities courses can range from informative speeches of explanation to individual and team debates. Some presentations may involve performance, with students expressing artistic content.

Informative Speeches of Description and Analysis

Often in the arts and humanities, students prepare informative presentations (see Chapter 23) in which they explain the relevance of an historical or contemporary person or event; a genre or school of philosophical thought; or a piece of literature, music, or art. For example, an art history professor may require students to discuss the artist Bernini's contribution to St. Peter's Cathedral in Rome. Visual aids are often a key part of such presentations; here, audiences would expect to see relevant reproductions and photographs.

Presentations That Compare and Contrast

Another common assignment in the arts and humanities is to compare and contrast events, stories, people, or artifacts in order to highlight similarities or differences. For example, you might compare two works of literature from different time periods or two historical figures or works of art. These presentations may be informative or persuasive in nature. Presentations that compare and contrast include the following items:

1. *Thesis statement* outlining the connection between the events, stories, people, or artifacts

2. *Discussion of main points,* including several examples that highlight similarities and differences

3. *Concluding evaluative statement* about the comparison (e.g., if the presentation is persuasive, why one piece of literature was more effective than another; if informative, a restatement of similarities and differences)

Debates

Often students will engage in debates on opposing ideas, historical figures, or philosophical positions. In a history class, for example, students might argue whether sixteenth-century women in Western Europe experienced a Renaissance. The speaker must present a brief assertion (two to three minutes) about the topic; the opposing speaker then responds with a position. Whatever side of an issue you address, prepare a well-composed argument with strong supporting evidence.

QUICK TIP

Be Prepared to Lead a Discussion
Many students taking arts and humanities courses must research a question and then lead a classroom discussion on it. For example, a student of English may lead a discussion on Anton Chekov's play, The Cherry Orchard. *The speaker would be expected to provide a synopsis of the plot, theme, and characters and offer an analysis of the play's meaning. For directions on leading a discussion, see Chapter 31.*

Preparing Effective Arts and Humanities Presentations

Good presentations in the arts and humanities help the audience to think of the topic in a new way by providing an original interpretation of it. A presentation on the historical significance of Reconstruction after the Civil War of 1861–1865, for example, will be more effective if you offer a new way of viewing the topic rather than reiterating what other people have said or what is already generally accepted knowledge. A debate on two philosophical ideas will be most effective when you assert issues and arguments that are different from those that the audience has thought of before. Because many speaking events in the arts and humanities call for interpretation, the more original the interpretation (while remaining logical and supported by evidence), the more compelling the presentation will be for the audience.

31   Education Courses

In education courses (including subfields such as curriculum and instruction, physical education, secondary and elementary education, and education administration), the most common speaking assignments focus on teaching and related instructional tasks, such as giving a lecture or demonstrating an activity. In a mathematics education course, you may give a mini-lecture on a particular geometric theorem. In a learning-styles course, you may tailor an activity to a variety of different learners.

Delivering a Lecture

A **lecture** is an informational speech for an audience of student learners. Standard lectures range from fifty minutes to an hour and a half in length; a *mini-lecture presentation*, designed to give students an opportunity to synthesize information in a shorter form, generally lasts about fifteen to twenty minutes. Typically, lectures include the following:

1. A clear introduction of the topic (see Chapter 15)
2. Statement of the central idea of the lecture
3. Statement of the connection to previous topics covered
4. Discussion of the main points
5. Summary of the lecture and preview of the next assigned topic

Facilitating a Group Activity

In the **group activity presentation**, the speaker describes an activity to be completed following a lecture. Typically this short presentation includes the following:

1. A brief review of the main idea of the lecture
2. An explanation of the goal of the activity
3. Directions on carrying out the activity
4. A preview of what students will gain from the activity and what the discussion following it will cover

Facilitating a Classroom Discussion

In the **classroom discussion presentation**, the speaker leads a discussion following a lecture, offering brief preliminary remarks and then guiding the discussion as it proceeds.

1. Begin by outlining critical points to be covered.
2. Prepare several general guiding questions to launch the discussion.
3. Prepare relevant questions and examples for use during the discussion.

QUICK TIP

Make Education Presentations Interactive
Good education presentations engage students in the learning process by posing frequent questions and eliciting answers. Begin a lecture by posing a question about the topic, for example, and allow time for discussion. Avoid delivering monologues and focus instead on encouraging class participation.

Preparing Effective Education Presentations

Good presentations in education are marked by clear organization, integration of the material into the broader course content, and student-friendly supporting material.

- *Organize material logically.* Presentations in education must be tightly organized so that the audience can easily access information. Thus, pay careful attention to selecting an organizational pattern (see Chapters 13 and 24). The simpler the organizational structure, the better. Use organizing devices such as preview statements and transitions to help listeners follow ideas in a lecture, for example (see Chapter 12). Provide clear and logical directions for group activities.

- *Integrate discussion to overall course content.* Describe how the lecture for the day relates to the previous day's lecture. In a discussion or group activity, make clear connections between students' comments and other topics that have been raised or will be raised later in the course.

- *Tailor examples and evidence to the audience.* Good educational presentations use familiar examples and evidence that the audience can grasp easily. The successful instructor will not support an idea with a statistical proof, for example, unless students are trained in statistics. Use familiar examples that will enhance learning (see section on analogies in Chapter 23); try to choose examples that are close to the students' experiences.

32 Nursing and Allied Health Courses

Speaking assignments in nursing and allied health courses—physical therapy, occupational therapy, radiology, pharmacy, and other areas of health care—range from *reviews of research articles* in professional journals to *reports on community service projects* in a clinical setting. Students are assigned a mix of individual and team presentations that do the following:

- Instruct clients on health care practices and techniques
- Describe plans of care to medical teams
- Communicate patient status at change of shifts
- Make policy recommendations to managers

Visual aids such as PowerPoint slides may be required; certain courses also entail preparation of individual or team poster sessions (see Chapter 26).

The Community Service Learning Project

In a **community service learning project**, students learn about and help address a need or problem in a community agency, such as may exist in an adult daycare center, a mental-health facility, or a burn center. Typically, presentations about your participation in these projects should include the following:

- Description of the community agency and its client base
- Overview of the service project and your role in it
- Description of your accomplishments
- Report of any problems encountered
- Relationship of service learning to course content
- Summary of what you learned

Treatment Plan Reports

The ability to communicate information about patients or clients is important for all health care providers. Either individually or as part of a health care team, persons in the helping professions often evaluate patients' conditions and outline plans of treatment. One form of treatment plan, called the **case conference**, includes the following:

- Description of patient status
- Explanation of the disease process

- Steps in the treatment regimen
- Goals for patient and family
- Plans for patient's care at home
- Review of financial needs
- Assessment of resources available

The **shift report** is a concise overview of the patient's status and needs, which is delivered to the oncoming caregiver. It includes the following information:

- Patient name, location, reason for care
- Current physical status
- Day on clinical pathway for particular diagnosis
- Pertinent psychosocial data, including plans for discharge and involvement of family
- Care needs (physical, hygiene, activity, medication, nutritional)

Policy Recommendation Report

In the *policy recommendation report*, the speaker recommends the adoption of a new (or modified) health practice or policy, such as introducing a new treatment regimen at a burn center. This report (sometimes assigned as part of a capstone course) addresses the following:

- Review of existing policy or practice
- Description of proposed policy recommendation
- Review of the existing scientific literature on the policy recommendation
- Plan of action for implementing the policy or practice

Preparing Effective Presentations in Nursing and Allied Health Courses

Good presentations in health-related courses accurately communicate scientific information while simultaneously assessing practical conditions. Depending on the audience (e.g., patient or staff), communication will shift from therapeutic/empathetic to more matter-of-fact, and instructors will expect to see these shifts of tone reflected in your presentations. They will also want you to support any assertions and recommendations with the relevant scientific literature and other reports containing evidence of effective clinical practice.

Instructors will expect you to do the following:

- Use **evidence-based practice (EBP)** based on current research findings for all assignments.
- Apply concepts in the literature to your work with patients.
- Evaluate the results of your interventions.

33 | Business Courses and Business Presentations

The curriculum of most business courses mimics the demands and challenges of the real world. Students typically practice speaking assignments from sales presentations and proposals to crisis response presentations. Thus, this chapter discusses oral presentations common to the business world that may also be assigned in business courses. In addition, it will explain the *case study,* which is unique to the classroom environment.

QUICK TIP

Build Career Skills

Approach your business presentation assignments as a way to build critically important career skills. Many prospective employers will ask about such classroom experience, and you will deliver similar presentations throughout your business career. Entry-level employees with superior oral presentation skills tend to get promoted sooner than their co-workers.

Case Study Presentations

To help students understand the potential complexities of real-world business situations, instructors often require them to report orally on case studies, either alone or in teams. A **case study** is a detailed analysis of a real (or realistic) business situation. Students are typically expected to consider the case study carefully and then report on the following items:

1. Description/overview of the major issues involved in the case
2. Statement of the major problems and issues involved
3. Identification of any relevant alternatives to the case
4. Presentation of the best solutions to the case, with a brief explanation of the logic behind them

5. Recommendations for implementing the solutions, along with acknowledgment of any impediments

Sales Presentations

A **sales presentation** attempts to lead a potential buyer to purchase a service or a product described by the presenter. The general purpose of sales presentations is to persuade.

Audience

The audience for a sales presentation depends on who has the authority to make the purchase under consideration. Some sales presentations are invited by the potential buyer. Others are "cold sales" in which the presenter/seller approaches a first-time potential buyer with a product or a service. In some cases the audience might be an intermediary—a community agency's office manager, for example, who then makes a recommendation to the agency director.

Sales presentations are most successful when you clearly show how the product or service meets the needs of the potential buyer and you demonstrate how it surpasses other options available.

Organization

Due to its inherently persuasive nature, plan on organizing a sales presentation as you would a persuasive speech. Suitable patterns include the motivated sequence, comparative advantage, and problem-solution or problem-cause-solution models (see Chapter 24). The comparative advantage pattern works well when the buyer must choose between competing products and seeks reassurance that the product being presented is indeed superior. The problem-solution or problem-cause-solution pattern is especially effective when selling to a buyer who needs a product to solve a problem.

With its focus on audience needs, the motivated sequence (sometimes called the *basic sales technique*) offers an excellent means of appealing to buyer psychology. To use it to organize a sales presentation, do the following:

1. Draw the potential buyer's attention to the product.
2. Isolate and clarify the buyer's need for the product.
3. Describe how the product will satisfy the buyer's need.
4. Invite the buyer to purchase the product.

> **QUICK TIP**
>
> ***Adapt the Motivated Sequence to the Selling Situation***
> *When making a sales presentation following the motivated*
> *sequence, the extent to which you focus on each step depends*
> *on the nature of the selling situation. In cold-call sales*
> *situations, consider spending more time discovering the*
> *potential buyer's needs. For invited sales presentations, spend*
> *more time detailing the characteristics of the product and*
> *showing how it will satisfy the buyer's needs.*

Proposals

Organizations must constantly make decisions based on whether to modify or adopt a product, procedure, or policy. Such information is routinely delivered as a **proposal presentation**. Proposals may be strictly informative, as when a facilities manager provides information to his or her superiors. Often, proposals are persuasive in nature, with the presenter arguing in favor of one course of action over another.

Audience

The audience for a proposal can vary from a single individual to a large group; the individual or individuals have primary or sole decision-making responsibility. Because many proposals seek to persuade listeners, careful adaptation to the audience is critical to an effective presentation.

Organization

A proposal can be quite lengthy and formally organized or relatively brief and loosely structured. Organize lengthy proposals as follows:

1. Introduce the issue.
2. State the problem.
3. Describe the method by which the problem was investigated.
4. Describe the facts learned.
5. Offer explanations and an interpretation of the findings.
6. Offer recommendations.

Organize brief proposals as follows:

1. State your recommendations.
2. Offer a brief overview of the problem.
3. Review the facts on which the recommendations are based.

Staff Reports

A **staff report** informs managers and other employees of new developments that affect them and their work, or reports on the completion of a project or task.

Audience

The audience for a staff report is usually a group, but it can be an individual. The recipients of a staff report then use the information to implement new policy, to coordinate other plans, or to make other reports to other groups.

Organization

Formal staff reports are typically organized as follows:

1. State the problem or question under consideration (sometimes called a "charge" to a committee or a subcommittee).
2. Provide a description of procedures and facts used to address the issue.
3. Discuss the facts that are most pertinent to the issue.
4. Provide a concluding statement.
5. Offer recommendations.

Progress Reports

A **progress report** is similar to a staff report, with the exception that the audience can include people *outside* the organization as well as within it. A progress report updates clients or principals on developments in an ongoing project. On long-term projects, such reports may be given at designated intervals or at the time of specific task completions. On short-term projects, reports can occur daily.

Audience

The audience for a progress report might be a group of clients or customers, developers and investors, next-line supervisors, company officers, media representatives, or same-level co-workers. Progress reports are commonplace in staff meetings in which subcommittees report on their designated tasks. Audience questions are common at the end of progress reports (see Appendix B on handling question-and-answer sessions).

Organization

Organize a progress report as follows:

1. Briefly review progress made up to the time of the previous report.
2. Describe new developments since the previous report.
3. Describe the personnel involved and their activities.
4. Detail the time spent on tasks.
5. Explain supplies used and costs incurred.
6. Explain any problems and their resolution.
7. Provide an estimate of tasks to be completed for the next reporting period.

Crisis-Response Presentations

Crisis-response presentations (also called "crisis communication") are meant to reassure an organization's various audiences (its "publics") and restore its credibility in the face of an array of threats, such as contaminated products, layoffs, chemical spills, or bankruptcy. These are often conveyed via media such as television and radio.

Audience

Crisis-response presentations may target one, several, or multiple audiences. A personnel manager may address a group of disgruntled engineers unhappy over a new policy. Seeking to allay fears of ruin and shore up stockholder confidence, the CEO of an embattled corporation may target anxious employees and shareholders alike.

Organization

A variety of strategies exists for organizing a crisis presentation, ranging from simple denial to admitting responsibility for a crisis and asking forgiveness.[1] Familiarity with a range of *image restoration strategies* will allow the speaker to select those techniques that best apply to the situation at hand.[2] In essence, the crisis-response presentation is based on persuasion and argument. Sound reasoning and evidence are essential to its effectiveness. Depending on the issue and audience(s) involved, use one or another of the organizational patterns described in Chapter 24, especially problem-solution and refutation.

QUICK TIP

Stick to Ethical Ground Rules

As in public speeches, the ethical standards of trustworthiness, respect, responsibility, and fairness (see Chapter 2) must infuse any business or professional presentation you deliver. **Business and professional ethics** *define how people within a company or profession integrate the "ethical ground rules" into their policies and practices. Such ethics also involve complying with legal standards and adherence to internal rules and regulations.*[3]

---

34 Presenting in Teams

Team presentations are oral presentations prepared and delivered by a group of three or more individuals. Regularly assigned in the classroom and frequently delivered in the workplace, successful team presentations require close cooperation and planning.

Working in Teams

When preparing and delivering a successful team presentation, you must keep in mind the guidelines you would use in an individual presentation, along with additional strategies for working effectively *with others*, as a team. This chapter discusses the specifics of planning team presentations; for guidelines on incorporating group communication and problem-solving techniques into your team presentations, see Chapter 35.

Analyze the Audience and Set Goals

Even if the topic is assigned and the audience consists solely of the instructor and classmates, consider their interests and needs with respect to the topic and how you can meet them. Then establish goals for the presentation that you can all agree upon.

Assign Roles and Tasks

First, designate a *team leader* to help guide coordination among members, beginning with the selection of roles and tasks. Assign team members to various aspects of the research, perhaps selecting different team members to present the introduction, body of the presentation, and conclusion, or other responsibilities. Set firm time limits for each portion of the presentation.

QUICK TIP

Be Mindful of Your Nonverbal Behavior
During a team presentation, the audience's eyes will fall on everyone involved, not just the person speaking. Thus any signs of disinterest or boredom by a team member will be easily noticed. Give your full attention to the other speakers on the team and project an attitude of interest toward audience members.

Establish Transitions Between Speakers

Work out transitions between speakers ahead of time—for example, whether one team member will introduce every speaker or whether each speaker will introduce the next speaker upon the close of his or her presentation. The quality of the presentation will depend in great part on smooth transitions between speakers.

Coordinate the Presentation Aids

Consider assigning one person the job of coordinating templates for slides or other visuals. Doing so will ensure each presentation aid is consistent in color, font size, and overall style. The team can also decide to assign a single individual the task of presenting the aids as another team member speaks. If this is the case, be sure that the team member presenting the aids or showing the slides remains unobtrusive so as not to distract the audience from the speaker.

Rehearse the Presentation Several Times

Together with the whole group, members should practice their portions of the presentation, with any presentation aids they will use, in the order they will be given in the final form. Rehearse several times, until the presentation proceeds smoothly, using the techniques for rehearsal described in Chapter 19.

QUICK TIP

For Maximum Impact, Consider the Presenters' Strengths
Audiences become distracted by marked disparities in style, such as hearing a captivating speaker followed by an extremely dull one. If you are concerned about an uneven delivery, consider choosing the person with the strongest presentation style and credibility level for the opening. Put the more cautious presenters in the middle of the presentation. Select another strong speaker to conclude the presentation.[1]

Panels, Symposiums, and Forums

Panels, symposiums, and forums are group discussions in which multiple speakers share their expertise with an audience; forums are convened specifically to discuss issues of public interest.

Panel Discussions

In this type of discussion, a group of people (at least three, and generally not more than nine) discusses a topic in the presence of an audience. Panel discussions do not feature formally prepared speeches. Instead, they require the presence of a skilled chairperson or **moderator** to direct the discussion.

When preparing remarks for a panel discussion, consider the following:

* What is the agenda for the discussion?
* Who is your audience?
* What aspects of the topic will the other participants address?
* Will questions from the audience be permitted during the discussion or deferred until the panel has ended?

Symposia

A **symposium** is a formal meeting at which several speakers (usually three to five) deliver short speeches on the same topic. Symposia are organized to inform audiences about different aspects of a topic or offer contrasting viewpoints. Sometimes the symposium concludes with a question-and-answer period; at other times, it is followed by a panel discussion among symposium participants.

When preparing a presentation for a symposium, consider the following:

- What aspects of the topic will the other participants address?
- In what order will the speakers address the audience?
- What are your time constraints?
- Who is your audience?
- Will you engage in questions and answers with the other speakers, or just with the audience?

Forums

A **forum** is an assembly for the discussion of issues of public interest. Forums can take place in a physical space, such as a town hall, or online, in moderated Web chats and other forms of virtual forums. Forums may feature a panel or a symposium, followed by an extensive question-and-answer period by the audience. One well-known forum is the *town*

 CHECKLIST: Team Presentation Tips

✓ Establish in writing each team member's responsibilities regarding content and presentation aids.

✓ Determine how introductions will be made—all at once at the beginning or having each speaker introduce the next one.

✓ Practice introductions and transitions to create a seamless presentation.

✓ Establish an agreed-upon set of hand signals to indicate when a speaker is speaking too loud or soft, too slow or fast.

✓ Assign someone to manage the question-and-answer session.

✓ Rehearse the presentation with presentation aids several times from start to finish.

hall meeting, in which citizens deliberate on issues of importance to the community.

When participating in public forums (not as a featured speaker, but as a member of the audience), consider the following:

- Organize your thoughts as much as possible in advance by jotting down your question or comment on a piece of paper.

- Do not duplicate someone else's questions or comments unless it adds to the discussion.

- Use no more time than necessary to make your points.

- If appropriate, include a call to action at the conclusion of your comments.

35 Communicating in Groups

Most of us will spend a substantial portion of our educational and professional lives participating in **small groups** or teams[1] (usually between three and twenty people); and many of the experiences we have as speakers, in the classroom, workforce, and in virtual groups online, occur in a group setting. Groups often report on the results they've achieved, and some groups form solely for the purpose of coordinating oral presentations (see Chapter 34 on team presentations). Thus understanding how to work cooperatively within a group setting is a critical skill.

Focus on Goals

How well or poorly you meet the objectives of the group—whether it is to coordinate a team presentation or to decide on a policy—is largely a function of how closely you keep sight of the group's goals and avoid behaviors that detract from these goals. Setting an **agenda** can help participants stay on track by identifying items to be accomplished during a meeting; often it will specify time limits for each item.[2]

Adopt Productive Roles

In a group, you will generally assume dual roles, such as a task role and an interpersonal role. **Task roles** are the hands-on roles that directly relate to the group's accomplishment of its objectives. Examples include "recording secretary" (takes notes) and "moderator" (facilitates discussion).[3] Members also adopt various **interpersonal roles**, or styles of interacting in the group, such as "the harmonizer" (smoothes out tension) and "the gatekeeper" (keeps the discussion moving and gets everyone's input).[4]

Task and interpersonal roles help the group achieve its mission. Conversely, **counterproductive roles** such as "floor hogger" (not allowing others to speak), "blocker" (being overly negative about group ideas; raising issues that have been settled), and "recognition seeker" (acts to call attention to oneself rather than to group tasks) do not help further the group's goals and should be avoided.

Center Disagreements around Issues

Whenever people come together to consider an important issue, conflict is inevitable. But conflict doesn't have to be destructive. In fact, the best decisions are usually those that emerge from productive conflict.[5] In *productive conflict,* group members clarify questions, challenge ideas, present counterexamples, consider worst-case scenarios, and reformulate proposals. Productive conflict centers disagreements around issues rather than personalities. In *person-based conflict,* members argue with one another instead of about the issues, wasting time and impairing motivation; *issues-based conflict* allows members to test and debate ideas and potential solutions. It requires each member to ask tough questions, press for clarification, and present alternative views.[6]

Resist Groupthink

For a group to be truly effective, members eventually need to form a *collective mind,* that is, engage in communication that is critical, careful, consistent, and conscientious.[7] At the same time, they must avoid **groupthink**, the tendency to accept information and ideas without subjecting them to critical analysis.[8] Groups prone to groupthink typically exhibit these behaviors:

- Participants reach a consensus and avoid conflict so as to not hurt others' feelings, but without genuinely agreeing.
- Members who do not agree with the majority feel pressured to conform.
- Disagreement, tough questions, and counterproposals are discouraged.
- More effort is spent justifying the decision than testing it.

QUICK TIP

Optimize Decision Making in Groups
Research suggests that groups can reach the best decisions by adopting two methods of argument: **devil's advocacy** *(arguing for the sake of raising issues or concerns about the idea under discussion) and* **dialectical inquiry** *(devil's advocacy that goes a step further by proposing a countersolution to the idea).[9] Both approaches help expose underlying assumptions that may be preventing participants from making the best decision. As you lead a group, consider how you can encourage both methods of argument.*

Be a Participative Team Leader

When called upon to lead a group, bear in mind the four broad styles of leadership and select the *participative model*:

- *Autocratic* (leaders make decisions and announce them to the group)
- *Consultive* (leaders make decisions after discussing them with the group)
- *Delegative* (leaders ask the group to make the decision)
- *Participative* (leaders make decisions with the group)[10]

Research suggests that often the most effective leader is participative, that is, one who facilitates a group's activities and interaction in ways that lead to a desired outcome.

Set Goals

As a leader, aim to be a catalyst in setting and reaching goals in collaboration with other group members. It is your responsibility to ensure that each group member can clearly identify the group's purpose(s) and goal(s).

Encourage Active Participation

Groups tend to adopt solutions that receive the largest number of favorable comments, whether these comments emanate from one individual or many. If only one or two members

CHECKLIST: Guidelines for Setting Group Goals

✓ Identify the problem.

✓ Map out a strategy.

✓ Set a performance goal.

✓ Identify resources necessary to achieve the goal.

✓ Recognize contingencies that may arise.

✓ Obtain feedback.

participate, it is their input that sets the agenda, whether or not their solution is optimal.[11] When you lead a group, take these steps to encourage group participation:

- *Directly ask members to contribute.* Sometimes one person, or a few people, dominates the discussion. Encourage others to contribute by redirecting the discussion in their direction ("Patrice, we haven't heard from you yet" or "Juan, what do you think about this?").

- *Set a positive tone.* Some people are reluctant to express their views because they fear ridicule or attack. Minimize such fears by setting a positive tone, stressing fairness, and encouraging politeness and active listening.

- *Make use of devil's advocacy and dialectical inquiry.* Raise pertinent issues or concerns, and entertain solutions other than the one under consideration.

Use Reflective Thinking

To reach a decision or solution that all participants understand and are committed to, guide participants through the six-step process of reflective thinking shown in Figure 35.1 on the following page, which is based on the work of educator John Dewey.[12]

Step 1 Identify the Problem
- What is being decided upon?

Group leader summarizes problem, ensures that all group members understand problem, and gains agreement from all members.

Step 2 Conduct Research and Analysis
- What information is needed to solve the problem?

Conduct research to gather relevant information.
Ensure that all members have relevant information.

Step 3 Establish Guidelines and Criteria
- Establish criteria by which proposed solutions will be judged.

Reach criteria through consensus and record criteria.

Step 4 Generate Solutions
- Conduct brainstorming session.

Don't debate ideas; simply gather and record all ideas.

Step 5 Select the Best Solution
- Weigh the relative merits of each idea against criteria. Select one alternative that can best fulfill criteria.

If more than one solution survives, select solution that best meets criteria.
Consider merging two solutions if both meet criteria.
If no solution survives, return to problem identification step.

Step 6 Evaluate Solution
- Does the solution have any weaknesses or disadvantages?
- Does the solution resemble the criteria that were developed?
- What other criteria would have been helpful in arriving at a better solution?

FIGURE 35.1 Making Decisions in Groups: John Dewey's Six-Step Process of Reflective Thinking

Appendices

A Citation Guidelines

Instructors will often require that you include a bibliography of sources with your speech (see Chapters 4 and 9). You can document sources by following documentation systems such as *Chicago*, APA, MLA, CSE, and IEEE.

Chicago Documentation

Two widely used systems of documentation are outlined in *The Chicago Manual of Style*, Fifteenth Edition (2003). The first, typically used by public speakers in a variety of disciplines, provides for bibliographic citations in endnotes or footnotes. This method is illustrated below. The second form employs an author-date system: Sources are cited in the text with full bibliographic information given in a concluding list of references. For information about the author-date system—and more general information about *Chicago*-style documentation—consult the *Chicago Manual*, Chapters 16 and 17.

1. BOOK BY A SINGLE AUTHOR   Give the author's full name, followed by a comma. Then italicize the book's title. In parentheses, give the city of publication, followed by a colon; the publisher's name, followed by a comma; and publication date. Place a comma after the closing parenthesis; then give page numbers from which your paraphrase or quotation is taken.

   1. Eric Alterman, *What Liberal Media? The Truth about Bias and the News* (New York: Basic Books, 2003), 180–85.

2. BOOK BY MULTIPLE AUTHORS

   2. Bill Kovach and Tom Rosenstiel, *The Elements of Journalism: What Newspeople Should Know and the Public Should Expect*, rev. ed. (New York: Three Rivers Press, 2007), 57–58.

3. EDITED WORK WITHOUT AN AUTHOR

   3. Joseph B. Atkins, ed., *The Mission: Journalism, Ethics, and the World* (Ames: Iowa State University Press, 2002), 150–57.

   3. Jonathan Dube, "Writing News Online," in *Shop Talk and War Stories: American Journalists Examine Their Profession,* ed. Jan Winburn (Boston: Bedford/St. Martin's, 2003), 202.

4. ENCYCLOPEDIA OR DICTIONARY   If the citation is from an online reference work, add the URL (Internet address) and the access date.

4. *Encyclopedia Britannica,* s.v. "Yellow Journalism," http://www.britannica.com/eb/article-9077903/yellow-journalism (accessed October 17, 2007).

5. ARTICLE IN A MAGAZINE

5. John Leo, "With Bias toward All," *U.S. News & World Report,* March 18, 2002, 8–9.

6. ARTICLE IN A JOURNAL   Give the author's full name; the title of the article in quotation marks; the title of the journal in italics; the volume and issue numbers; the year of publication in parentheses, followed by a colon; and the pages used. If the journal article was found online, give the URL, and if timeliness is an issue, the date of access.

6. Tom Goldstein, "Wanted: More Outspoken Views: Coverage of the Press Is Up, but Criticism Is Down," *Columbia Journalism Review* 40, no. 4 (2001): 144–45.

6. Tom Goldstein, "Wanted: More Outspoken Views: Coverage of the Press Is Up, but Criticism Is Down," *Columbia Journalism Review* 40, no. 4 (2001), http://backissues.cjrarchives.org/year/01/6/goldsteinpresscrit.asp (accessed October 29, 2007).

7. ARTICLE IN A NEWSPAPER

7. Felicity Barringer, "Sports Reporting: Rules on Rumors," *New York Times,* February 18, 2002, sec. C.

8. WEB SITE   Give the name of the author (if available; if not, list the site's owner if there is one); the title of the page in quotation marks, followed by a comma; the title of the Web site; and the site's URL. The date you accessed the site is optional; if you include it, add it in parentheses at the end.

8. FAIR (Fairness & Accuracy in Reporting), "Challenging Hate Radio: A Guide for Activists," http://www.fair.org/index.php?page=112 (accessed September 21, 2007).

9. E-MAIL MESSAGE

9. Grace Talusan, e-mail message to author, March 20, 2005.

10. E-MAIL DISCUSSION LIST MESSAGE

10. Ola Seifert, e-mail to Society of Professional Journalists mailing list, August 23, 2002, http://f05n16.cac.psu.edu (accessed September 14, 2005).

11. NEWSGROUP MESSAGE Include the author's full name, the phrase "message to," followed by the newsgroup name, posting date, and URL. Date of access is optional.

11. Jai Maharaj, message to alt.journalism.newspapers. newsgroup, November 11, 2002, http://groups.google.com (accessed December 19, 2005).

12. ENTRY IN A BLOG

12. Virginia Heffernan, comment on "Finding Harmony in YouTube's Cacophony of Sounds," The Medium: The Way We Watch Now Blog, comment posted May 1, 2009, http://themedium.blogs .nytimes.com/ (accessed May 6, 2009).

13. ELECTRONIC DATABASE

13. Mark J. Miller, "Tough Calls: Deciding When a Suicide Is Newsworthy and What Details to Include Are among Journalism's More Sensitive Decisions," *American Journalism Review* 24, no. 10 (2002): 43, http://infotrac.galegroup.com (accessed March 1, 2005).

14. GOVERNMENT DOCUMENT

14. U.S. Congress, *The Electronic Freedom of Information Improvement Act: Hearing before the Subcommittee on Technology and the Law of the Committee on the Judiciary, 1992* (Washington, DC: GPO, 1993), 201.

15. PERSONAL COMMUNICATION

15. Soo Jin Oh, letter to author, August 13, 2005.

16. INTERVIEW

16. Walter Cronkite, interview by Daniel Schorr, *Frontline*, PBS, April 2, 1996.

17. VIDEO RECORDING

17. *All the President's Men*, VHS, directed by Alan J. Pakula (Burbank, CA: Warner Brothers, 1976).

18. SOUND RECORDING

18. Noam Chomsky, *Case Studies in Hypocrisy,* read by Noam Chomsky (AK Press, 2000).

18. Antonio Vivaldi, *The Four Seasons,* conducted by Seiji Ozawa, Telarc CD-80070.

APA Documentation

Most disciplines in the social sciences—psychology, anthropology, sociology, political science, education, and economics—use the author-date system of documentation established by the American Psychological Association (APA). This citation style highlights dates of publication because the currency of published material is of primary importance in these fields.

In the author-date system, use an author or organization's name in a signal phrase or parenthetical reference within the main text to cite a source.

For example, you could cite Example 1 on p. 272 with the author's name in a signal phrase as follows:

Rabin (1999) states that an increase in environmental stresses increases the chances for contracting common types of influenza by 12%.

Or with a parenthetical reference as follows:

One study found that environmental stress increased the chances for contracting common types of influenza by 12% (Rabin, 1999).

Each in-text citation refers to an alphabetical references list that you must create.

For more information about APA format, see the *Publication Manual of the American Psychological Association,* Sixth Edition (2010). The guide advises users to omit retrieval dates for content that is in permanent form, such as published journal articles, and to provide the DOI (digital object identifier) for that content. If no DOI is available, list the home page URL of the content's publisher. Including the database in which the content was sourced is not recommended, as this can be subject to change.

The numbered entries that follow introduce and explain some conventions of this citation style using examples related to the topic of stress management. All titles and subtitles of books, references, and government documents are italicized, but only the first words are capitalized; all other words are lowercased. All titles of journals and magazines are also italicized, but follow the standard rules of capitalization. Subtitles of these sources, however, are not italicized and follow the APA rules for capitalizing titles of books, references, and government documents.

1. BOOK BY A SINGLE AUTHOR Begin with the author's last name and initials, followed by the date of publication in parentheses. Next, italicize the book's title, and end with the place of publication, including city and state or country, and the publisher.

Rabin, B. S. (1999). *Stress, immune function, and health: The connection*. New York, NY: Wiley-Liss.

2. BOOK BY MULTIPLE AUTHORS OR EDITORS

Williams, S., & Cooper, L. (2002). *Managing workplace stress: A best practice blueprint*. New York, NY: Wiley.

3. ARTICLE IN A REFERENCE WORK If an online edition of the reference work is cited, give the retrieval date and the URL. Omit end punctuation after the URL.

Kazdin, A. E. (2000). Stress. In *Encyclopedia of psychology* (Vol. 7, pp. 479–489). New York, NY: Oxford University Press.

Biofeedback. (2007). In *Encyclopedia Britannica Online.* Retrieved from http://www.britannica.com/eb/article-9079253

4. GOVERNMENT DOCUMENT

U.S. Department of Health and Human Services. (1997). *Violence in the workplace: Guidelines for understanding and response*. Washington, DC: U.S. Government Printing Office.

5. JOURNAL ARTICLE Begin with the author's last name and initials followed by the date of publication in parentheses. Next, list the title of the article and italicize the title of the journal in which it is printed. Then give the volume number, italicized, and the issue number in parentheses if the journal is paginated by issue. End with the inclusive page numbers of the article. For an article found online, include the issue number, regardless of how the journal is paginated. If a DOI number is given, add "doi:" and the number after the end period of the citation. Otherwise, add "Retrieved from" and the URL for an open-content article, or for the journal home page for subscription-only content.

Dollard, M. F., & Metzer, J. C. (1999). Psychological research, practice, and production: The occupational stress problem. *International Journal of Stress Management, 6*(4), 241–253.

Hardie, E.A., Crtichley, C., & Swann, K. (2007, June 12). Self-coping complexity: The role of relational, individual, and collective self-aspects and corresponding coping styles in stress and health. *Current Research in Social Psychology, 12*(10), 134–150. Retrieved from http://www.uiowa.edu /~grpproc/crisp/crisp12_10.pdf

Corrigan, P. W., Kuwabara, S. A., & O'Shaughnessy, J. (2009). The public stigma of mental illness and drug addiction. *Journal of Social Work 9*(2), 137–147. doi: 10.1177/1468017308101818

6. MAGAZINE ARTICLE

Cobb, K. (2002, July 20). Sleepy heads: Low fuel may drive brain's need to sleep. *Science News, 162,* 38.

7. NEWSPAPER ARTICLE

Goode, E. (2002, December 17). The heavy cost of chronic stress. *The New York Times,* p. D1.

Goode, E. (2002, December 17). The heavy cost of chronic stress. *The New York Times.* Retrieved from http://www.nytimes.com

8. UNSIGNED NEWSPAPER ARTICLE

Stress less: It's time to wrap it up. (2002, December 18). *Houston Chronicle,* p. A1.

9. DOCUMENT FROM A WEB SITE

Centers for Disease Control. (1999, January 7). *Stress . . . at work.* Retrieved January 6, 2005, from http://www.cdc.gov/niosh /stresswk.html

10. PERSONAL WEB SITE   Simply note the site in your speech:

Dr. Wesley Sime's stress management page is an excellent resource (http://www.unl.edu/stress/mgmt/).

11. ELECTRONIC MAILING LIST MESSAGE

Greenberg, G. (2002, May 26). Re: Job Stress & Mortality: Psychosomatic Med, U-T Houston [Electronic mailing list message]. Retrieved from http://list.mc.duke.edu/cgi-bin/wa?A2=ind0205&L=oem-announce&P=R13114&1=-3&0=A&T=0

12. NEWSGROUP, ONLINE FORUM, OR DISCUSSION GROUP MESSAGE

Dimitrakov, J. (2001, February 21). Immune effects of psychological stress [Online discussion group message]. Retrieved from http://groups.google.com/groups?q=stress&start=40&hl=en&lr=&ie=UTF-8&selm=3A9ABDE4%40MailAndNews.com&rnum=44

13. BLOG POST

Bellemare, S. A. (2009, April 27). A peek into my sketchbook [Web log message]. Retrieved from http://www.poppytalkhandmadeartists.blogspot.com/

14. E-MAIL MESSAGE   Simply note the message in your speech:

An e-mail message from the staff of AltaVista clarifies this point (D. Emanuel, personal communication, May 12, 2005).

15. MATERIAL FROM AN ONLINE DATABASE

Waring, T. (2002). Stress management: A balanced life is good for business. *Law Society Journal, 40,* 66–68. Retrieved from http://www.lawsociety.com.au

16. ABSTRACT FROM AN INFORMATION SERVICE OR ONLINE DATABASE

Viswesvaran, C., Sanchez, J., & Fisher, J. (1999). The role of social support in the process of work stress: A meta-analysis. *Journal of Vocational Behavior, 54,* 314–334. Abstract retrieved from http://www.elsevier.com

17. PERSONAL INTERVIEW   Simply note the interview in your speech:

During her interview, Senator Cole revealed her enthusiasm for the new state-funded stress management center (M. Cole, personal communication, October 7, 2005).

MLA Documentation

Created by the Modern Language Association, MLA documentation style is fully outlined in the *MLA Handbook for Writers of Research Papers,* Seventh Edition (2009). Disciplines that use MLA style include English literature, the humanities, and various foreign languages.

In MLA format, you document materials from other sources with in-text citations that incorporate signal phrases and parenthetical references.

For example, you could cite Example 1 below with the author's name in a signal phrase as follows:

Berg notes that "'Chicano' is the term made popular by the Mexican American civil rights movement in the 1960s and 1970s" (6).

Or with a parenthetical reference as follows:

The term "Chicano" was "made popular by the Mexican American civil rights movement in the 1960s and 1970s" (Berg 6).

Each in-text citation refers to an alphabetical works-cited list that you must create.

The sample citations given here all relate to a single topic: film appreciation and criticism.

1. BOOK BY A SINGLE AUTHOR   Citations for most books are arranged as follows: (1) the author's name, last name first; (2) the title and subtitle, italicized; and (3) the city of publication, an abbreviated form of the publisher's name, and the date. Each of these three pieces of information is followed by a period and one space. End the citation with the medium of publication (*Print*) and a period.

Berg, Charles Ramírez. *Latino Images in Film: Stereotypes, Subversion, and Resistance.* Austin: U of Texas P, 2002. Print.

2. BOOK BY MULTIPLE AUTHORS OR EDITORS   Give the first author's name, last name first, then list the name(s) of the other author(s) in regular order with a comma between authors and the word *and* before the last one. The final name in a list of editors is followed by a comma and "ed." or "eds."

Hill, John, and Pamela Church Gibson, eds. *The Oxford Guide to Film Studies.* New York: Oxford UP, 1998. Print.

3. ARTICLE IN A REFERENCE WORK   If the citation is to an online version of the work, give the author, article title, and name of the Web site. Then add the publisher or sponsor of the site, the date of publication or last update, the medium (*Web*), and the date you accessed the work (day, month, year). End with a period.

Katz, Ephraim. "Film Noir." *The Film Encyclopedia*. 4th ed. 2001.
    Print.

"Auteur Theory." *Encyclopaedia Britannica Online*. Encyclopaedia
    Britannica, 2007. Web. 22 Oct. 2007.

4. GOVERNMENT DOCUMENT

United States. Cong. House. Committee on the Judiciary. *National*
    Film Preservation Act of 1996. 104th Cong., 2nd sess. H.
    Rept. 104–558. Washington: GPO, 1996. Print.

United States. Cong. House. Committee on House Administration.
    Library of Congress Sound Recording and Film Preservation
    Programs Reauthorization Act of 2008. 110th Cong., 2nd sess.
    H. Rept. 110–683. *GPOAccess, Congressional Reports*. Web.
    15 Jan. 2009.

5. MAGAZINE ARTICLE   If you are citing the article from an online edition of the magazine, after the title of the article, add the name of the Web site in italics, followed by a period. Then add the publisher or sponsor of the site, the date of publication, the medium (*Web*), and the date you accessed the article.

Ansen, David. "Lights! Action! Cannes!" *Newsweek* 19 May 1997:
    76–79. Print.

Ansen, David. "Boomer Files: 7,714 Movies, and Counting."
    Newsweek. Newsweek, 29 Oct. 2007. Web. 3 Nov. 2007.

6. JOURNAL ARTICLE   If an article is accessed online through a database service, after the publication information, add the name of the database in italics, followed by a period. Then give the medium (*Web*) and your date of access. End with a period.

Kingsley-Smith, Jane E. "Shakespearean Authorship in Popular
    British Cinema." *Literature-Film Quarterly* 30.3 (2002):
    159–61. Print.

Holcomb, Mark. "A Classic Revisited: *To Kill a Mockingbird*." *Film*
    Quarterly 55.4 (2002): 34-40. *JSTOR*. Web. 22 Oct. 2007.

7. NEWSPAPER ARTICLE   If you are citing a newspaper article found online, after the title of the article, give the name of the newspaper's Web site, followed by a period. Then specify the publisher or sponsor of the site, the date of publication, the medium consulted (*Web*), and the date you accessed the article.

Sebastian, Pamela. "Film Reviews Have a Delayed Effect on Box-
    Office Receipts, Researchers Say." *Wall Street Journal* 13 Nov.
    1997: A1+. Print.

Dargis, Manohla. "Unblinking Eye, Visual Diary: Warhol's Films."
    New York Times. New York Times, 21 Oct. 2007. Web. 30 Oct.
    2007.

8. NEWSPAPER EDITORIAL

"The Edgy Legacy of Stanley Kubrick." Editorial. *New York Times*
    10 Mar. 1999: A18. Print.

9. ONLINE SCHOLARLY PROJECT OR REFERENCE DATABASE

"Origins of American Animation." *American Memory*. Lib. of Cong.
    31 Mar. 1999. Web. 26 June 2003.

10. PERSONAL OR COMMERCIAL WEB SITE

Last, Kimberly. *007*. Kimberly Last, n.d. Web. 18 Oct. 2007.

"American Beauty." *Crazy for Cinema*. N.p., n.d. Web. 24 Oct. 2003.

11. POSTING OR COMMENT ON A BLOG   Give the author's name; the title of the post or comment in quotation marks (if there is no title, use the description *blog post* or *blog comment*, not italicized); the title of the blog, italicized; the sponsor of the blog (if there is none, use *N.p.*); the date of the most recent update; the medium (*Web*); and the date of access.

Scola, Nancy. "And the White House Tweets Back." *techPresident*.
    Personal Democracy Forum, 5 May 2009. Web. 5 May 2009.

12. ARTICLE IN AN ONLINE PERIODICAL

Taylor, Charles. "The Pianist." *Salon.com*. Salon Media Group,
    27 Dec. 2002. Web. 1 Jan. 2005.

13. POSTING TO A DISCUSSION GROUP

Granger, Susan. "Review of *The Cider House Rules*." *Rotten Tomatoes*. IGN Entertainment, 30 Mar. 2000. Web. 2 Oct. 2000.

14. E-MAIL MESSAGE

Boothe, Jeanna. "Re: Top 100 Movies." Message to the author. 16 Feb. 2005. E-mail.

15. SINGLE-ISSUE CD-ROM, DISKETTE, OR MAGNETIC TAPE

"Pulp Fiction." *Blockbuster Movie Trivia*. 3rd ed. New York: Random, 1998. CD-ROM.

16. WORK OF ART OR PHOTOGRAPH

Christenberry, William. *Coleman's Café*. 1971. Ektacolor Brownie Print. Hunter Museum of Art, Chattanooga.

17. INTERVIEW

Sanderson, Andrew. Telephone interview. 12 June 2002.

CSE Documentation

The CSE (Council of Science Editors) style is most frequently used in the fields of biology and environmental science. The current CSE style guide is *Scientific Style and Format: The CSE Manual for Authors, Editors, and Publishers,* Seventh Edition (2006). Publishers and instructors who require the CSE style do so in three possible formats: a citation sequence superscript format, a name-year format, or a citation-name format, which combines aspects of the other two systems.

- If you use the citation-sequence superscript format, number and list the references in the sequence in which they are first cited in the speech.

- If you use the name-year format, list the references, unnumbered, in alphabetical order.

- If you use the citation-name format, arrange references alphabetically and number the list sequentially.

In the following examples, all of which refer to environmental issues, you will see that the citation-sequence format calls for listing the date after the publisher's name in references for books and after the name of the periodical in references for articles. The name-year format calls for listing the date immediately after the author's name in any kind of reference. Notice also the absence of a comma after the author's last name, the absence of a period after an initial, and the absence of underlining in titles of books or journals.

1. BOOK BY ONE AUTHOR   Be sure to list the total number of pages in the book.

Citation-Sequence

1 Leggett JK. The carbon war: global warming and the end of the oil era. New York: Routledge; 2001. 341 p.

Name-Year

Leggett JK. 2001. The carbon war: global warming and the end of the oil era. New York: Routledge. 341 p.

2. BOOK BY TWO OR MORE AUTHORS

Citation-Sequence

2 Goldstein IF, Goldstein M. How much risk?: a guide to understanding environmental health hazards. New York: Oxford Univ Pr; 2002. 304 p.

Name-Year

Goldstein IF, Goldstein M. 2002. How much risk?: a guide to understanding environmental health hazards. New York: Oxford Univ Pr. 304 p.

3. JOURNAL ARTICLE   If citing a journal on the Internet, add the medium, date cited, and the URL. Also give the DOI code if available. Omit end punctuation after a URL or DOI.

Citation-Sequence and Citation-Name

3 Brussard PF, Tull JC. Conservation biology and four types of advocacy. Conserv Biol. 2007; 21(1):21–24.

3 Brussard PF, Tull JC. Conservation biology and four types of advocacy. Conserv Biol. [Internet]. 2007 [cited 2007 Oct 22]; 21 (1):21–24. Available from http://www. blackwell-synergy.com/toc/cbi/21/1doi:10.1111/ j.1523-1739.2006.00640.x

Name-Year

Brussard PF, Tull JC. 2007. Conservation biology and four types of advocacy. Conserv Biol. 21(1):21–24.

Brussard PF, Tull JC. 2007. Conservation biology and four types of advocacy. Conserv Biol [Internet]. 2007 [cited 2007 Oct 22]; 21 (1):21–24. Available from http://www .blackwell-synergy.com/toc/cbi/21/1 doi:10.1111/ j.1523-1739.2006.00640.x

4. MAGAZINE ARTICLE

Citation-Sequence and Citation-Name

[4] Wilcott B. Art for Earth's sake. Mother Jones 2000 Jun:16.

Name-Year

Wilcott B. 2000 June. Art for Earth's sake. Mother Jones:16.

5. NEWSPAPER ARTICLE

Citation-Sequence and Citation-Name

[5] Parson EA. Moving beyond the Kyoto impasse. New York Times 2001 Jul 1; Sect A:23(col 1).

Name-Year

Parson EA. 2001 Jul 1. Moving beyond the Kyoto impasse. New York Times; Sect A:23(col 1).

6. WEB SITE For material found on a Web site, give the author's name (if any) and the title of the material, followed by "Internet" in brackets. Add the place of publication, the publisher, date of publication, followed by the date of citation in brackets. Add "Available from:" and the URL.

Citation-Sequence and Citation-Name

[6] Water Pollution Control: Watershed Management Cycle [Internet]. Nashville: Tennessee Department of Environment and Conservation; 2007 [cited 2007 Oct 23]. Available from: http://www.tennessee.gov/environment/wpc/watershed/ cycle.shtml

Name-Year

Water Pollution Control: Watershed Management Cycle [Internet] 2007.
  Nashville: Tennessee Department of Environment and Conservation.
  [cited 2007 Oct 23]. Available from: http://www.tennessee.gov/
  environment/wpc/watershed/cycle.shtml

7. **E-MAIL MESSAGE** CSE recommends mentioning personal communications in text, but not listing them in the list of references. An explanation of the material should go in the "Notes."

. . .(2003 e-mail from Maura O'Brien to me; unreferenced, see
  "Notes").

8. **E-MAIL DISCUSSION LIST OR NEWSGROUP MESSAGE**

8 Affleck-Asch W. Three hundred pesticides to be withdrawn in
  Europe [discussion list on the Internet]. 2002 Dec 2, 6:37 pm
  [cited 2003 Jan 2]. [about 8 paragraphs]. Available from:
  http://www.mail-archive.com/ecofem%40csf.colorado.edu

IEEE Documentation

The Institute of Electrical and Electronics Engineers (IEEE) style requires that references appear at the end of the text, not in alphabetical order but in the order in which the references are cited in the text. A bracketed reference number beginning with *B* precedes each entry. For speakers, this means creating a bibliography of sources listed in the order in which they were cited in the speech (this is done in bibliographies for speeches in any format). For more information on IEEE documentation, check the *IEEE Standards Style Manual* online at http://standards.ieee.org/guides/style/index.html.

1. **BOOK**

[B1] Vorpérian, V., *Fast Analytical Techniques for Electrical and
  Electronic Circuits.* New York: Cambridge University Press,
  2002, p. 462.

2. **PERIODICAL**

[B2] Brittain, J. C., "Charles F. Scott: A pioneer in electrical power
  engineering," *IEEE Industry Applications Magazine,* vol. 287,
  no. 6, pp. 6–8, Nov./Dec. 2000.

3. WEB PAGE

[B3] Harnack, A., and Kleppinger, E., "Beyond the MLA Handbook: Documenting Electronic Sources on the Internet" [Online style sheet] (June 1996), Available at: http://english.ttu .edu.kairos/1.2/

B Question-and-Answer Sessions

Deftly fielding questions is a final critical component of making a speech or a presentation. As the last step in preparing your speech, anticipate and prepare for questions the audience is likely to pose to you. Write these questions down, and practice answering them. Spend time preparing an answer to the most difficult question that you are likely to face. The confidence you will gain from smoothly handling a difficult question should spill over to other questions.[1]

Protocol during the Session

As a matter of courtesy, call on audience members in the order in which they raise their hands. Consider the following guidelines:

- *Repeat or paraphrase the question* ("The question is 'Did the mayor really vote against . . .'"). This will ensure that you've heard it correctly, that others in the audience know what you are responding to, and that you have time to reflect upon and formulate an answer. Note that there are a few exceptions to repeating the question, especially when the question is hostile. One expert suggests that you should always repeat the question when speaking to a large group; when you're in a small group or a training seminar, however, doing so isn't necessary.[2]

- *Initially make eye contact with the questioner; then move your gaze to other audience members.* This makes all audience members feel as though you are responding not only to the questioner but to them as well.

- *Remember your listening skills.* Give questioners your full attention, and don't interrupt them.

- *Don't be afraid to pause while formulating an answer.* Many speakers feel they must feed the audience instantaneous responses; this belief sometimes causes them to say things that they later regret. This is especially the case in media interviews (see Appendix C). Pauses that seem long to you may not appear lengthy to listeners.

- *Keep answers concise.* The question-and-answer session is not the time to launch into a lengthy treatise on your favorite aspect of a topic.

Handling Hostile and Otherwise Troubling Questions

When handling hostile questions, do not get defensive. Doing so will damage your credibility and only encourage the other person. Maintain an attitude of respect, and stay cool and in control. Attempt to defuse the hostile questioner with respect and goodwill. Similarly, never give the impression that you think a question is stupid or irrelevant, even if it clearly is.

- *Do not repeat or paraphrase a hostile question.* This only lends the question more credibility than it is worth. Instead, try to rephrase it more positively[3] (e.g., in response to the question "Didn't your department botch the handling of product X?" you might respond, "The question was 'Why did product X experience a difficult market entry?' To that I would say that . . .").

- *If someone asks you a seemingly stupid question, do not point that out.* Instead, respond graciously.[4]

Ending the Session

Never end a question-and-answer session abruptly. As time runs out, alert the audience that you will take one or two more questions and then must end. The session represents one final opportunity to reinforce your message, so take the opportunity to do so. As you summarize your message, thank your listeners for their time. Leave an air of goodwill behind you.

Preparing for Mediated Communication

The underlying principles described throughout this guide will stand you in good stead as you prepare to communicate through an electronic medium such as television, radio, or the videoconference. These speaking situations do present some unique challenges, however.

Speaking on Television

On television, you are at the mercy of reporters and producers who will edit your remarks to fit their time frame. Therefore, before your televised appearance, find out as much as you can about the speech situation—for example, how long you will be on camera and whether the show will be aired live or taped. You may need to convey your message in *sound bite* form—succinct statements that summarize your key points in twenty seconds or less.

Eye Contact, Body Movements, and Voice

The question of where to direct your gaze is critical in televised appearances, as is controlling body movement and voice. The following are some guidelines:

- Don't play to the camera. In a one-on-one interview, focus on the interviewer. Do not look up or down or tilt your head sideways; these movements will make you look uncertain or evasive.[1]
- If there is an audience, treat the camera as just another audience member, glancing at it only as often as you would at any other individual during your remarks.
- If there is only you and the camera, direct your gaze at it as you speak.
- Keep your posture erect.
- Exaggerate your gestures slightly.
- Project your voice, and avoid speaking in a monotone.

Dress and Makeup

To compensate for the glare of studio lights and distortions caused by the camera, give careful consideration to dress and grooming:

- Choose dark rather than light-colored clothing. Dark colors such as blue, gray, green, and brown photograph better than lighter shades.

- Avoid stark white, because it produces glare.
- Avoid plaids, dots, and other busy patterns because they tend to jump around on the screen.
- Avoid glittering jewelry, including tie bars.
- Wear a little more makeup than usual because bright studio lights tend to make you look washed out.

Speaking on Radio: The Media Interview

The following are guidelines for preparing for media interviews on the radio. These same guidelines can be applied to the television interview.

- Know the audience and the focus of the program. What subjects does the broadcast cover? How long will the interview be? Will it be taped or live?
- Brush up on background information and have your facts ready. Assume that the audience knows little or nothing about the subject matter.
- Use the interviewer's name during the interview.
- Prepare a speaking outline on notecards for the interview. Remember that the microphone will pick up the sound of papers being shuffled.
- Remember that taped interviews may be edited. Make key points in short sentences, and repeat them using different words.[2] Think in terms of sound bites.
- Anticipate questions that might arise, and decide how you will answer them.
- Use transition points to acknowledge the interviewer's questions and to bridge your key message points, such as "I am not familiar with that, but what I can tell you is . . ."; "You raise an interesting question, but I think the more important matter is . . ."[3]
- Avoid the phrase "No comment." It will only exaggerate a point you are trying to minimize. Instead, say "I am not at liberty to comment/discuss. . . ."

Speaking on the Videoconference

Videoconferencing integrates video and voice to connect students and instructors in remote sites with each other in real time. To deliver an online presentation, prepare as you would for one on-site, but pay particular attention to good diction, delivery, and dynamic body language.[4]

- Look into the camera to create eye contact; speak directly to the long-distance audience.

- To prevent video "ghosting" (pixilation), avoid sudden, abrupt, or sweeping movements.

- To compensate for audio delays, speak and move a little more slowly and deliberately than normal.

- Wear pale, solid colors and avoid flashy jewelry (see additional tips on dress on pages 284–85, "Speaking on Television").

- Prepare visual aids following the principles described in Chapter 21.[5]

D Tips for Non-Native Speakers of English

In addition to the normal fear of being at center stage, non-native speakers of English face the burden of worrying about delivering a speech in a non-native language. If English is your first language, remind yourself of how difficult it would be for you to deliver a speech in another language. As you listen to a non-native speaker, place yourself in his or her shoes. If necessary, politely ask questions for clarification.

If you are a non-native speaker of English, think about public speaking as an opportunity to learn more about the English language and how to use it. As you listen to your classmates' speeches, for example, you will gain exposure to spoken English. Practicing your speech will give you time to work on any accent features you want to improve.[1] Research shows that thinking positively about preparing speeches actually *reduces anxiety* and helps you prepare a better speech. So tell yourself that by studying public speaking you will find many good opportunities to improve your English and become a better communicator of English. In addition, by spending time writing and outlining your speech, you will gain confidence in your written language skills. Here are a few tips to get you started:

- *Take your time and speak slowly.* This will give your listeners time to get used to your voice and to focus on your message.

- *Identify English words that you have trouble saying.* Practice saying these words five times. Pause. Then say the words again five times. Progress slowly until the word becomes easier to pronounce.

- *Avoid using words that you don't really have to use, such as jargon* (see Chapter 16). Learn to use a thesaurus to find synonyms—words that mean the same thing—that are simpler and easier to pronounce.

- *Offer words from your native language to emphasize your points.* This will help the audience to better appreciate your native language and accent. For example, the Spanish word *corazón* has a lyrical quality that makes it sound much better than its English counterpart, "heart." Capitalize on the beauty of your native tongue.

Learn by Listening

Listening is the key to learning a language. Using textbooks to study usage and grammar is important, but it is through spoken language—hearing it and speaking it—that we gain fluency.

Listening to the speeches of colleagues or classmates, as well as those broadcast by television channels such as C-Span, can help you hone the skills you need to become a better speaker. Nearly all college libraries own many videocassettes and other recorded materials made specifically for ESL (English as a second language) speakers such as yourself, and the reference librarian will be happy to locate them for you. The Internet also offers many helpful listening resources. Among the many sites you can find is the *Talking Merriam Webster English Dictionary* (at www.webster.com/). This online dictionary allows you to hear the correct pronunciations of words.

Broaden Your Listeners' Perspectives

Consider sharing a personal experience with the audience. Stories from other lands and other ways of life often fascinate listeners. Unique cultural traditions, eyewitness accounts of newsworthy events, or tales passed down orally from one generation to the next are just some of the possibilities. Depending on the goal of your speech, you can use your experiences as supporting material for a related topic or as the topic itself.

One freshman public-speaking student from Poland related what life for her was like after the fall of communism in 1989. She described how goods she had never seen before suddenly flooded the country. A wondrous array of fruit and meat left the most vivid impression on the then 11-year-old; both had been nearly impossible to find under the old regime. Her audience was fascinated with her firsthand account of historical events, and the speaker found that sharing her unique experiences boosted her confidence.

Practice with an Audio Recorder

Most experts recommend that you prepare for delivering your first speech (as well as for subsequent speeches) by practicing with an audio recorder.[2] Non-native speakers may wish to pay added attention to pronunciation and articulation as they listen. *Pronunciation* is the correct formation of word sounds. *Articulation* is the clarity or forcefulness with which the sounds are made, regardless of whether they are pronounced correctly. It is important to pay attention to and work on both areas.

Because languages vary in the specific sounds they use and the way these sounds are produced by the vocal chords, each of us will speak a non-native language a bit differently than do native speakers. That is, we speak with some sort of accent. This should not concern you in and of itself. What is important is identifying which specific features of your pronunciation, if any, seriously interfere with your ability to make yourself understandable. Listening to your speech with an audio recorder or videotape, perhaps in the presence of a native speaker, will allow you to identify trouble spots. Once you have identified which words you tend to mispronounce, you can work to correct the problem. If possible, try to arrange an appointment with an instructor to help you identify key linguistic issues in your speech practice recording. If instructors are unavailable, try asking a fellow student.

Use Vocal Variety

Non-native speakers may be accustomed to patterns of vocal variety—volume, pitch, rate, and pauses—that are different from a native English speaker. The pronunciation of English depends on learning how to combine a series of about forty basic sounds (fifteen vowels and twenty-five consonants) that together serve to distinguish English words from one another. Correct pronunciation also requires that the speaker learn proper word stress, rhythm, and intonation or pitch.[3] As you

> **QUICK TIP**
>
> **Check for Correct Articulation**
> As you listen to your recording, watch also for your articulation of words. ESL students whose first languages don't differentiate between the /sh/ sound and its close cousin /ch/, for example, may say "share" when they mean "chair" or "shoes" when they mean "choose."[4] It is important therefore that you also check to make sure that you are using the correct meaning of the words you have selected for your speech.

practice your speeches, pay particular attention to these facets of delivery. Seek feedback from others, including your teacher, making sure that your goal of shared meaning can be met when you do deliver your speech.

Counteract Problems in Being Understood

Virtually everyone who learns to speak another language will speak that language with an accent. What steps can you take when your accent will make your oral presentation difficult for the audience to understand?

In the long term, interacting with native speakers in everyday life will help enormously. With immersion, non-native speakers can begin to stop translating things word for word and start thinking in English. Using an audio recorder and practicing your speech in front of others are also very important.

But what if your experience with English is limited and you must nonetheless give an oral presentation? Robert Anholt, a scientist and the author of *Dazzle 'Em with Style: The Art of Oral Scientific Presentation*, suggests the following:

- Practice the presentation often, preferably with a friend who is a native English speaker.

- Learn the presentation almost by heart.

- Create strong presentation aids that will convey most of the story by themselves, even if your voice is hard to understand.[5]

Glossary

abstract language Language that is general or nonspecific.

active listening A multistep, focused, and purposeful process of gathering and evaluating information.

ad hominem fallacy A logical fallacy that targets the person instead of the issue at hand in an attempt to discredit an opponent's argument. See also *logical fallacy*.

advanced searching Narrowing results in a Web search beyond basic search commands (also called *field searching*).

after-dinner speech A speech that is likely to occur before, after, or during a formal dinner; a breakfast or lunch seminar; or other type of business, professional, or civic meeting.

agenda A document identifying the items to be accomplished during a meeting.

agora In ancient Greece, a public square or marketplace. See also *forum* and *public forum*.

alliteration The repetition of the same sounds, usually initial consonants, in two or more neighboring words or syllables.

almanac A reference work that contains facts and statistics in many categories or on a given topic, including those that are related to historical, social, political, and religious subjects.

analogy An extended metaphor or simile that compares an unfamiliar concept or process with a more familiar one in order to help the listener understand the one that is unfamiliar. See also *imagery*.

anaphora A rhetorical device in which the speaker repeats a word or phrase at the beginning of successive phrases, clauses, or sentences.

anecdote A brief story of an interesting, humorous, or real-life incident that links back to the speaker's theme.

antithesis A rhetorical device in which two ideas are set off in balanced (parallel) opposition to each other.

appeal to tradition A logical fallacy suggesting that something is true because traditionally it has been true. See also *logical fallacy*.

architecture design review A type of oral presentation which enables the audience to visualize an architectural design.

argument A stated position, with support, for or against an idea or issue; contains the core elements of claim, evidence, and warrants.

articulation The clarity or forcefulness with which sounds are made, regardless of whether they are pronounced correctly.

atlas A collection of maps, text, and accompanying charts and tables.

attitude Our general evaluations of people, ideas, objects, or events.

audience analysis The process of gathering and analyzing demographic and psychological information about audience members.

audience-centered Focused on the needs, attitudes, and values of the audience.

average Information calculated on the basis of typical characteristics.

bandwagoning A logical fallacy that uses (unsubstantiated) general opinion as its (false) basis. See also *logical fallacy*.

begging the question A logical fallacy in which what is stated cannot help but be true, even though no evidence has been presented. See also *logical fallacy*.

beliefs The ways in which people perceive reality or determine the very existence or validity of something.

biased language Any language that relies on unfounded assumptions, negative descriptions, or stereotypes of a given group's age, class, gender, disability, and geographic, ethnic, racial, or religious characteristics.

blog Short for "Weblog," an online personal journal.

body (of speech) The part of the speech in which the speaker develops the main points intended to fulfill the speech's purpose.

body language The bodily activity of the speaker and the meaning the audience assigns to this activity.

brainstorming A problem-solving technique that involves the spontaneous generation of ideas; includes making lists, using word association, and mapping topics.

brief example A single illustration of an idea, item, or event being described.

business and professional ethics Defines how individuals within a company or a profession integrate ethical ground rules into policies, practices, and decision making.

call to action A challenge to audience members to act in response to a speech; placed at the conclusion of a persuasive speech.

canned speech A speech used repeatedly and without sufficient adaptation to the rhetorical speech situation.

canons of rhetoric A classical approach to speechmaking in which the speaker divides a speech into five parts: invention, arrangement, style, memory, and delivery.

captive audience An audience required to attend.

case conference An oral report prepared by health-care professionals evaluating a patient's condition and outlining a treatment plan.

case study A detailed illustration of a real or hypothetical business situation.

causal (cause-effect) pattern of arrangement A pattern of organizing speech points in order of causes and then in order of effects, or vice versa.

causal reasoning Offering a cause-and-effect relationship as proof of a claim.

central processing A mode of processing a persuasive message that involves thinking critically about the contents of the message and the strength and quality of the speaker's arguments.

channel The medium through which the speaker sends a message, such as sound waves, air waves, and so forth.

chart A method of representing data and their relationship to other data in a meaningful form. Several different types of charts are helpful for speakers: flow charts, organization charts, and tabular charts (tables).

cherry-picking Selectively presenting only those facts and statistics that buttress one's point of view while ignoring competing data.

chronological pattern of arrangement A pattern of organizing speech points in a natural sequential order; used when describing a series of events in time or when the topic develops in line with a set pattern of actions or tasks.

circle pattern of arrangement A pattern of organizing speech points so that one idea leads to another, which leads to a third, and so forth, until the speaker arrives back at the speech thesis.

claim The declaration of a state of affairs in which a speaker attempts to prove something by providing evidence and reasoning.

claim of fact An argument that focuses on whether something is or is not true or whether something will or will not happen.

claim of policy An argument that recommends that a specific course of action be taken, or approved, by an audience.

claim of value An argument that addresses issues of judgment.

classroom discussion presentation A type of oral presentation in which the speaker presents a brief overview of the topic under discussion and introduces a series of questions to guide students through the topic.

cliché An overused phrase such as "burning the midnight oil" or "He works like a dog."

closed-ended question A question designed to elicit a small range of specific answers supplied by the interviewer.

co-culture A community of people whose perceptions and beliefs differ significantly from those of other groups within the larger culture.

code-switching The selective use of dialect within a speech.

colleagues within the field audience An audience of persons who share the speaker's knowledge of the general field under question but who may not be familiar with the specific topic under discussion.

colloquial expression An informal expression characterized by regional variations of speech. See also *idiom*.

common knowledge Information that is likely to be known by many people and is therefore in the public domain; the source of such information need not be cited in a speech.

community service learning project A project in which someone learns about and helps to address a need or problem in a community.

comparative advantage pattern A pattern of organizing speech points so that the speaker's viewpoint or proposal is shown to be superior to one or more alternative viewpoints or proposals.

conclusion (of speech) The part of the speech in which the speaker reiterates the speech theme, summarizes main points, and leaves the audience with something about which to think or act.

concrete language Nouns and verbs that convey specific (as opposed to abstract) meaning.

connotative meaning The individual associations that different people bring to bear on a word.

context The situation that created the need for a speech; influences the speaker, the audience, or the occasion, and affects the message of the speech.

conversation stoppers Speech that discredits, demeans, or belittles.

coordinate points Ideas that are given the same weight in an outline and are aligned with one another; thus Main Point II is coordinate with Main Point I.

coordination and subordination The logical placement of ideas (in an outline, essay, or speech) relative to their importance to one another. Ideas that are coordinate are given equal weight. An idea that is subordinate to another is given relatively less weight.

copyright A legal protection afforded original creators of literary or artistic works.

counterproductive roles Negative interpersonal roles adopted by group members.

Creative Commons An organization that allows creators of works to decide how they want other people to use their copyrighted works.

crisis-response presentation A type of oral presentation in which the speaker seeks to reassure an organization's various audiences ("publics") and restore its credibility in the face of potentially reputation-damaging situations.

cultural intelligence The willingness to learn about other cultures and gradually reshape one's thinking and behavior in response to what one has learned.

decoding The process of interpreting a message.

defamatory speech Speech that potentially harms an individual's reputation at work or in the community and is thus subject to legal action. See also *reckless disregard for the truth*.

defensive listening A poor listening behavior in which the listener reacts defensively to a speaker's message.

definition by example Defining something by providing an example of it.

definition by negation Defining something by explaining what it is not.

definition by synonym Defining something by comparing it with another term that has an equivalent meaning. For example: A friend is a comrade, or a buddy.

definition by word origin (etymology) Defining something by providing an account of a word's history.

delivery The vocal and nonverbal behavior that a speaker uses in a public speech; one of the five canons of rhetoric.

delivery cues Brief reminder notes or prompts placed in the speaking outline that can refer to transitions, timing, speaking rate and volume, presentation aids, quotations, statistics, and difficult-to-pronounce or remember names or words.

demographics Statistical characteristics of a given population. Characteristics typically considered in the analysis of audience members include age, gender, ethnic or cultural background, socioeconomic status (including income, occupation, and education), and religious and political affiliation.

denotative meaning The literal or dictionary definition of a word.

devil's advocacy Arguing for the sake of raising issues or concerns about the idea under discussion.

diagram A schematic drawing that explains how something works or how it is constructed or operated; useful in simplifying and clarifying complicated procedures, explanations, and operations.

dialect A distinctive way of speaking associated with a particular region or social group.

dialectical inquiry Devil's advocacy that goes a step further by proposing a countersolution to an idea.

dialogic communication Sharing ideas through dialogue.

dignity The feeling that one is worthy, honored, or respected as a person.

direct quotation Statement made verbatim—word for word—by someone else. Direct quotations should always be acknowledged in a speech.

disinformation The deliberate falsification of information.

DLP (digital light processing) projector A projector designed for computer images that is equipped with an illumination, or light source, in its own case, thereby eliminating the need for an overhead projector.

domain The suffix at the end of a Web address that describes the nature of the Web site: business/commercial <.com>, educational <.edu>, government <.gov>, military <.mil>, network <.net>, or nonprofit organization <.org>.

dyadic communication Communication between two people, as in a conversation.

eight by eight rule Rule of design suggesting having no more than eight lines or bullet points per slide or other kind of visual aid.

either-or fallacy A logical fallacy stated in terms of two alternatives only, even though there are additional alternatives.

encoding The process of organizing a message, choosing words and sentence structure, and verbalizing the message.

encyclopedia A reference work that summarizes knowledge found in original form elsewhere and provides an overview of subjects.

engineering design review An oral presentation that provides information on the results of an engineering design project.

ethos The Greek word for "character." According to the ancient Greek rhetorician Aristotle, audiences listen to and trust speakers if they exhibit competence (as demonstrated by the speaker's grasp of the subject matter) and good moral character.

eulogy A speech whose purpose is to celebrate and commemorate the life of someone while consoling those who are left behind; typically delivered by close friends and family members.

evidence Supporting material that provides grounds for belief.

evidence-based practice An approach to medical treatment in which caregivers make decisions based on current research and "best practices."

example (as form of support) An illustration whose purpose is to aid understanding by making ideas, items, or events more concrete and by clarifying and amplifying meaning.

expert or insider audience An audience of persons with an intimate knowledge of the topic, issue, product, or idea being discussed.

expert testimony Any findings, eyewitness accounts, or opinions by professionals who are trained to evaluate or report on a given topic; a form of supporting material.

explanatory research presentation A type of oral presentation focusing on studies that attempt to analyze and explain a phenomenon; frequently delivered in social scientific fields.

extended example Multifaceted illustration of the idea, item, or event being described, thereby getting the point across and reiterating it effectively.

fact book See *almanac.*

facts Documented occurrences, including actual events, dates, times, places, and people involved.

fairness An ethical ground rule; making a genuine effort to see all sides of an issue; being open-minded.

fair use doctrine Legal guidelines permitting the limited use of copyrighted works without permission for the purposes of scholarship, criticism, comment, news reporting, teaching, and research.

feedback Audience response to a message, which can be conveyed both verbally and nonverbally through gestures. Feedback from the audience often indicates whether a speaker's message has been understood.

field study presentation A type of oral presentation typically delivered in the context of science-related disciplines in which the speaker provides (1) an overview of the field research, (2) the methods used in the research, (3) an analysis of the results of the research, and (4) a time line indicating how the research results will be used going forward.

figures of speech Expressions, such as metaphors, similes, analogies, and hyperbole, in which words are used in a nonliteral fashion.

First Amendment The amendment to the U.S. Constitution that guarantees freedom of speech. ("Congress shall make no law abridging the freedom of speech.")

fixed-alternative question A closed-ended question that contains a limited choice of answers, such as "Yes," "No," or "Sometimes."

flip chart A large (27–34 inch) pad of paper on which a speaker can illustrate speech points.

flowchart A diagram that shows step-by-step the progression through a procedure, relationship, or process.

font A set of type of one size and face.

forum In ancient Rome, a public space in which people gathered to deliberate about the issues of the day. See also *agora* and *public forum.*

frequency A count of the number of times something occurs.

full-sentence transition A signal to listeners, in the form of a declarative sentence, that the speaker is turning to another topic.

gender Social or psychological sense of self as male or female.

general speech purpose A statement of the broad speech purpose that answers the question, "Why am I speaking on this topic for this particular audience and occasion?" Usually the general speech purpose is to inform, to persuade, or to celebrate or com-memorate a special occasion. See also *specific speech purpose.*

graph A graphical representation of numerical data. Graphs neatly illustrate relationships among components or units and demonstrate trends. Four major types of graphs are line graphs, bar graphs, pie graphs, and pictograms.

group activity presentation An oral presentation that intro-duces students to an activity and provides them with clear direc-tions for its completion.

groupthink The tendency of a group to accept information and ideas without subjecting them to critical analysis.

handout Printed material that conveys information that is either impractical to give to the audience in another manner or intended to be kept by audience members after a presentation.

hasty generalization A logical fallacy in which an isolated instance is used to make an unwarranted general conclusion. See also *logical fallacy.*

hate speech Any offensive communication—verbal or nonverbal—directed against people's race, ethnicity, religion, gender, disabil-ity, or other characteristics. Racist, sexist, or ageist slurs, gay bashing, and cross burnings are all forms of hate speech.

hierarchy of needs A classic model of human action developed by Abraham Maslow based on the principle that people are motivated to act on the basis of their needs.

hypothetical example An illustration of something that could happen in the future if certain events were to occur.

identification A feeling of commonality with another. Effective speakers attempt to foster a sense of identification between themselves and audience members.

idiom Language specific to a certain region or group of people. See also *colloquial expression.*

imagery Colorful and concrete words that appeal to the senses. See also *analogy, metaphor,* and *simile.*

indentation In an outline, the plotting of speech points to indi-cate their weight relative to one another; subordinate points are placed underneath and to the right of higher-order points.

individual debate format A debate in which one person takes a side against another.

individual search engine A search engine that compiles its own database of Web pages, such as Google or AltaVista. See also *meta-search engine.*

information Data set in a context for relevance.

informative speech A speech providing new information, new insights, or new ways of thinking about a topic. The general pur-pose of an informative speech is to increase the audience's understanding and awareness of a topic.

integrity The quality of being incorruptible; unwillingness to compromise for the sake of personal expediency.

internal preview An extended transition that alerts audience members to ensuing speech content.

internal summary An extended transition that draws together important ideas before proceeding to another speech point.

interpersonal roles Types of roles or styles of interacting in a group that facilitate group interaction.

introduction (of speech) The first part of a speech, in which the speaker establishes the speech purpose and its relevance to the audience, and previews the topic and the main points.

invective Abusive speech.

invisible Web The portion of the World Wide Web that includes pass-protected sites, documents behind firewalls, and the contents of proprietary databases. General search engines usually fail to find this portion of the Web.

jargon Specialized terminology developed within a given endeavor or field of study.

key-word outline The briefest form of outline; uses the smallest possible units of understanding associated with a specific point to outline the main and supporting points.

lavaliere microphone A microphone that attaches to a lapel or a collar.

lay audience An audience of persons lacking specialized knowledge of the general field related to the speaker's topic and of the topic itself.

lay testimony Firsthand findings, eyewitness accounts, or opinions from nonexperts such as eyewitnesses.

lazy speech A poor speech habit in which the speaker fails to properly articulate words.

LCD (liquid crystal display) panel A device connected to a computer used to project slides stored in the computer.

learning styles Preferred ways of processing information; one learning theory model suggests visual, aural, read/write, and kinesthetic modes of learning.

lecture An informational speech to an audience of student learners.

library portal An entry point to a large collection of research and reference information that has been selected and reviewed by librarians.

listening The conscious act of receiving, comprehending, interpreting, and responding to messages.

listening distraction Anything that competes for a listener's attention. The source of the distraction may be internal or external.

logical fallacy A statement that is based on an invalid or deceptive line of reasoning. See also *ad hominem argument, appeal to tradition, bandwagoning, begging the question, either-or fallacy, hasty generalization, non sequitur,* and *slippery slope.*

logos The Greek rhetorician Aristotle used this term to refer to persuasive appeals to reason and logic.

main points Statements that express the key ideas and major themes of a speech. Their function is to make claims in support of the thesis statement.

malapropism The inadvertent use of a word or phrase in place of one that sounds like it.

mass communication Communication that occurs between a speaker and a large audience of unknown people. The receivers of the message are not present with the speaker or are part of such an immense crowd that there can be little or no interaction between speaker and listener. Television, radio news broadcasts, and mass rallies are examples of mass communication.

mean The sum of the scores divided by the number of scores; the arithmetic (or computed) average.

median A type of average that represents the center-most score in a distribution; the point above and below which 50 percent of the scores fall.

message The content of the communication process—thoughts and ideas put into meaningful expressions. A message can be expressed both verbally (through the sentences and points of a speech) and nonverbally (through eye contact and gestures).

metaphor A figure of speech used to make implicit comparisons without the use of "like" or "as" (e.g., "Love is a rose"). See also *imagery.*

meta-search engine A search engine that searches a variety of individual search engines simultaneously. Examples include MetaCrawler and Dogpile. See also *individual search engine.*

methods/procedure presentation An oral presentation describing and sometimes demonstrating an experimental or mathematical process, including the conditions under which it can be applied; frequently delivered in scientific and mathematics related fields.

misinformation Information that is false.

mixed audience An audience composed of a combination of persons—some with expert knowledge of the field and topic and others with no specialized knowledge.

mode A type of average that represents the most frequently occurring score(s) in a distribution.

model A three-dimensional, scale-size representation of an object such as a building.

moderator A person who presides over a discussion or meeting.

motivated sequence A five-step process of persuasion, developed by Alan Monroe, that begins with arousing attention and ends with calling for action.

multimedia A single production that combines several media (stills, sound, video, text, and data).

mumbling Slurring words together at low volume and pitch so they are barely audible.

narrative A story based on personal experiences or imaginary incidents. See also *story*.

narrative organizational pattern A pattern of organizing speech points so that the speech unfolds as a story with characters, plot, and setting. In practice, this pattern often is combined with other organizational patterns.

noise Anything that interferes with the communication process between a speaker and audience so that the message cannot be understood; source may be external (in the environment) or internal (psychological factors).

non sequitur ("does not follow") A logical fallacy in which the conclusion is not connected to the reasoning. See also *logical fallacy*.

nonverbal immediacy Acts that create the perception of psychological closeness between the speaker and audience members.

operational definition Defining something by describing what it does. For example: A computer is something that processes information.

oral scientific presentation A type of oral presentation following the model used in scientific investigations, including an introduction, description of methods, results, and conclusion; commonly found in the disciplines of science and mathematics.

oratory In classical terms, the art of public speaking.

original research presentation See *oral scientific presentation*.

overhead transparency An image on a transparent background that can be viewed by projection.

paid inclusion The practice of paying a fee to a search engine company for inclusion in its index of possible results, without a guarantee of ranking.

paid placement The practice of paying a fee to a search engine company to guarantee a higher ranking within its search results.

pandering Identifying with values not one's own in order to win approval from an audience.

panel discussion A type of oral presentation in which a group of persons (at least three, and generally not more than nine) discusses a topic in the presence of an audience and under the direction of a moderator.

parallel form The statement of equivalent speech points in similar grammatical form and style.

parallelism The arrangement of words, phrases, or sentences in similar grammatical and stylistic form. Parallel structure can help the speaker emphasize important ideas in the speech.

paraphrase A restatement of someone else's statements or written work that alters the form or phrasing but not the substance of that person's ideas.

pathos The Greek rhetorician Aristotle used this term for appeals to emotion. Such appeals can get the audience's attention and stimulate a desire to act but must be used ethically.

pauses Strategic elements of a speech used to enhance meaning by providing a type of punctuation, emphasizing a point, drawing attention to a key thought, or just allowing listeners a moment to contemplate what is being said.

percentage The quantified portion of a whole.

performance anxiety A feeling of anxiety that occurs the moment one begins to perform.

periodical A regularly published magazine or journal.

peripheral processing A mode of processing a persuasive message that does not consider the quality of the speaker's message, but is influenced by such non-content issues as the speaker's appearance or reputation, certain slogans or one-liners, and obvious attempts to manipulate emotions. Peripheral processing of messages occurs when people lack the motivation or the ability to pay close attention to the issues.

persuasive speech A speech whose goal is to influence the attitudes, beliefs, values, or acts of others.

phrase outline A delivery outline that uses a partial construction of the sentence form of each point, instead of using complete sentences that present the precise wording for each point.

pitch The range of sounds from high to low (or vice versa) determined by the number of vibrations per unit of time; the more vibrations per unit (also called *frequency*), the higher the pitch, and vice versa.

plagiarism The act of using other people's ideas or words without acknowledging the source.

policy/program evaluation report A report on a policy/program's mission, a description of its accomplishments and how they were measured, and conclusions on how well or poorly the policy/program has met its stated objectives.

poster A large (36″ × 56″), bold, two-dimensional design incorporating words, shapes, and, if desired, color, placed on an opaque backing; used to convey a brief message or point forcefully and attractively.

poster session A format for the visual presentation of posters, arranged on freestanding boards, containing a display summarizing a study or issue for viewing by participants at professional conferences. The speaker prepares brief remarks and remains on hand to answer questions as needed.

preparation anxiety A feeling of anxiety that arises when a speaker begins to prepare for a speech, at which point he or she might feel overwhelmed at the amount of time and planning required.

pre-performance anxiety A feeling of anxiety experienced when a speaker begins to rehearse a speech.

pre-preparation anxiety A feeling of anxiety experienced when a speaker learns he or she must give a speech.

presentation aid(s) Objects, models, pictures, graphs, charts, video, audio, or multimedia used to illustrate speech points.

presentational speaking A type of oral presentation in which individuals or groups deliver reports addressing colleagues, clients, or customers within a business or professional environment.

previews Transitions that tell the audience what to expect next.

preview statement Statement included in the introduction of a speech in which the speaker identifies the main speech points.

primary research Original or firsthand research, such as interviews and surveys. See also *secondary research.*

problem-cause-solution pattern of arrangement A pattern of organizing speech points so that they demonstrate (1) the nature of the problem, (2) reasons for the problem, and (3) proposed solution(s).

problem-solution pattern of arrangement A pattern of organizing speech points so that they demonstrate the nature and significance of a problem first, and then provide justification for a proposed solution.

progress report A report that updates clients or principals on developments in an ongoing project.

pronunciation The correct formation of word sounds.

prop Any live or inanimate object used by a speaker as a presentation aid.

propaganda Information represented in such a way as to provoke a desired response.

proposal presentation A type of business or professional presentation in which the speaker provides information needed for decisions related to modifying or adopting a product, procedure, or policy.

prototype A model of a design.

public discourse Open conversation or discussion in a public forum.

public domain Bodies of work, including publications and processes, available for public use without permission; not protected by *copyright* or patent.

public forum Any space (physical or virtual) in which people gather to voice their ideas about public issues.

public speaking A type of communication in which a speaker delivers a message with a specific purpose to an audience of people who are present during the delivery of the speech. Public speaking always includes a speaker who has a reason for speaking, an audience that gives the speaker its attention, and a message that is meant to accomplish a purpose.

public-speaking anxiety Fear or anxiety associated with a speaker's actual or anticipated communication to an audience.

qualitative research Research in which the emphasis is placed on observing, describing, and interpreting behavior.

quantitative research Research in which the emphasis is placed on statistical measurement.

questionnaire A written survey designed to gather information from a pool of respondents.

reasoning Logical explanation of a claim by linking it to evidence. See also *warrant.*

receiver The recipient of a source's message; may be an individual or a group of people.

reckless disregard for the truth A quality of defamatory speech that is legally liable. See also *defamatory speech.*

reference librarian A librarian trained to help library users locate information resources.

refutation organizational pattern A pattern of organizing speech points in which each main point addresses and then refutes (disproves) an opposing claim to a speaker's position.

request for funding presentation A type of oral presentation providing evidence that a project, proposal, or design idea is worth funding; frequently delivered in technical fields such as engineering, computer science, and architecture.

research presentation An oral presentation describing original research undertaken by the speaker, either alone or as part of a team; it is frequently delivered in the fields of science and social science.

respect To feel or show deferential regard. For the ethical speaker, respect ranges from addressing audience members as unique human beings to refraining from rudeness and other forms of personal attack.

responsibility A charge, trust, or duty for which one is accountable.

restate-forecast form A type of transition in which the speaker restates the point just covered and previews the point to be covered next.

review of academic article A type of oral presentation in which the speaker reports on an article or study published in an academic journal.

review of the literature presentation A type of oral presentation in which the speaker reviews the body of research related to a given topic or issue and offers conclusions about the topic based on this research; frequently delivered in social scientific fields.

rhetoric A term with multiple meanings, all of which relate to aspects of human communication and encompass the art of public speaking.

rhetorical device A technique of language to achieve a desired effect.

rhetorical question A question that does not invite actual responses, but is used to make the listener or the audience think.

rhetorical situation The circumstances that call for a public response; in broadest terms, consideration of the audience, occasion, and overall speech situation when planning a speech.

roast A humorous tribute to a person; one in which a series of speakers jokingly poke fun at the individual being honored.

roman numeral outline An outline format in which main points are enumerated with roman numerals (I, II, III); supporting points with capital letters (A, B, C); third-level points with Arabic numerals (1, 2, 3); and fourth-level points with lowercase letters (a, b, c).

rules of engagement Standard of conduct for communicating with others in the public arena.

sales presentation A type of oral presentation that attempts to lead a potential buyer to purchase a service or product described by the presenter.

sans serif typeface A typeface that is blocklike and linear and is designed without tiny strokes or flourishes at the top and bottom of each letter.

scale question A closed-ended question that measures the respondent's level of agreement or disagreement with specific issues.

scanning A technique for creating eye contact with audiences; the speaker moves his or her gaze across an audience from one listener to another and from one section to another, pausing to gaze briefly at each individual.

secondary research Published facts and statistics, texts, documents, and any other information not originally collected and generated by the researcher. See also *primary research.*

selective perception A psychological principle that posits that listeners pay attention selectively to certain messages and ignore others.

sentence outline An outline in which each main and supporting point is stated in sentence form and in precisely the way the speaker wants to express the idea; generally used for working outlines.

serif typeface A typeface that includes small flourishes, or strokes, at the top and bottom of each letter.

shared meaning The mutual understanding of a message between speaker and audience. Shared meaning occurs in varying degrees. The lowest level of shared meaning exists when the speaker has merely caught the audience's attention. As the message develops, depending on the encoding choices by the source, a higher degree of shared meaning is possible.

shift report Oral report by a health-care worker that concisely relays patient status and needs to incoming caregivers.

signposts Conjunctions or phrases (such as "next," "in the first case," etc.) that indicate *transitions* between supporting points.

simile A figure of speech used to compare one thing with another by using the words "like" or "as" (e.g., "He works like a dog"). See also *imagery.*

slippery slope A logical fallacy in which one instance of an event is offered as leading to a series of events or actions. See also *logical fallacy.*

small group A collection of between three and twenty people.

small group communication Communication involving a small number of people who can see and speak directly with one another, as in a business meeting.

social news site(s) Web sites dedicated to specific kinds of news or entertainment (e.g., Digg, Daytripper, Campus Reader).

socioeconomic status (SES) A demographic variable that includes income, occupation, and education.

source The person who creates a message, also called a *sender.* The speaker transforms ideas and thoughts into messages and sends them to a receiver, or an audience.

source qualifier A brief description of the source's qualifications.

source reliability The qualities that determine the value of a source, such as the author's background and reputation, the reputation of a publication, the source of data, and how recent the reference is.

spatial pattern of arrangement A pattern of organizing main points in order of their physical proximity or direction relative to each other; used when the purpose of a speech is to describe or explain the physical arrangement of a place, a scene, or an object.

speaker credibility The quality that reveals that a speaker has a good grasp of the subject, displays sound reasoning skills, is honest and nonmanipulative, and is genuinely interested in the welfare of audience members; a modern version of *ethos.*

speaking extemporaneously A type of delivery that falls somewhere between impromptu and written or memorized deliveries. Speakers delivering an extemporaneous speech prepare well and practice in advance, giving full attention to all facets of the speech—content, arrangement, and delivery alike. Instead of memorizing or writing the speech word for word, they speak from an outline of key words and phrases.

speaking from manuscript A type of delivery in which the speaker reads the speech verbatim—that is, from prepared written text that contains the entire speech, word for word.

speaking from memory A type of delivery in which the speaker puts the entire speech, word for word, into writing and then commits it to memory.

speaking impromptu A type of delivery that is unpracticed, spontaneous, or improvised.

speaking outline A delivery outline to be used when practicing and actually presenting a speech.

speaking rate The pace at which a speech is delivered. The typical public speech occurs at a rate slightly less than 120 words per minute.

specialized search engine A search engine that searches for information only on specific topics. Also called *vertical search engine* or *vortal*.

special occasion speech A speech whose general purpose is to entertain, celebrate, commemorate, inspire, or set a social agenda.

specific speech purpose A refined statement of purpose that zeroes in more closely than the general purpose on the goal of the speech. See also *general speech purpose*.

speech of acceptance A speech made in response to receiving an award. Its purpose is to express gratitude for the honor bestowed on the speaker.

speech of inspiration A speech whose purpose is to inspire or motivate the audience to consider positively, reflect on, and sometimes even to act on the speaker's words.

speech of introduction A short speech whose purpose is defined by two goals: to prepare or "warm up" audience members for the speaker and to motivate them to listen to what the speaker has to say.

speech of presentation A speech whose purpose is twofold: to communicate the meaning of the award and to explain why the recipient is receiving it.

staff report A report that informs managers and other employees of new developments relating to personnel that affect them and their work.

statistics Quantified evidence; data that measure the size or magnitude of something, demonstrate trends, or show relationships with the purpose of summarizing information, demonstrating proof, and making points memorable.

story An account of events. See also *narrative*.

style The specific word choice, sentence structure, and rhetorical devices (techniques of language) that speakers use to express their ideas.

subject (Web) directory A searchable database of Web sites organized by categories (e.g., Yahoo! Directory).

subordinate points Ideas subordinate to others that are given relatively less weight. In an outline, they are indicated by their indentation below the more important points.

summary Part of a conclusion to a speech; a restatement of points covered.

supporting material Examples, narratives, testimony, facts, and statistics that support the speech thesis and form the speech.

supporting points Information (examples, narratives, testimony, and facts and statistics) that clarifies, elaborates, and verifies the speaker's assertions.

symposium A formal meeting at which several speakers deliver short speeches on the same topic.

table A systematic grouping of data or numerical information in column form.

talking head A speaker who remains static, standing stiffly behind a podium, and so resembles a televised shot of a speaker's head and shoulders.

target audience Those individuals within the broader audience who are most likely to be influenced in the direction the speaker seeks.

task roles Types of roles that directly relate to the accomplishment of the objectives and missions of a group. Examples include "Recording secretary" and "Moderator."

team debate format A debate in which a team of two or more people opposes a second team, with each person having a speaking role.

team presentation A type of oral presentation prepared and delivered by a group of three or more people.

testimony Firsthand findings, eyewitness accounts, and opinions by people, both lay (nonexpert) and expert.

thesis statement The theme, or central idea, of a speech that serves to connect all the parts of the speech in a single line. The main points, supporting material, and conclusion all relate to the thesis.

toast A brief tribute to a person or an event being celebrated.

topical pattern of arrangement A pattern of organizing main points as subtopics or categories of the speech topic.

topic mapping A brainstorming technique in which words are laid out in diagram form to show categorical relationships among them; useful for selecting and narrowing a speech topic.

transitions Words, phrases, or sentences that tie speech ideas together and enable a speaker to move smoothly from one point to the next.

trustworthiness The quality of displaying both honesty and dependability.

typeface A specific style of lettering, such as Arial, Times Roman, or Courier. Typefaces come in a variety of fonts, or sets of sizes (called the "point size"), and upper and lower cases.

values Our most enduring judgments about what is good and bad in life, as shaped by our culture and our unique experiences within it.

videoconferencing Synchronized visual and audio communication between two or more remote locations.

virtual library A collection of library holdings available online.

visualization An exercise for building confidence in which the speaker, while preparing for the speech, closes his or her eyes and envisions a series of positive feelings and reactions that will occur on the day of the speech.

vocal fillers Unnecessary and undesirable sounds or words used by a speaker to cover pauses in a speech or conversation. Examples include "uh," "hmm," "you know," "I mean," and "it's like."

vocal variety The variation of volume, pitch, rate, and pauses to create an effective delivery.

voice A feature of verbs in written and spoken text that indicates the subject's relationship to the action; verbs can be either active or passive.

volume The relative loudness of a speaker's voice while giving a speech.

voluntary audience As opposed to a captive audience, an audience whose members have chosen to attend.

warrant The link between a claim and evidence. See also *reasoning*.

word association A brainstorming technique in which one writes down ideas as they come to mind, beginning with a single word.

working bibliography A running list of speech sources with relevant citation information; used to create a final bibliography or reference list for a speech.

working outline A preparation or rough outline using full sentences in which the speaker firms up and organizes main points and develops supporting points to substantiate them.

Notes

CHAPTER 1

1. Vickie K. Sullivan, "Public Speaking: The Secret Weapon in Career Development," *USA Today*, 133 (May 2005): 24.

2. Ronald Alsop, "Poor Writing Skills Top M.B.A. Recruiter Gripes," *The Wall Street Journal* (January 17, 2006).

3. D. Uchida, M. J. Cetron, and F. McKenzie, "What Students Must Know to Succeed in the 21st Century," special report (World Future Society) based on "Preparing Students for the 21st Century," a report on a project by the American Association of School Administrators, 1996.

4. For a discussion of Daniel Yankelovich's three-step process by which public judgments occur, see Yankelovich, *Coming to Public Judgment*.

5. W. Barnett Pearce, "Toward a National Conversation About Public Issues," in *The Changing Conversation in America: Lectures from the Smithsonian*. ed. William F. Eadie and Paul E. Nelson (Thousand Oaks, CA: Sage, 2002) 16.

6. Robert Perrin, "The Speaking-Writing Connection: Enhancing the Symbiotic Relationship," *Contemporary Education* 65 (1994): 2.

7. William Avram, "Public Speaking," *Compton's Online Encyclopedia*. Retrieved June 10, 2000, from www.comptons.com/encyclopedia/.

8. Lloyd F. Bitzer, "The Rhetorical Situation," *Philosophy and Rhetoric* (Winter 1968): 1–14.

CHAPTER 3

1. James C. McCroskey, "Classroom Consequences of Communication Anxiety," *Communication Education* 26 (1977): 27–33; James C. McCroskey, "Oral Communication Apprehension: A Reconceptualization," in *Communication Yearbook* 6, ed. M. Burgoon (Beverly Hills: Sage, 1982), 136–70; Virginia P. Richmond and James C. McCroskey, *Communication Apprehension, Avoidance, and Effectiveness*, 5th ed. (Boston: Allyn & Bacon, 1998).

2. Adapted from James C. McCroskey, "Oral Communication Apprehension: A Summary of Recent Theory and Research," *Human Communication Research* 4 (1977): 79–96.

3. Ibid.

4. David-Paul Pertaub, Mel Slater, and Chris Barker, "An Experiment on Public Speaking Anxiety in Response to Three Different Types of Virtual Audience," *Presence: Teleoperators and Virtual Environments* 11 (2002): 678–80.

5. Joe Ayres, "Coping with Speech Anxiety: The Power of Positive Thinking," *Communication Education* 37 (1988): 289–96; Joe Ayres, "An Examination of the Impact of Anticipated Communication and Communication Apprehension on Negative Thinking, Task-Relevant Thinking, and Recall," *Communication Research Reports* 9 (1992): 3–11.

6. S. Hu and Joung-Min Romans-Kroll, "Effects of Positive Attitude toward Giving a Speech on the Cardiovascular and Subjective Fear Responses during Speech in Speech Anxious Subjects," *Perceptual and*

Motor Skills 81, no. 2 (1995): 609–10; S. Hu, T. R. Bostow, D. A. Lipman, S. K. Bell, and S. Klein, "Positive Thinking Reduces Heart Rate and Fear Responses to Speech-Phobic Imagery," *Perceptual and Motor Skills* 75, no. 3, pt. 2 (1992): 1067–76.

7. M. T. Motley, "Public Speaking Anxiety Qua Performance Anxiety: A Revised Model and Alternative Therapy," *Journal of Social Behavior and Personality* 5 (1990): 85–104.

8. Joe Ayres, C. S. Hsu, and Tim Hopf, "Does Exposure to Performance Visualization Alter Speech Preparation Processes?" *Communication Research Reports* 17 (2000): 366–74.

9. Joe Ayres and Tim S. Hopf, "Visualization: Is It More than Extra-Attention?" *Communication Education* 38 (1989): 1–5.

10. Herbert Benson and Miriam Z. Klipper, *The Relaxation Response* (New York: HarperCollins, 2000).

11. Laurie Schloff and Marcia Yudkin, *Smart Speaking* (New York: Plume, 1991), 91–92.

12. Lars-Gunnar Lundh, Britta Berg, Helena Johansson, Linda Kjellén Nilsson, Jenny Sandberg, and Anna Segerstedt, "Social Anxiety is Associated with a Negatively Distorted Perception of One's Own Voice," *Cognitive Behavior Therapy* 31 (2002): 25–30.

CHAPTER 4

1. *The Compact Edition of the Oxford English Dictionary*, 1971 ed., 2514.

2. Cited in Edward P. J. Corbett, *Classical Rhetoric for the Modern Student* (New York: Oxford University Press, 1990).

3. Rebecca Rimel, "Policy and the Partisan Divide: The Price of Gridlock," speech given at the Commonwealth Club in San Francisco, November, 2004. Retrieved May 10, 2007 from the Pew Charitable Trusts Web site, www.pewtrusts.org

4. Susan Grogan Faller, Steven E. Gillen, and Maureen P. Haney, "Rights Clearance and Permissions Guidelines," paper prepared by law firm of Greenebaum Doll & McDonald, Cincinnati, Ohio, 2002.

5. W. Barnett Pearce, "Toward a National Conversation About Public Issues," in William F. Eadie and Paul E. Nelson, eds., *The Changing Conversation in America: Lectures from the Smithsonian* (Thousand Oaks, CA: Sage, 2002), 16.

6. W. Gudykunst, S. Ting-Toomey, S. Suweeks, and L. Stewart, *Building Bridges: Interpersonal Skills for a Changing World* (Boston: Houghton Mifflin, 1995), 92.

7. Ibid.

8. Michael Josephson, personal interview, May 10, 1996.

9. Ibid.

10. Rebecca Moore Howard, "A Plagiarism Pentimento," *Journal of Teaching Writing* 11 (1993): 233.

11. Skyscraper Museum Web site. Retrieved June 26, 2002, from www.skyscraper.org.

12. "How to Recognize Plagiarism," Indiana University Bloomington School of Education Web site. Retrieved June 16, 2002, from www.indiana.edu/.

13. United States Copyright Office Web site on copyright at www.copyright.gov, including works classified as literary, musical, dramatic,

choreographic, pictorial, graphic, sculptural, audiovisual, sound recording, and architectural.

14. Steven E. Gillen, "Rights Clearance and Permissions Guidelines," paper prepared by the law firm Greenebaum Doll & McDonald, Cincinnati, Ohio, 2002.

15. United States Copyright Office Web site on copyright, section on Fair Use. Retrieved February 19, 2005, from www.copyright.gov/fls/fl102.html.

CHAPTER 5

1. Kathy Thompson, Pamela Leintz, Barbara Nevers, and Susan Witkowski, "The Integrative Listening Model: An Approach to Teaching and Learning Listening," *Journal of General Education* 53 (2004): 225–46.

2. Andrew Wolvin and C. Coakley, *Listening,* 4th ed. (Dubuque, IA: Wm. C. Brown, 1992), 28.

3. M. Burley-Allen, *Listening: The Forgotten Skill: A Self-teaching Guide* (New York: Wiley, 1995). M. G. Eskaros, "Fine-tune your listening skills," *Hydrocarbon Processing* 83 (2004).

4. H. E. Chambers, *Effective Communication Skills for Scientific and Technical Professionals* (Cambridge, MA: Perseus Publishing, 2001).

5. Philip Vassallo, "Dialogue: Speaking to Listen: Listening to Speak," *ETC* (Fall 2000): 306–13.

6. S. Golen, "A Factor Analysis of Barriers to Effective Listening," *Journal of Business Communication* 27 (1990): 25–36.

7. Thanks to Barry Antokoletz of New York City College of Technology for suggesting the inclusion of these strategies.

8. Thomas E. Anastasi Jr., *Listen! Techniques for Improving Communication Skills,* CBI series in Management Communication (Boston: CBI Publishing, 1982), 35.

9. Ibid.

10. "Listening Factoids." Retrieved March 28, 2006, from www.listen.org/Templates/factoids.htm; Thomas E. Anastasi Jr., *Listen! Techniques for Improving Communication* (Boston: CBI Publishing, 1982), 35.

CHAPTER 6

1. James C. McCroskey, Virginia P. Richmond, and Robert A. Stewart, *One on One: The Foundations of Interpersonal Communication* (Englewood Cliffs, NJ: Prentice Hall, 1986).

2. Daniel O'Keefe notes that although attitudes and behavior are "generally consistent," there are "a large number of possible moderating variables," including the relative demands of the behavior, whether there is a vested position, and others. Daniel J. O'Keefe, *Persuasion: Theory & Research,* 2nd ed. (Thousand Oaks, CA: Sage, 2002), 17.

3. Ibid.

4. "Crafting a Communications Project." Biodiversity Project, March 2003. Retrieved July 10, 2007, from www.biodiversityproject.org/EF%20Kit/EFCraftingcommunication.

5. James C. McCroskey et al., *One-on-One: The Foundation of Interpersonal Communication* (Englewood Cliffs, NJ: Prentice Hall, 1986), 76.

6. Herbert Simon, *Persuasion in Society* (Thousand Oaks, CA: Sage, 2001), 385–87.

7. Kenneth Burke, *A Rhetoric of Motives* (Berkeley, CA: University of California Press, 1969).

8. Nick Morgan, *Working the Room: How to Move People to Action through Audience-Centered Speaking* (Cambridge, MA: Harvard Business School Press, 2003).

9. J. G. Melton, *Encyclopedia of American Religions*, 7th ed. (Detroit: Gale Research, 1999).

10. Daniel Canary and K. Dindia, eds., *Sex Differences and Similarities in Communication* (Mahwah, NJ: Lawrence Erlbaum, 1998).

11. "Facts for Features," Newsroom, U.S. Census Bureau Web site, May 29, 2007. Retrieved June 5, 2007, from www.census.gov/Press-Release/www/releases/archives/facts_for_features_special_editions/010102.html.

12. Ibid.

13. "Foreign-Born Population by Sex, Age, and World Region of Birth: 2003," Foreign-Born Population of the United States American Community Survey–2003 Special Tabulation (ACS-T-2), Table 3.1a. Retrieved June 5, 2007, from U.S. Census Bureau Web site, www.census.gov/population/www/socdemo/foreign/acst2.html.

14. Richard D. Lewis, *When Cultures Collide: Leading across Cultures*, 3rd ed. (Boston: Intercultural Press-Nicholas Brealey International, 2005), 27.

15. E. D. Steele and W. C. Redding, "The American Value System: Premises for Persuasion," *Western Speech* 26 (1962): 83–91; Robin M. Williams Jr., *American Society: A Sociological Interpretation*, 3rd ed. (New York: Alfred A. Knopf, 1970).

16. Inter-University Consortium for Political and Social Research, World Values Survey, 1981–1984 and 1990–1993 (Irvine CA: Social Science Data Archives, University Libraries, University of California, 1997).

17. Rushworth M. Kidder, *Shared Values for a Troubled World: Conversations with Men and Women of Conscience* (San Francisco: Jossey-Bass, 1994).

CHAPTER 8

1. Richard F. Corlin, "The Coming Golden Age of Medicine," *Vital Speeches of the Day* 68, no. 18 (2002).

2. Risa Lavizzo-Mourey, "Childhood Obesity: The Killer Threat Within," *Vital Speeches of the Day* 70, no. 13 (2004): 396–400.

3. Quoted in K. Q. Seelye, "Congressman Offers Bill to Ban Cloning of Humans," *New York Times*, March 6, 1997, sec. A:3.

4. Mark Turner, *The Literary Mind* (New York: Oxford University Press, 1996).

5. Barack Obama, "The Great Need of the Hour," Atlanta, GA, January 20, 2008. Accessed on October 23, 2008 from www.barackobama.com/2008/01/20/remarks_of_senator_barack_obam_40.php

6. Earle Gray, "Want to be a Leader? Start Telling Stories," *Canadian Speeches* 16, no. 6 (2003): 75(2).

7. Testimony of Derek P. Ellerman to Subcommittee on Human Rights and Wellness, Committee on Government Reform, United States House of Representatives, July 8, 2004 (Polaris Project). Retrieved Mar. 15, 2005, from www.polarisproject.org/polarisproject/news_p3/DPETestimony_p3.htm.

8. Rodney Reynolds and Michael Burgoon, "Evidence," in *The Persuasion Handbook: Developments in Theory and Practice*, ed. J. P. Dillard and M. Pfau (Thousand Oaks, CA: Sage, 2002), 427–44.

9. J. C. Reinard, "The Empirical Study of the Persuasive Effects of Evidence: The Status After Fifty Years of Research," *Human Communication Research* 15 (1988): 3–59.

10. Steve Jobs, Worldwide Developers Conference (WWDC) Keynote Address, June 11, 2007, at San Francisco's Moscone West. Retrieved from http://www.apple.com/quicktime/qtv/mwsf07/.

11. U.S. Census Bureau American Factfinder, Profile of General Demographic Characteristics 2000, Geographic Area Colorado, factfinder .census.gov/servlet/QTTable?_bm=n&_lang=en&qr_name=DEC_2000 _SF1_U_DP1&ds_name=DEC_2000_SF1_U&geo_id=04000US08.

12. Sara Kehaulani Goo, "Airbus Hopes Big Plane Will Take Off, Beat Boeing." *Washington Post*, Sunday, December 19, 2004. Retrieved May 13, 2005, from www.washingtonpost.com/wp-dyn/articles/A9900-2004Dec18 .html.

13. Centers for Disease Control and Prevention, "Births to Youngest Teens at Lowest Levels in Almost 60 Years." Retrieved May 13, 2005, from www.cdc.gov/od/oc/media/pressrel/r041115.htm.

14. Bureau of Transportation Statistics, "Airlines On-Time Performance in April Better Than March but Slips from Previous Year," June 4, 2007. Retrieved June 4, 2007, from www.bts.gov/press_releases/2007/ dot055_07/html/dot055_07.html.

15. Center on Budget and Policy Priorities Web site, "Behind the Numbers: An Examination of the Tax Foundation's Tax Day Report," April 14th, 1997. Retrieved June 7, 2005, from www.cbpp.org/taxday .htm.

16. Roger Pielke Jr., "The Cherry Pick," *Ogmius: Newsletter for the Center for Science and Technology Research* 8 (May 2004). Retrieved May 24, 2005 from http://sciencepolicy.colorado.edu/ogmius/archives/ issue_8/index.html.

CHAPTER 9

1. Robert G. Torricelli, *Quotations for Public Speakers: A Historical, Literary, and Political Anthology* (New Brunswick, NJ: Rutgers University Press, 2002).

2. Robert J. Morgan, *Nelson's Complete Book of Stories, Illustrations, and Quotes: The Ultimate Contemporary Resource for Speakers* (Nashville: Thomas Nelson, 2000).

CHAPTER 10

1. Susan Gilroy, "The Web in Context: Virtual Library or Virtual Chaos?" Lamont Library of the Harvard College Library Web site. Retrieved May 5, 2005, from hcl.harvard.edu/lamont/resources/guides/.

2. Elizabeth Kirk, "Evaluating Information Found on the Internet" (The Sheridan Libraries of the Johns Hopkins University), last modified February 12, 2002. Retrieved May 4, 2005, from www.library.jhu.edu/ researchhelp/general/evaluating/index.html.

3. See, for instance, recommendations made by librarians at University of California Berkeley Teaching Library Internet Workshops, www.lib.berkeley.edu/TeachingLib/Guides/Internet/MetaSearch.html (accessed May 10, 2005).

4. Jorgen J. Wouters, "Searching for Disclosure: How Search Engines Alert Consumers to the Presence of Advertising in Search Results," *Consumer Reports WebWatch*, November 8, 2004. Retrieved May 7, 2005, from www.consumerwebwatch.org/dynamic/search-report-disclosureabstract.cfm.

CHAPTER 11

1. Ralph Underwager and Hollida Wakefield, "The Taint Hearing," *IPT* 10 (1998). Originally presented at the 13th Annual Symposium in Forensic Psychology, Vancouver, BC (April 17, 1997). Retrieved September 1, 2007, from www.ipt-forensics.com/journal/volume10/j10_7.htm#en0.

2. Institute for Writing and Rhetoric, "Sources and Citation at Dartmouth College," May 2008, produced by The Committee on Sources, www.dartmouth.edu/~writing/sources/sources-citation.html.

CHAPTER 12

1. Gordon H. Bower, "Organizational Factors in Memory," *Cognitive Psychology* 1 (1970): 18–46.

2. E. Thompson, "An Experimental Investigation of the Relative Effectiveness of Organization Structure in Oral Communication," *Southern Speech Journal* 26 (1960): 59–69.

3. R. G. Smith, "Effects of Speech Organization upon Attitudes of College Students," *Speech Monographs* 18 (1951): 292–301.

4. H. Sharp Jr. and T. McClung, "Effects of Organization on the Speaker's Ethos," *Speech Monographs* 33 (1966): 182ff.

CHAPTER 13

1. PBS, "Life on the Internet Timeline," www.pbs.org/internet/timeline/index.html.

2. Anita Taylor, "Tales of the Grandmothers: Women and Work." *Vital Speeches of the Day* 71, no. 7 (2005): 209–12.

3. Sonja K. Foss and Karen A. Foss, *Inviting Transformation: Presentational Speaking for a Changing World* (Prospect Heights, IL: Waveland Press, 1994).

CHAPTER 14

1. Mark B. McClellan, speech presented at the fifth annual David A. Winston lecture, Washington, DC, October 20, 2003. Retrieved August 14, 2005, from www.fda.gov/oc/speeches/2003/winston1020.html.

CHAPTER 15

1. Ron Hoff, *I Can See You Naked*, rev. ed. (Kansas City: Andrews McMeel, 1992), 41.

2. William Safire, *Lend Me Your Ears: Great Speeches in History* (New York: W.W. Norton, 1992), 676.

3. Bas Andeweg and Jap de Jong, "May I Have Your Attention? Exordial Techniques in Informative Oral Presentations," *Technical Communication Quarterly* 7, no. 3 (Summer 1998): 271–84.

4. W. Lee, "Communication about Humor as Procedural Competence in Intercultural Encounters," in *Intercultural Communication: A Reader,* 7th ed., ed. L. A. Samovar and R. E. Porter (Belmont, CA: Wadsworth, 1994), 373.

5. Kenneth Burke, *A Rhetoric of Motives* (Berkeley: University of California Press, 1950).

6. Marvin Runyon, "No One Moves the Mail like the U.S. Postal Service," *Vital Speeches of the Day* 61, no. 2 (November 1, 1994): 52–55.

7. Robert L. Darbelnet, "U.S. Roads and Bridges," *Vital Speeches of the Day* 63, no. 12 (April 1, 1997): 379.

8. Andeweg and de Jong, 271.

9. Holger Kluge, "Reflections on Diversity," *Vital Speeches of the Day* 63, no. 6 (January 1, 1997): 171–72.

10. Elpidio Villarreal, "Choosing the Right Path," speech delivered to the Puerto Rican Legal Defense and Education Fund Gala in New York City, October 26, 2006, *Vital Speeches of the Day* 72, no. 26 (2007): 784–86.

11. Hillary Rodham Clinton, "Women's Rights Are Human Rights," speech delivered to the United Nations Fourth World Conference on Women, Beijing, China, September 5, 1995.

CHAPTER 16

1. Robert Harris, "A Handbook of Rhetorical Devices," July 26, 2002, *Virtual Salt* Web site. Retrieved August 5, 2002, from www.virtualsalt.com/rhetoric.htm.

2. Peggy Noonan, *Simply Speaking: How to Communicate Your Ideas with Style, Substance, and Clarity* (New York: Regan Books, 1998), 51.

3. Dan Hooley, "The Lessons of the Ring," *Vital Speeches of the Day* 70, no. 20 (2004): 660–63.

4. James E. Lukaszewski, "You Can Become A Verbal Visionary," speech delivered to the Public Relations Society of America, Cleveland, Ohio, April 8, 1997. Executive Speaker Library, www.executive-speaker.com/lib_moti.html.

5. Joseph Biden's Vice-Presidential Acceptance Speech, Aug. 28, 2008, www.cnn.com/2008/POLITICS/08/27/biden.transcript/

6. Loren J. Naidoo and Robert G. Lord, "Speech imagery and perceptions of charisma: The mediating role of positive affect. *The Leadership Quarterly* 19:3 (2008): 283–96.

7. Ibid, phrase taken from President Franklin Delano Roosevelt's 1933 inaugural address.

8. Andrea Lunsford and Robert Connors, *The St. Martin's Handbook,* 3rd ed. (New York: St. Martin's Press, 1995), 101.

9. L. Clemetson and J. Gordon-Thomas, "Our House Is on Fire," *Newsweek* 137 (June 11, 2001), 50.

10. Andrew C. Billings, "Beyond the Ebonics Debate: Attitudes About Black and Standard American English," *Journal of Black Studies,* 36 (2005): 68–81.

11. Sylvie Dubois, "Sounding Cajun: The Rhetorical Use of Dialect in Speech and Writing," *American Speech* 77, no. 3 (2002): 264–87.

12. Quoted in Alsion Mitchell, "State of the Speech: Reading Between the Lines," *New York Times,* February 2, 1997, E5.

13. *The Concise Oxford Dictionary of Linguistics* (Oxford University Press, 1997).

14. Remarks of President-Elect Barack Obama: Election Night Chicago, IL, November 4, 2008 www.barackobama.com/2008/11/04/remarks_of_presidentelect_bara.php

15. Cited in William Safire, *Lend Me Your Ears: Great Speeches in History* (New York: W.W. Norton, 1992), 22.

16. Lunsford and Connors, *St. Martin's Handbook,* 345.

CHAPTER 17

1. James C. McCroskey, *An Introduction to Rhetorical Communication,* 8th ed. (Englewood Cliffs, NJ: Prentice Hall, 2001), 273.

2. Robbin Crabtree and Robert Weissberg, *ESL Students in the Public Speaking Classroom: A Guide for Teachers* (Boston: Bedford/St.Martin's, 2000), 24.

CHAPTER 18

1. Susan Berkley, "Microphone Tips." *Great Speaking* ezine 4, no. 7 (2002). Retrieved September 1, 2002, from the Great Speaking Web site www.antion.com.

2. Kyle James Tusing and James Price Dillard, "The Sounds of Dominance: Vocal Precursors of Perceived Dominance during Interpersonal Influence," *Human Communication Research* 26 (2000): 148–71.

3. Walt Wolfram, "Everyone Has an Accent," *Teaching Tolerance Magazine,* Fall 2000, 18. Retrieved April 16, 2006 from www.tolerance.org/teach/magazine/features.jsp?p=0&is=17&ar=186.

CHAPTER 19

1. Reid Buckley, *Strictly Speaking: Reid Buckley's Indispensable Handbook on Public Speaking* (New York: McGraw-Hill, 1999), 204.

2. Achim Nowak, *Power Speaking: The Art of the Exceptional Public Speaker* (New York: Allworth Communications, 2004).

3. Buckley, *Strictly Speaking,* 209.

4. J. P. Davidson, "Shaping an Image That Boosts Your Career," *Marketing Communications* 13 (1988): 55–56.

5. Albert Mehrabian, *Silent Messages* (Belmont, CA: Wadsworth, 1981); Mike Allen, Paul L. Witt, and Lawrence R. Wheeless, "The Role of Teacher Immediacy as a Motivational Factor in Student Learning: Using Meta-Analysis to Test a Causal Model," *Communication Education* 55, no. 6 (2006): 21–31.

CHAPTER 20

1. Richard E. Mayer, *Multimedia Learning* (Cambridge University Press, 2001); Edward R. Tufte, *Visual Explanations: Images and Quantities, Evidence and Narrative* (Cheshire, CT: Graphics Press, 1997).

2. Mayer, *Multimedia Learning.*

3. Mayer, *Multimedia Learning.*

4. Adapted from "Using Overhead Transparencies" by Lenny Laskowski. Retrieved May 5, 2006, from www.ljlseminars.com/transp.htm; and "Using Overhead Projectors," by Media Services, Robert A. L. Mortvedt Library, Pacific Lutheran University. Retrieved May 5, 2006, from www.plu.edu/~libr/workshops/multimedia/overhead.html.

CHAPTER 21

1. Edward Tufte, "PowerPoint is Evil," *Wired* 11 (2003). Retrieved May 10, 2006, from www.wired.com/wired/archive/11.09/ppt2_pr.html.

2. Julie Terberg, "Font Choices Play a Crucial Role in Presentation Design," *Presentations Magazine*, April 2005. Retrieved May 8, 2006, from www.presentations.com/presentations/creation/article_display.jsp?vnu_content_id=1000875169.

3. Ibid.

4. Cheryl Currid, *Make Your Point: The Complete Guide to Successful Business Presentations Using Today's Technology* (Rocklin, CA: Prima Publishing, 1995).

CHAPTER 23

1. With thanks to Barry Antokoletz, NYC College of Technology, for these comments.

2. Vickie K. Sullivan, "Public Speaking: The Secret Weapon In Career Development," *USA Today*, May 2005 133 no. 2720, p. 24(2).

3. Howard K. Battles and Charles Packard, *Words and Sentences*, bk. 6 (Lexington, MA: Ginn & Company, 1984), 459.

4. Katherine E. Rowan, "A New Pedagogy for Explanatory Public Speaking: Why Arrangement Should Not Substitute for Invention," *Communication Education* 44 (1995): 236–50.

5. Ibid.

6. S. Kujawa and L. Huske, *The Strategic Teaching and Reading Project Guidebook*, rev. ed. (Oak Brook, IL: North Central Regional Educational Laboratory, 1995).

7. Shawn M. Glynn et al., "Teaching Science with Analogies: A Resource for Teachers and Textbook Authors," National Reading Research Center, Instructional Resource no. 7, Fall 1994, 19.

8. Tina A. Grotzer, "How Conceptual Leaps in Understanding the Nature of Causality Can Limit Learning: An Example from Electrical Circuits," paper presented at the annual conference of the American Educational Research Association, New Orleans, LA, April 2000. Retrieved June 17, 2005, from the Project Zero Web site, Harvard University Graduate School of Education, pzweb.harvard.edu/Research/UnderCon.htm.

9. Neil D. Fleming and C. Mills, "Helping Students Understand How They Learn," *Teaching Professor* 7, no. 4 (1992).

10. E. Thompson, "An Experimental Investigation of the Relative Effectiveness of Organization Structure in Oral Communication," *Southern Speech Journal* 26 (1966): 59–69.

CHAPTER 24

1. Richard E. Petty and John T. Cacioppo, *Communication and Persuasion: Central and Peripheral Routes to Attitude Change* (New York: Springer-Verlag, 1986).

2. Kathleen Reardon, *Persuasion in Practice* (Newbury Park, CA: Sage Publications, 1991), 210.

3. Russel H. Fazio, "How Do Attitudes Guide Behavior?" in *The Handbook of Motivation and Cognition: Foundations of Social Behavior*, ed. Richard M. Sorrentino and E. Tory Higgins (New York: Guilford, 1986).

4. Elpidio Villarreal, "Choosing the Right Path," speech delivered to the Puerto Rican Legal Defense and Education Fund Gala in New York

City, October 26, 2006, *Vital Speeches of the Day* 72, no. 26 (2007): 784–86.

5. Kim Witte and Mike Allen, "A Meta-analysis of Fear Appeals: Implications for Effective Public Health Campaigns," *Health Education and Behavior* 27 (2000): 591–615.

6. Joseph R. Priester and Richard E. Petty, "Source Attributions and Persuasion: Perceived Honesty as a Determinant of Message Scrutiny," *Personality and Social Psychology Bulletin* 21 (1995): 637–54.

See also Kenneth G. DeBono and Richard J. Harnish, "Source Expertise, Source Attractiveness, and the Processing of Persuasive Information: A Functional Approach," *Journal of Personality and Social Psychology* 55 (1987): 541.

7. B. Soper, G. E. Milford, and G. T. Rosenthal, "Belief When Evidence Does Not Support the Theory," *Psychology and Marketing* 12 (1995): 415–22, cited in Stephen M. Kosslyn and Robin S. Rosenberg, *Psychology: The Brain, the Person, the World* (Boston, MA: Allyn & Bacon, 2004), 330.

8. Richard Petty and John T. Cacioppo, "The Elaboration Likelihood Model of Persuasion," in *Advances in Experimental Social Psychology* 19, ed. L. Berkowitz (San Diego: Academic Press, 1986), 123–205; Richard Petty and Duane T. Wegener, "Matching versus Mismatching Attitude Functions: Implications for Scrutiny of Persuasive Messages," *Personality and Social Psychology Bulletin* 24 (1998): 227–40.

9. Richard M. Perloff, *The Dynamics of Persuasion: Communication Attitudes in the 21st Century* (Mahwah, NJ: Lawrence Erlbaum, 2003), 137.

10. Dennis S. Gouran, "Attitude Change and Listeners' Understanding of a Persuasive Communication," *Speech Teacher* 15 (1966): 289–94; J. P. Dillard, "Persuasion Past and Present: Attitudes Aren't What They Used to Be," *Communication Monographs* 60 (1966): 94.

11. James C. McCroskey, *An Introduction to Rhetorical Communication*, 6th ed. (Englewood Cliffs, NJ: Prentice Hall, 1993).

12. Ibid.

13. Edward P. J. Corbett, *Classical Rhetoric for the Modern Student*, 3rd ed. (New York: Oxford University Press, 1990).

14. S. Morris Engel, *With Good Reason: An Introduction to Informal Fallacies*, 6th ed. (Boston: Bedford/St. Martin's, 2000), 191.

15. Jennifer Aaker and Durairaj Maheswaran, "The Impact of Cultural Orientation on Persuasion," *Journal of Consumer Research* 24 (December 1997): 315–28.

16. Jennifer L. Aaker, "Accessibilty or Diagnosticity? Disentangling the Influence of Culture on Persuasion Processes and Attitudes," *Journal of Consumer Research* 26 (March 2000): 340–57.

17. Kristine L. Fitch, "Cultural Persuadables," *Communication Theory* 13 (February 2003): 100–123.

18. Ibid.

19. Jennifer L. Aaker and Patti Williams, "Empathy versus Pride: The Influence of Emotional Appeals across Cultures," *Journal of Consumer Research* 25 (1998): 241–61.

20. Ibid.

21. Ibid.

22. Herbert Simon, *Persuasion in Society* (Thousand Oaks, CA: Sage Publications, 2001), 385–87.

23. Alan Monroe, *Principles and Types of Speeches* (Chicago: Scott, Foresman, 1935).

24. Ibid.

CHAPTER 25

1. Roger E. Axtell, *Do's and Taboos of Public Speaking: How to Get Those Butterflies Flying in Formation* (New York: Wiley, 1992), 150.

2. Ellen A. Kim, "How to Make a Memorable Oscar Speech," Feb. 27, 2005 MSNBC, at www.msnbc.msn.com/id/6983108/.

3. Transcript of Barack Obama's Comedy Roast at Al Smith Dinner in New York, Oct. 16, 2008, About.com: Political Humor Web site, at politicalhumor.about.com/od/barackobama/a/obama-al-smith.htm.

CHAPTER 26

1. For a review, see Priscilla S. Rogers, "Distinguishing Public and Presentational Speaking," *Management Communication Quarterly* 2 (1988): 102–15; Frank E. X. Dance, "What Do You Mean 'Presentational' Speaking?" *Management Communication Quarterly* 1 (1987): 270–81.

2. With continuing thanks to Michal Dale of Southwest Missouri State University's Department of Communication.

CHAPTER 27

1. Robert Anholt, *Dazzle 'Em with Style: The Art of Oral Scientific Presentation* (New York: W. H. Freeman and Company, 1994).

CHAPTER 28

1. Deanna P. Daniels, "Communicating across the Curriculum and in the Disciplines: Speaking in Engineering," *Communication Education* 51 (July 2002): 3.

2. Ibid.

3. Ibid.

4. Office of Naval Research Web site. "Tips for Preparing and Delivering Scientific Talks and Using Visual Aids." Retrieved January 1, 2001, from www.onr.navy.mil/onr/speak/.

5. Frederick Gilbert Associates. "Power-Speaking Tips." Retrieved August 30, 2000, from www.powerspeaking.com/powerspeaking/pstips.cfm.

CHAPTER 29

1. James M. Henslin, *Sociology: A Down-to-Earth Approach,* 5th ed. (Boston: Allyn & Bacon, 2001), 139.

2. William E. Thompson and James V. Hickey, *Society in Focus: An Introduction to Sociology,* 2nd ed. (New York: HarperCollins, 1966), 39.

CHAPTER 33

1. William L. Benoit, *Accounts, Excuses, and Apologies: A Theory of Image Restoration Strategies* (Albany: State University of New York Press, 1995).

2. Ibid.

3. Business for Social Responsibility Web site, "Business Ethics," copyright 2001–2002. Retrieved October 2, 2002, from www.bsr.org/BSRResources/WhitePaperDetail.conf.

CHAPTER 34

1. Lin Kroeger, *The Complete Idiot's Guide to Successful Business Presentations* (New York: Alpha Books, 1997), 113.

CHAPTER 35

1. H. Dan O'Hair, James S. O'Rourke, and Mary John O'Hair, *Business Communication: A Framework for Success* (Cincinnati: South-Western, 2001).

2. H. Dan O'Hair, Gustav Friedrich, and Lynda Dixon, *Strategic Communication for Business and the Professions,* 4th ed. (Boston: Houghton Mifflin, 2002).

3. K. D. Benne and P. Sheats, "Functional Roles of Group Members," *Journal of Social Issues* 4 (1948): 41–49.

4. Ibid.

5. M. Afzalur Rahim, *Managing Conflict in Organizations,* 3rd ed. (Westport, CT: Greenwood Publishing Group, 2001).

6. Dan O'Hair, Gustav Friedrich, John Wiemann, and Mary Wiemann, *Competent Communication,* 2nd ed. (New York: St. Martin's, 1997).

7. Geoffrey A. Cross, "Collective Form: An Exploration of Large-Group Writing," *Journal of Business Communication* 37 (2000): 77–101.

8. Irving Lester Janis, *Groupthink: Psychological Studies of Policy Decisions and Fiascoes* (Berkeley: University of California Press, 1982).

9. Ibid.

10. Victor H. Vroom and Philip Yetton, *Leadership and Decision Making* (Pittsburgh: University of Pittsburgh Press, 1973); C. Pavitt, "Theorizing about the Group Communication-Leadership Relationship: Input-Process-Output and Functional Models," in *Handbook of Group Communication Theory and Research,* ed. Lawrence R. Frey, Dennis S. Gouran, and Marshall Scott Poole (Thousand Oaks, CA: Sage, 1999), 313–34.

11. L. Richard Hoffman and Norman R. F. Maier, "Valence in the Adoption of Solutions by Problem-Solving Groups: Concept, Method, and Results," *Journal of Abnormal and Social Psychology* 69 (1964): 264–71.

12. John Dewey, *How We Think* (Boston: D. C. Heath Co., 1950).

APPENDIX B

1. Patricia Nelson (page revised Nov. 3, 1999). "Handling Questions and Answers." Toastmasters International, Edmonton and Area. Retrieved September 1, 2000, from www.ecn.ab.ca/toast/qa.html.

2. Diane DiResta, *Knockout Presentations: How to Deliver Your Message with Power, Punch, and Pizzazz* (Worcester, MA: Chandler House Press, 1998), 236.

3. Ibid., 237.

4. Lillian Wilder, *Talk Your Way to Success* (New York: Eastside Publishing, 1986), 279.

APPENDIX C

1. Patricia Nelson (page revised Nov. 3, 1999). "Handling Questions and Answers." Toastmasters International, Edmonton and Area. Retrieved September 1, 2000, from www.ecn.ab.ca/toast/qa.html.

2. Daria Price Bowman, *Presentations: Proven Techniques for Creating Presentations that Get Results* (Holbrook, MA: Adams Media, 1998), 177.

3. Oklahoma Society of CPAs (OSCPA), "Tips for Successful Media Interviewing." Retrieved June 10, 2006, from www.oscpa.com/?757.

4. Diane Howard, "Guidelines for Videoconference Presentations, Performances, and Teaching," Retrieved June 10, 2006, from dianehoward.com.

5. Some tips adapted from AT&T Education Web site, "Videoconferencing." Retrieved June 13, 2006, from www.kn.pacbell.com/wired/vidconf/compressedVid.html.

APPENDIX D

1. E. Flege, J. M. Munro, and I. R. A. McKay, "Factors Affecting Strength of Perceived Foreign Accent in a Second Language," *Journal of the Acoustical Society of America* 97 (1995): 312.

2. The content in this section is based on Robbin Crabtree and Robert Weissberg, *ESL Students in the Public Speaking Classroom*, 2nd ed. (Boston: Bedford/St. Martins, 2003), 23.

3. M. C. Florez, "Improving Adult ESL Learners' Pronunciation Skills," *National Clearinghouse for ESL Literacy Education*, 1998. Retrieved April 10, 2000, from www.cal.org/NCLE/DIGESTS/Pronun.htm.

4. Ibid.

5. Robert Anholt, *Dazzle 'Em with Style: The Art of Oral Scientific Presentation* (New York: W. H. Freeman & Co, 1994), 156.

Acknowledgments

Text Credits

Joe Ayers and Tim S. Hopf. "Visualization: Is It More than Extra-Attention?" From *Communication Education*, 38 (1989): 1–5. Reprinted by permission of Taylor & Francis Ltd. www.informaworld.com.

Steven Soderbergh. Excerpt from Oscar Acceptance Speech. Originally published in *How to Make a Memorable Oscar Speech* by Ellen A. Kim. Posted February 27, 2005, on MSNBC Web site, www.msnbc.com. Used by permission of the Academy of Motion Picture Arts and Sciences and Mr. Steven Soderbergh.

Photo Credits

From Source to Speech, pages 54 & 55. Screenshots of Brooklyn Public Library Info Bridge Search pages copyright © Brooklyn Public Library. Reprinted by permission.

From Source to Speech, page 55. Abstract of article from Psychological Reports by Isabelle Golmier. Copyright 2007 by Ammons Scientific, Ltd. Reproduced with permission of Ammons Scientific Ltd. in the format Textbook via Copyright Clearance Center.

From Source to Speech, page 68. From The Big Picture by Edward Jay Epstein. Copyright © 2005 by E.J.E. Publications, Ltd., Inc. Used by permission of Random House, Inc.

From Source to Speech, page 70. Peg Tyre And Sarah Staveley-O'Carroll. "How To Fix School Lunch" From Newsweek, August 8, 2005. Copyright © 2005 Newsweek, Inc. www.newsweek.com. All rights reserved. Used by permission and protected by the Copyright Laws of the United States. The printing, copying, redistribution, or retransmission of the Material without express written permission is prohibited.

From Source to Speech, page 70. Photo of chef Jamie Oliver from Newsweek, August 8, 2005. Reprinted by permission from Rex USA.

From Source to Speech, page 77. News release reprinted courtesy of NASA.

Figure 10.1, page 78. DMOZ Open Directory Search page. Copyright © 2010 Netscape. All Rights Reserved. Used with permission.

From Source to Speech, page 80. Screenshot of Anders Cullhed homepage. http://nobelprize.org/nobel_prizes/literature/articles/cullhed/index.html. Copyright © 2010 The Nobel Foundation. Reprinted by permission of Nobelprize.org and permission of the author.

Figure 10.2, page 82. Advanced Search page reprinted by permission of GOOGLE™. GOOGLE is a trademark of Google Inc.

From Source to Speech, page 87. Screenshot of Institute of Medicine Web site (www.iom.edu). Copyright © 2010 National Academy of Sciences. All rights reserved.

Index

SAMPLE SPEECHES

Informative Speeches

Persuasive Speeches

Special Occasion Speeches

VISUAL GUIDES

QUICK TIPS

CHECKLISTS

CONTENTS